The Miraculous 16th Karmapa

Incredible Encounters with the Black Crown Buddha

THE MIRACULOUS 16TH KARMAPA

Incredible Encounters
with the Black Crown Buddha

Compiled by
NORMA LEVINE

ཨ་ཁྲིད་ཨེ་ཝཾ་ཆོས་ལྡན་ལ་ས་འཛིན༎
SHANG SHUNG PUBLICATIONS

May the passing obstacles to the fullness of activity of the buddhas' representative in our world, the great Karmapa, Ogyen Trinley Dorje, soon be removed! And may he have the freedom to perform the sacred activity of the Karmapas! Convinced that our own ignorance and negativity is a key factor in this removal, I wish and pray that we may all progress in that direction.

Karmapa Khyenno!

KATIA HOLMES
How the Karmapa Transformed and Saved My Life

© 2013 Norma Levine
Shang Shung Publications
Merigar
58031 Arcidosso (GR)
Italy
www.shangshungpublications.org
info@shangshungpublications.org

Interior design: Paul Cimiz
Cover design: Vince Sneed, *tangentdesign.co.UK*
Front cover photo: HH Karmapa at age 16 in the meditation of Karma
Pakshi, the 2nd Karmapa, courtesy of Norma Levine
Back cover photo: HH Karmapa bestowing Vajra Crown ceremony at
Dakpo Kagyu Ling, courtesy of Ward Holmes
Copy editing: Kathy McGrane, Trinley Walker, Kathy Cullen, Giorgio
Dall'Orto

ISBN: 978-88-7834-133-3

Contents

The Karmapa

The Sixteenth Gyalwa Karmapa Rangjung Rigpe Dorje was not like other Dharma teachers; he gave very few formal Dharma teachings. Sometimes he did give the Vajra Crown ceremony, but often he would just simply sit with people, and his aura was so powerful that merely by being there he touched their lives in unparalleled ways. Some of his students have told me how just to be in his presence, or even outside his room, would clear the fog and confusion of disturbing emotions within their minds. They describe him as majestic: a magnificent, spiritual king of immense stature, whom everyone revered. His spiritual power was enormous; in his presence everyone became biddable and their minds were calm.

His influence as a spiritual leader extended beyond the Kagyu school: he maintained connections across all traditions and lineages of Tibetan Buddhism. In this age of degeneration when both the world at large and the Kagyu lineage face so many difficulties and even threats to their very existence, his guidance and leadership are sorely missed. Sadly, he was only fifty eight years old when he passed away. He died too young. Often, I wish that he were alive today to see the fruits of his activities in the lives of his students; how they have grown and matured in their Dharma practice. Their continued diligence and commitment to practice is the greatest gift that they can offer him.

In conclusion, I would like to thank Ms Levine for compiling this collection. Many of these accounts are highly personal and subjective, yet they form an important contribution to the record of the life and work of the Sixteenth Gyalwa Karmapa. He entered paranirvana more than thirty years ago, and yet, those who knew him still remember him with awe and tremble at the memory.

17th Karmapa Ogyen Trinley Dorje,
Dharamsala, Himachal Pradesh, India
6th October, 2012

Publisher's Note

His Holiness the 16th Karmapa was one of the most important masters of Tibetan Buddhism of the 20th century. He played a crucial role in bringing the precious ancient teachings of Vajrayana to the West, and was a spiritual father to thousands of practitioners, in the East as well as in the Western world.

Chögyal Namkhai Norbu, the founder of Shang Shung Publications, has been recognized as a reincarnation of an important master by the 16th Karmapa. Moreover, it was due to repeated requests by His Holiness that Chögyal Namkhai Norbu started to give teachings in the West. The publication of this book is a way of honouring the close relationship of these two masters. We sincerely hope that all practitioners of Tibetan Buddhism, irrespective of their affiliation, are inspired by the stories recounted in this book and that all good qualities of the Karmapa, such as pure love, great kindness and profound insight, plant their seeds within us and manifest in full.

This book is the result of Norma Levine's tireless efforts to collect and edit the stories presented here. We have decided to keep the editing to minimum and preserve as much as possible the individual style of several authors, some of whom are not native English speakers.

Last but not least, we did extensive research trying to identify the persons who took the photos included in this book. In many cases, however, our attempts were unsuccessful. Should you have information regarding the photographers marked as "unknown," we kindly ask you to contact us at *photos@shangshungpublications. org* so that we can include this data in future editions of this book.

May this work bring benefit to all sentient beings!

Editor's Introduction
Norma Levine

IT WAS 1976 WHEN I first heard the name Karmapa. From his monastery in Sikkim, he was making a tour of Europe, including my home town of Hay-on-Wye on the Welsh borders, invited by the first Buddhists I ever met. We were told he would be touring in a big maroon bus large enough to carry his entourage of monks and menagerie of birds.

The preparations required were extraordinary. Most memorable was the construction of a large wooden throne, built to exact specifications, covered in exquisite silk brocade. We were told it had to be suitable for a great spiritual king.

Now picture his long maroon bus with gold Tibetan lettering wending its way carefully through the narrow lanes towards a farmhouse in the Black Mountains. I watched a middle-aged, broadly-built man descend regally from the gold brocaded front seat, helped by his attendants. He paused for a long moment to look around at the welcoming group holding white offering scarves and reciting his mantra "Karmapa Khyenno," then upwards towards the hills to the skyline, and smiled at the universe with every cell in his body. Thick clouds of juniper smoke filled the air as an offering to the great 16th Gyalwang Karmapa.

When I met him I was barely a Buddhist. My first and lasting impression was of a natural force, like thunder or lightning masquerading in a human body. Clearly he was not an ordinary human being.

His body seemed unlike flesh and blood. He was as pure as the elements: wind, water, earth, air and space. A photograph taken of him a few years later would show a blur of multi-coloured lights instead of a solid body. It was said to indicate his realization of *shunyata* or emptiness (see p. 143).

His expression changed constantly like clouds shifting across the sky. Sometimes he smiled with delight like a child, sometimes he stared wrathfully black as thunder. The force of his presence alone brought a hushed silence. How did one talk to him, I wondered? I was struck dumb by his massive presence.

The Karmapa was known as the Black Hat Lama of Tibet. The Hat, which his attendant carried in a silk hat box, was a spiritual crown marking Karmapa as the Buddha of Activity for the Dark Age.

It is said that that in another epoch and dimension the Karmapa was crowned by celestial enlightened women known as dakinis. This "naturally arising" Black Crown, said to be woven from the hair of dakinis, was always on his head, but could only be seen by the pure in heart. For the vast majority unable to see this crown, the 15th-century Chinese Emperor Yongle, a disciple of the Karmapa, made a material replica for everyone to see. During the Black Crown ceremony the Karmapa places the Black Hat on his head and embodies the bodhisattva of compassion, Chenrezig. It is said to plant the seed of enlightenment in those who witness it.

He brought the Black Hat on his tour and performed the ceremony anywhere he was requested—in large private houses, squats, village halls, and even in the tiny room in a Welsh farmhouse where I first witnessed it.

The throne took up more than half the space of the shrine room

HH 1 6th Karmapa, Vajra Crown ceremony. (Photographer unknown)

whose walls were already covered in sacred representations of deities on scrolls. The rest was occupied by the Karmapa's monks and their ritual instruments. To this day none of us can comprehend how seventy-five people could also have sat in a room measuring 12 by 12 feet. It seemed to become a cathedral-like space.

Karmapa occupied the throne completely. He had a spiritual dignity that made it his rightful seat, just as the lion proclaims his natural dominion. His eyes seemed to cover all directions and dimensions: the people crammed together bursting out the doorway into the sitting room, the house, the Black Mountains, right out through space and beyond time.

The impact of the Karmapa on our lives was difficult to measure because it is impossible to pinpoint exactly what causes events to happen. We had entered his sacred mandala in which events happen with perfect synchronicity. We had also become part of an ancient lineage of miraculous history—one of the oldest and most revered in Tibet.

When the spiritual King came to town my life started to go in another direction, on every level—just like that.

Reading an account of miracles from a Tibetan text makes it seem mythical, but if we look at the history of the Karmapas and expand our mind to understand what a buddha is, it becomes more like sacred history.

Sacred history tells us that the first Karmapa, born in 1110 CE, was known as Dusum Khyenpa or Knower of the Three Times, a name given to him because he was believed to have gone beyond the relativity of time. Past, present and future dissolved because he had achieved the highest state of meditation in which all boundaries are realized to be fabrications.

His great bequest to spiritual history was his ability to recognize his own future reincarnation, thus establishing for the first time an infallible, continuous reincarnation lineage in which he could draw upon his clairvoyance to guide beings in the present. Since then the Karmapas were frequently called upon to identify other reincarnate Lamas. To foretell his own reincarnation he would write a prediction letter before passing away and give it secretly to a trusted disciple to be opened at the right time. This letter would tell the time and place of his birth and the names of his parents, as well as the special natural signs that would occur. The letter is infallible proof that it is the spiritual lineage that reincarnates and not a dynastic blood line.

The Karmapas also managed to maintain their purely spiritual status against the manipulation of powerful political overlords.

Statue of Dusum Khyenpa, the first Karmapa shown at the opening ceremony of Karmapa 900 in Bodh Gaya. (Copyright Maia Saabye Christensen)

The 4th Karmapa was invited by the Mongolian Khan to reside with him but he refused, maintaining his activity was to move around.

It was the fourth Karmapa, Rolpe Dorje (1340–1383) who started what became known as the Great Encampment, or Garchen in Tibetan, a massive nomadic caravan, which carried teachings and empowerments to people in remote regions of Tibet. These encampments were integral to the activity of the Karmapa signifying his freedom to connect with people and spread the dharma. It was felt that to receive the full benefit of the Karmapa's blessing, people had to see his face.

In its heyday during the time of the 7th Karmapa, the Encampment numbered 10,000 people and contained all the facilities of a real city with education for monks and lay people; and developed a school of painting known as Karma Gadri. Even animals and beggars had a place in the encampment. People who saw it were so impressed by its extent and variety, it became known as the Ornament of the World. The Encampment came to a tragic end in the time of the tenth Karmapa, Chöying Dorje, when the entire caravan of monks, nuns and laypeople was surrounded by the combined force of the Mongols under Gushri Khan and an army from Central Tibet, and massacred.

Although some of the Karmapas were gurus to the Emperors of China, they chose to be free from the constraints of politics in order to perform their spiritual activity. When the Emperor of China requested the 5th Karmapa to remain with him in his court, the Karmapa declined. He decided not to use the backing of the Ming dynasty to make his sect politically dominant, rather he proclaimed the need for religious freedom with a multiplicity of schools, thus neatly sidestepping Chinese political strategies.

Throughout their history, the Karmapas adroitly transformed every manoeuvre to ensnare them and use their power for political purposes, into peace and harmony. They were mahasiddhas, not power-mongers; buddhas, not empire builders.

The 16th in the lineage of Karmapas was born in 1924, two years after the death of the 15th Karmapa, into an aristocratic family in East Tibet, where many of the previous Karmapas had been born. Various miraculous signs attended his birth. The sound of the Chenrezig mantra "OM MANI PADME HUNG" was heard coming from his mother's womb, and on the day of his birth many rainbows appeared in the sky. All the water in the offering bowls turned into milk. Like the Lord Buddha, the infant took seven steps saying, "Mother, mother, I am going away." Soon afterwards two of his heart sons, Situ Rinpoche and Jamgön Kongtrul Rinpoche, recognised the child in accordance with the precise descriptions left in the prediction letter of the 15th Karmapa.

In 1931, at the age of seven, he was ordained as a novice monk, and taken to Palpung monastery, the seat of the Tai Situ lineage, where he was enthroned. Afterwards, he bestowed the Black Hat ceremony for the first time. Once more multiple rainbows appeared and flowers fell from the heavens[1].

---

1 Nik Douglas and Meryl White, *Karmapa the Black Hat Lama of Tibet*, pp. 107–110.

HH Karmapa photo from a monastery in Darjeeling. (Courtesy of Ward Holmes)

Amongst all the accomplished yogis, scholars, noble selfless beings and nameless itinerant holy hermits that the secret methods of Vajrayana Buddhism produced in Tibet, the Karmapas were considered the supreme reincarnations. The stories of their miraculous powers were recounted orally from generation to generation. In *The Wondrous Activities of His Holiness the 16th Gyalwang Karmapa,* (p. 29) incidents first witnessed by the 16th Karmapa's General Secretary, Tenzin Namgyal, then narrated to a group of students and afterwards written down in 1989, illustrate how the oral tradition of miraculous tales gets transformed into sacred biography.

The stories told in this book form a part of that oral tradition. Tibetan accounts of the lives of the masters tend towards hagiography rather than biography. This is a genre that completely ignores the human side of the person and dwells entirely on supernormal attainments. The miracles recounted here are not emphasized to conceal the human being. These close-up encounters show the many facets of the 16th Karmapa's unique but entirely human personality. I have recorded them from those willing to share their experiences. Most are from Westerners who had meaningful contact with the 16th Karmapa either in India or during his three visits to the West.

Let's leave behind sacred history for a moment and jump into recent memory. The 16th Karmapa lived through one of the most turbulent times in the lineage's 900 year history. His ability to see the future clearly enabled him to make preparations for the Buddhist dharma in exile, well ahead of the Chinese invasion. In 1959 he escaped from Tibet through Bhutan to Sikkim with a large party of monks and followers carrying out what he was able to save of his vast collections of spiritual treasures.

Among these treasures was the most powerful symbol of his lineage, the Black Crown or Black Hat. Another was the axe that the 12th-century yogi, Milarepa, had used to construct and demolish the many houses that his guru Marpa obliged him to build in order to purify his negative deeds. The axe is an important element in the making of the Karmapa Black Pill which has the power to save or prolong life. There are many stories about the miraculous Black Pill, which Katia Holmes confirms from personal experience in her significant contribution, *How the Karmapa Transformed and Saved My Life* (p. 347).

The Karmapa and his followers settled in India, in Sikkim (1962), at that time an independent Buddhist kingdom with

1973. HH 16th Karmapa at Kalu Rinpoche's monastery in Sonada, West Bengal, India, with 4 heart sons, plus Kalu Rinpoche, Bokar Rinpoche and Beru Khyentse Rinpoche. (Photographer unknown)

a Chögyal, or dharma King. The Karmapa's monastery at Rumtek soon became known to 1960s spiritual seekers who came to find out for themselves what enlightenment really was. Among them was Michael Hollingshead (*The Man Who Turned on the World*, p. 69) whose story prefigures the Karmapa's historic meeting with the Hopi Indians in Arizona in 1974, movingly described in Steve Roth's, *When the Iron Bird Flies* (p. 181). Caroline Alioto (now Lama Palden), who writes of her experiences in *Emperor of Love*, (p. 131) was at that time married to a Bhutanese Lama and had heard of the Karmapa through her connections with the Bhutanese royal family. Lama Surya Das (born Jeffrey Miller in New York) spent many years in India, first in the early 1970s with his Hindu guru, Neem Karoli Baba, and then in Darjeeling at Kalu Rinpoche's monastery, and also in Sikkim at Rumtek Monastery for several month-long periods.

In the introduction to his stories in this book, he writes, "His Holiness the 16th Karmapa was the greatest lama I ever met. All the Himalayan lamas I knew were in awe of him and intimidated by his prodigious powers. He seemed to see through everyone and everything, and brooked no nonsense."

Like all the Karmapas before him the 16th remained non-political. He refused to get drawn into the newly formed Tibet cause. Although it caused some tension in his close friendship with the 14th Dalai Lama, he kept his distance from the politics in Dharamsala. His position was that the Tibetan freedom struggle was politics and he advised his centres in Europe and North America not to get involved[2]. Only by separating buddha-dharma from politics could he be free to manifest the spontaneous quality of the Karmapas' spiritual activity.

These early stories show the freedom both of 1960s Western culture and the 16th Karmapa. There is a quality of recognition on both sides as they meet. A similar occurrence took place when the Karmapa met the Indian Swami, Muktananda at his ashram near Bombay. The genuine expression of their love for each other is clear in the photos taken at the time. Their meeting is described in Didi Contractor's extraordinary account, *The Meeting of Mahasiddhas* (p. 87).

It was when the Karmapa first came on tour to the West in 1974, that our oral history really springs to life. Since the first emergence of Buddhism in the West in the late nineteenth century, many teachers had visited but none of his stature had ever walked the streets as freely as he did. He strode into foreign continents and

---

2 HH Dalai Lama stated his case in an unpublished interview with Mick Brown, March 2, 2001: "The Karmapa Rinpoche later, in talking to some of his centres in Europe and America, said the Tibetan freedom struggle is politics, and they should not be involved.

But it is necessary. It is buddha-dharma. But some people get the wrong impression, that this is something political, a struggle for a few officials' benefit: the Tibetan government's benefit. Later, I found in Europe and America that on 10th March (Freedom Day) some Tibetan Buddhist centres never participate. Every Tibetan joins in with this; it's the national struggle. But some centres are very reluctant, thinking this is politics."

1974. HH 16th Karmapa in San Francisco. (Photo courtesy of Steve Roth)

with fearless compassion, picked up his students from previous lives and moved them along the path of liberation from suffering.

Many people had supranormal experiences. When he embodied Chenrezig, some saw the white four-armed Chenrezig. When he gave an empowerment of the Medicine Buddha, all those in the room saw him as lapis lazuli, the colour of the Medicine Buddha (*Karmapa Becomes the Medicine Buddha* p. 347). To the 1960s generation desperately seeking salvation, he showed the way of yogic transformation. Many went into traditional three year retreat, and even became lamas, like Surya Das. Ken and Katia Holmes, who accompanied Karmapa on his tours, received direct transmission and teachings from him while translating or driving him from place to place (*Memories of the Buddha Karmapa,* p. 289) as did his drivers in the US, Steve Roth, Dale Brozosky and Ward Holmes.

He taught from ordinary life situations, using whatever arose to point out ultimate reality or the nature of mind. But, in fact, he himself embodied what's called the nature of mind. His very presence pointed out the state of naked awareness. For someone whose only language was Tibetan, he had a special ability to communicate completely with speakers of other languages, some of them hearing him in their own language. His love of birds led him to the doors of obscure bird breeders. Having directed his astounded drivers through back lanes with no signposts, no previous knowledge of the place he was in, no map and certainly no sat nav, he would then bargain for the best birds.

He left indelible memories with shopkeepers, breeders, department store managers, wherever he went. Several stories tell how he recognised certain birds as his students from a previous lifetime and how they would die in a meditative state.

When I started collecting these memories I was moved every time I heard how incredibly human he was in his super-humanness. "He gave me a way to see greatness," says Didi Contractor in *When Time and Eternity Met*, (p. 96). His laughter, his knowing remarks, his playfulness, his love of being driven at high speed, even his manner of dying, released the magical in the ordinary world.

I began to understand that greatness is not just miracles but also humanity. When his time came to die at the predicted age of fifty-eight, he was taken to hospital in Zion, Illinois. He had a combination of cancer, tuberculosis, pneumonia and diabetes but was cheerful and caring of those around him throughout. The doctors thought it was very strange that someone with his painful condition did not show pain. In fact there were times when all symptoms disappeared.

He said to his doctor, Mitchell Levy, "There is one thing that is very important for you to understand. If I am needed here to teach sentient beings, if I still have work to do here, then no disease will ever be able to overcome me. And if I am no longer really required to teach sentient beings, then you can tie me down and I will not stay on this earth."[3] An hour after his heart had stopped and 15 minutes after the doctors gave up trying to resuscitate, he seemed to come to life miraculously with perfectly normal blood pressure and warmth in his body.[4]

When he finally succumbed to death, he remained in meditation with his skin elastic and supple and heat from his heart just as it would be from a normal live body. The doctor attending him cried on seeing these miraculous signs.

He was born in the East but died in the West, seemingly a sign that his activity encompassed the whole world. Many of the stories in this book show that for his close disciples he never left at all but has continued to care for and protect them, appearing even in a physical form many years after leaving his body.

When I consider the stories in this book, they seem almost to belong to a golden age, when the Karmapa and the whole Western world were celebrating personal freedom. From my own

---

3 Reginald Ray, *Secrets of the Vajra World.*
4 See Introduction to Parinirvana, p. 278.

observations,[5] the 17th Karmapa has never known that freedom from the time he was recognised as Karmapa in Tibet at the age of seven. In Chinese controlled Tibet he was increasingly coming under pressure to denounce the Dalai Lama. Then his daring escape from Tibet to "freedom in exile" in India in 2000 resulted in another kind of imprisonment within a labyrinthine web of religious and political intrigue, accompanied by suspicion and innuendo on all sides and attempts in some of the media at defamation of character.

He has been stripped of his homeland, his family, and denied access to his monastic seat at Rumtek in Sikkim, where his sacred treasures and Black Hat are locked up. What was supposed to be a two day stopover at a monastery under construction in Dharamsala, while the Indian Government deliberated on the best place to settle him, has turned into twelve long years of intrigue, with no end in sight. Since his escape at the age of fourteen, he has been living within two rooms in a monastery belonging to a different Buddhist tradition, which is like housing the Archbishop of Canterbury in the Vatican. In order to travel outside the immediate area, he has to get permission well in advance from the Indian Government in Delhi.

The miracle of the 17th Karmapa is that he has shouldered the immense responsibilities of his office with humour, and majestic dignity; that he gives love to all, that he can still show humanity within the cramped quarters of what he now calls "a permanent hotel"[6] in which he does not possess even his own shrine room. He is a humble human being, a perfect bodhisattva, and already a great Karmapa.

---

5 The views expressed here are solely mine, based on my observations and research over many years. They are in no way intended to represent the views of the 17th Karmapa Ogyen Trinley Dorje or his Office of Administration.

6 HH Karmapa from Chod teachings October 28, 2012 at Dorzong Monastery. The "permanent hotel" is Gyuto Monastery which has provided rented accommodation for the past twelve years.

His Holiness the 16th Gyalwang Karmapa   His Holiness the 17th Gyalwang Karmapa

The 16th and 17th Karmapas. (Photographer unknown)

From all of us who contributed these stories, I would like to dedicate this book to the 17th Karmapa's personal freedom and the continuation of his lineage's vast unimpeded buddha activity.

Tibet and India

Black Crown Lama: the 16th Gyalwang Karmapa

by Lama Surya Das

Lama Surya Das (born Jeffrey Miller, 1950) is an American-born lama in the Tibetan Buddhist tradition. He is a poet, chant-master, spiritual activist and author of many popular works on Buddhism; a teacher and spokesperson for Buddhism in the West. He has long been involved in charitable relief projects in the Third World and in interfaith dialogue. Surya Das is a dharma heir of Nyoshul Khenpo Rinpoche, a Nyingma master of the non-sectarian Rime movement. His name, which means "Servant of the Sun" is a combination of Sanskrit (sūrya) and Hindi (das, from the Sanskrit dāsa), was given to him by the Hindu guru Neem Karoli Baba.

Tibetan Buddhism stresses the importance of a spiritual master, whom we call the Root Guru or heart-master. He or she is considered the root of all blessings, inspiration and encouragement, energy, edification and spiritual accomplishments (*siddhis*), and we take refuge in and rely on them every step along the path of awakened enlightenment. There are many different levels of teachers and of teacher-student and guru-disciple relationships. Master teachers are vital lineage holders in an unbroken line reaching back to the Buddha himself, like the flame being passed from one candle to the next.

One's own root lama is said to embody and transmit all the wisdom, compassion and dynamism of the entire lineage including all the buddhas and bodhisattvas, dakas and dakinis and dharma guardians, for—almost miraculously—given a little diligence and good karma, each of us can, through the sincere devotional practice known as Guru Yoga and related meditational practices, eventually realize union with the guru's own realized state, inseparable from the Buddha's enlightenment. Anyone can become as enlightened, wise and selfless, compassionate and loving, as the Buddha himself; this is Buddha's promise, dharma teaching and the entire Sangha's intention.

In our tradition, we consider the root guru as even kinder to us and more of a personal benefactor and mentor than the historical Buddha; for the personal teacher is the Buddha's representative appearing in human form to us, where we are, in this time and place. He or she hands over the entire dharma legacy of both knowledge and realization to us dedicated practitioners, introducing us to our own true buddha nature within our minds and hearts, leading us by the hand beyond the mire of conditioning and worldliness—karma and klesha—while pointing out what we are and can become. This is why the Kagyu lineage is often called the secret whispered oral lineage, being passed intimately from mouth to ear and from heart to heart in the process of spiritual transformation and awakening. Let those with ears to hear, listen. Let those who have eyes to see, know. Let those who know, enjoy.

A wise woman once told me, in my twenties when I was a Dharma student living in refugee villages in Nepal and Darjeeling, that any Dharma teacher must have at least four qualities:

knowledge, humility, kindness, and generosity. Immense spiritual knowledge, the humility not to declare it, and the kindness and generosity to pass it on to others.

As the oldest line of recognized tulkus (reincarnated lamas, or what the Chinese call "living buddhas") in Tibetan history, Gyalwang Karmapa, Rangjung Rigpai Dorje (1924–1981) exemplified these qualities, and so much more. He was my root guru, and the head lama of the Kagyu Lineage of Tibetan Buddhism. The Gyalwang Karmapa was the grand lama and reincarnate tulku ("emanation of the Buddha") in a line of successive reincarnations stretching back to Karmapa Dusum Khyenpa ("Knower of All Time and Space") in the eleventh century. The Tibetan name Gyalwang means, traditionally, Buddha or main Conqueror (Jina, in Sanskrit): as in conqueror of karma and worldly conditioning.

His Holiness helped keep intact our tradition in exile in Sikkim, India, and around the world during the Tibetan diaspora. He gathered together and educated its main tulkus, many of whom, old and young, he cared for over decades at Rumtek Monastery, where they could study and practice under the tutelage of grand masters led by Khenpo Thrangu and Lobpon Tenga Rinpoche among others.

HH 16th Karmapa with tulkus at Ka-Nying Shedrub Ling Monastery. (Photographer unknown)

He was also responsible for recognizing hundreds of tulkus born outside of Tibet as reincarnate lamas, a traditional duty and almost unique specialty of the Karmapas. As this book shows, he made a tremendous contribution and impact on Buddhism and spiritual practitioners in the West—especially on contemplatives, meditators, monastics, and yogis.

I first encountered His Holiness Karmapa at Kalu Rinpoche's monastery near Darjeeling, West Bengal, in the autumn of 1973, where he had come from Sikkim with a large and fascinating entourage of tulkus, monks and lamas to give Buddhist teachings and Tantric initiations over a period of several weeks. There is a terrific smiling photo of him from that glorious, sun-drenched day long ago with me right in front of him, which I still keep on my home altar. Later we would invite him to Woodstock, New York, and help him to establish an American monastery he named Karma Triyana Dharmachakra (KTD) atop Meads Mountain. I was also fortunate to be with him, study and serve him in New York City, Washington D.C., France, and Kathmandu, Nepal.

HH 16th Karmapa. (Photo courtesy of Dorothea Fischer)

His Holiness was the

greatest enlightened lama I ever met. I am certainly not alone in that assessment. Many lamas of his time were in awe of his all-seeing wisdom, endless compassion, prodigious powers of clairvoyance and prognostication, and particularly his obvious ability to see through people.

An elegant leader and diplomatic hierarch, he could stand beside Prime Minister Nehru and still look like a king.

Yet he could spontaneously express his feelings, tell jokes which cut close to the bone, and occasionally demonstrate iconoclastic crazy wisdom. He brooked no nonsense, nor suffered fools gladly. Once I saw him, displeased, pinch one of his monk-assistants so hard he left a black and blue bruise on his side beneath the arm.

Once in New York in 1980, at his center on West End and Eighty-Sixth street, he serenely stated to a room crowded with excited followers and visitors, "Your minds are like boiling pots." It could not have been truer.

An elegant, accomplished, and diplomatic spiritual leader and gentleman, he was also a mercurial character, demonstrating more vividly than most how buddha nature, enlightenment, or the Light comes through each of our personalities differently. Like water and ice, of the same nature, but in temporarily different states. We all have the same infinite, groundless and boundless, luminous buddha heart-mind—it's merely a matter of scope of realization. This was his teaching, which he lived and embodied, day and night, wherever he was. When I was with him—or even thinking of him now; I remember how he saw the buddha in each and all of us, which was how he lovingly helped us to see that in ourselves, and in each other too. This was his rare and sacred gift as a spiritual master.

His Holiness could be quite simple and straightforward as well. I've sat with him on the floor of his bedroom, with his maroon stocking feet stuck out while he leaned against his bed as if we were in a college dorm room at night, and discussed "the first king of America," as he called General George Washington—and other Western things which he'd scarcely heard of and wondered about. He pinched my right ear and asked me about Jews and where they came from (there were none in Tibet), and what kind of God they believed in.

People used to say that His Holiness could communicate with animals. His favorite hobby seemed to be collecting rare and exotic birds, which he kept wherever he went, especially in an aviary atop the multi-storied rooftop at his own Rumtek Monastery outside Gangtok, the capital of the old Himalayan principality of Sikkim (now part of India).

He used to teach the birds to chant again and again his name mantra, Karmapa Khyenno, and joked that they were "The returns of old monks who'd broken their vows." He was talking of course about reincarnation. He would laugh uproariously at times, and be heard several houses away.

These were some of the things we, his followers loved most about him, which helped us feel close to him, and even somewhat akin to him—his many genuinely extraordinary and special characteristics notwithstanding. The Karmapa, whom we called "YishinNorbu" in Tibetan—"All-Knowing Wish-Fulfilling Gem"—carried his own atmosphere with him, like a Pure Land/ Buddha Field, and transported us as well, in so very many ways. He seemed to see through everyone and everything. He was not a peaceful, Jesus-like guru, but more akin to the intense and even fierce Guru Rinpoche or Padma Sambhava, the intrepid Tantric master who brought Vajrayana Buddhism to Tibet in the year 712.

Yet he was always kind and gracious to me and the other Western dharma students, whom he seemed to enjoy playing with in a warm and avuncular manner. He was very intimate with us, touched us, pinched us, made us laugh and cry too. Once I asked his forgiveness for speaking out of turn to some other disciples in front of him, and he simply said, gently: "Nothing is difficult for me."

Guru Rinpoche, Tantric master of Tibet (Artist unknown)

In the early days at Rumtek Monastery, only ten years after the Karmapa and his school of Buddhism arrived in Sikkim, we few foreign pilgrims, seekers and students had almost unprecedented access to him. As long as one could manage to patiently navigate the winding course through tangled Indian bureaucracy and obtain the proper India visa and special permits necessary to visit Sikkim, one was free to go where one wanted and stay as many weeks or months as one could manage.

We would walk around the monastery grounds with His Holiness or hang out in his upstairs bedroom, perhaps with only the

HH 16th Karmapa in his room in Rumtek. (Copyright Lars Gammeltoft)

translators Achi or Ngodrup Burkhar accompanying His Holiness; or in his second-storey sitting room, with his cabinet of ancient and invaluable terma treasures on a shelf, full of blessed statues, dorjes, and other sacred relics from the Vajrayana lineage.

Now and then there would be a teaching or all day ritual with chanting, sacred music and lama-dances (*cham*), a tantric initiation (*wang*), or the highly symbolic Black Crown Ceremony for which he was famous, utilizing the jewel encrusted Black Vajra Crown—said to be woven of the hair of one hundred thousand dakinis—which was presented to the Fifth Karmapa by his disciple the Chinese Emperor Yongle around 1410. His Holiness is known as the incarnation of Chenrezig (Avalokitesvara, Kuan Yin), and transmits—especially through this particular ceremonial practice of the Black Vajra Crown—the vast and buoyant blessings of that Bodhisattva of impartial compassion and unconditional love.

At the inaugural ceremonies blessing the newly renovated Rumtek Monastery in the very early seventies, when several strong monks struggled and failed to pull up the pole with ropes, as customary; Gyalwang Karmapa raised the towering prayer-flag pole with his pointing finger, as many who were present that day have attested—one occasion among the many when he is reported to have performed miracles. The 16th Karmapa's ceremonial cremation and extensive funeral rites in 1981 at Rumtek were also marked by miraculous occurrences, including rainbows, extraordinary relics remaining in the ashes, and other signs seen by the entire multitude.

I myself may give little importance to such siddhis (miraculous powers), and consider them more like special effects and thus secondary to the main liberation and enlightenment story. And yet, given that they are a part of every generation's dharma lore since time immemorial and seemingly continue to occur since the time of Lord Buddha, twenty six hundred years ago—I feel there's no real need to ignore them. The Buddha himself said, of course, that he only performed miracles when necessary to inspire and edify those who needed such graphic demonstrations of inner accomplishments which were much more significant, and that one should never show off supernatural powers merely to impress others or for profit, fame, celebrity, etc.

In a similar vein, the tradition tells us not to talk about our spiritual dreams, visions, and meditation experiences and epiphanies—except to our teacher—in order to avoid giving rise to pride, dissipating the subtle inner energy, or providing others with material to produce conceptual obscurations. I speak of these things for the first time in forty years, venturing to put some of them in print here in honor of the powerful and profound lineage blessings of the Gyalwang Karmapas, to whom I owe so much.

Let me add here in this somewhat personal sharing that the Karmapa did demonstrate his superpowers to me on at least two occasions during the Seventies, although it was never apparent to me whether he did it intentionally or it simply happened, as part of our rich guru-disciple relationship. Once he appeared in a dream, his radiant face beaming like a full moon, and said directly to me: "I am always with you. Each of you will be in my heart through all my lifetimes. I belong to you, and you belong to me."

I myself, though devotionally inclined by nature, am generally quite skeptical; one man's mythology—like the archetypal Garden of Eden story—is another man's history, religion, or even science. Because the proof is there for me at least, I have chosen to share my experiences in a few of the stories that appear in this book. These are not miracles which words can fully express.

In 1981, on his death bed in a hospital outside Chicago, concerning his imminent death, the Karmapa looked right into the eyes of an inquiring disciple and said, simply: "Nothing happens." A Mahamudra instruction par excellence. The 16th Karmapa was not a bookish man, yet everything he did was a teaching. He helped us to see and experience the entire universe—outer, inner and subtlest—as (his) divine buddha activity, like cosmic dance, sublime sport, a dream, pageant and illusion.

The Karmapa conquered my heart and soul, mind and spirit. To have seen him for even a few moments in his naked Dharmakaya nature (true state) was to become his servant and disciple for life. To be with him felt as if there was nowhere else to go and nothing else to do: one felt like the perfect person in the perfect place enjoying the perfect teachings from the perfect time. His mantra is an essential Guru Yoga instruction: Karmapa Khyenno! (Master, turn toward me/be with me.)

These are a few joyful thoughts offered in reverent memory of my blessed and beloved guru-lama. Just to hear such a name as Karmapa is said to plant the seed of liberation.

May it be accomplished!

A Pointing Out
by Lama Surya Das

*H*is *Holiness often visits me in dreams and meditation, and I feel he is always with and in me. I found him sitting in my meditation box one evening during my first three year retreat in France, a year after he passed away in Zion, Illinois, in 1981. Not long afterwards he appeared to me again in an extraordinary clear light dream, predicting his rebirth by saying: "Tara will give birth to Tara on the eighth of the eighth month. Tell . . . Rinpoche."[1]*

His Holiness vouchsafed me what is perhaps my greatest vision during a small group Phowa *(consciousness transference yoga) empowerment in Carmel, NY, in the spring of 1977. I perceived him as Amitabha, the Buddha of Infinite Light, sitting beneath the Bodhi Tree in Bodhgaya and blazing beams into and out of me as if we were not separate entities—a vision of how things actually are, that I recall and recognize every day. This experience introduced me to the complete inseparability of myself and my root-lama—and moreover, to the genuine buddha-nature, the very buddhaness within— though it took me years to really process and internalize it.*

This is the first time I have spoken of these visitations and revelations. I do so only to honor the kind of teachings and transmission

---

1 The editor has not been able to clarify this prediction.

he promised us, his devoted disciples, and to remember what is possible through the lineage blessings of a true Master. These direct transmissions introduced me to Buddha Vision and highlighted what I call The Diamond Rule (of Vajrayana): to see the buddhaness, the radiant light, innate in everyone and everything.

One day I was sitting on the floor with His Holiness in his bedroom upstairs at Rumtek Monastery. Usually he met with us in his sitting room, where he sat on his rug-covered couch near shelves arrayed with precious buddhas and terma (rediscovered treasure) objects. This day I was ushered into his bedroom by Achi, his handsome Tibetan interpreter, and found the Master sitting on the floor with his legs outstretched and his back against his bed. I bowed and sat in front of him.

I don't remember what we talked about, but suddenly he pointed with his right hand at a Chenrezig tangka on the wall and I actually saw the edge of the Bodhisattva of Compassion's robes fluttering and glittering, sparkling and sizzling with blessings—which seemed to radiate directly from him through Karmapa and into me. Or was it vice versa?! I was filled with bliss as well as overawed beyond any other perceptions of my surroundings, and intuitively knew beyond knowing that Chenrezig and the Karmapa are one and the same as well as inseparable from my own heart.

After a few timeless, ineffable instants, things came back into focus—or should I say, the murk I think of as the normal, ordinary world—and we just kept chatting and joking.

His Holiness always seemed so light, youthful and carefree. But I'm the serious type of student, Serious Das—as my old girlfriend used to call me in the 1970s. I asked His Holiness about what had happened—or should I perhaps say, what I'd experienced. He just laughed, pulled and stroked my brown beard, saying "Karma Pakshi, Karma Pakshi!" (the name of the goateed Second Karmapa Lama) as he used to like to do. Then he said, quietly, as if musing: "It's all like a dream. Good dreams, bad dreams. Like a dream, a fantasy."

Then someone came to get His Holiness and I was sent away, back down to the pedestrian realms. Or so it seemed.

"Things are not what they appear to be, nor are they otherwise" — as it says in the Surangama Sutra. I've been chewing on this for decades.

Bowing to Buddha

Very early one morning in the mid-seventies, I was energetically performing full prostrations in front of the temple door at Rumtek, throwing myself down on the floor again and again while reciting the refuge prayers and chants. If I remember correctly, I was trying to complete a certain number of refuge and prostration practices of the Ninth Karmapa's *Mahamudra Ngondro*—which I did under the guidance of Kyabje Kalu Rinpoche—before I had to leave. I did that every morning during the week or two that I could spend at the monastery in the restricted zone of Sikkim. The rest of each day would be spent studying and practicing with the Kagyu tulku-regents there, who themselves were receiving instruction from the Karmapa and their illustrious abbots, Khenpo Thrangu Rinpoche and Tenga Rinpoche.

It was about four in the morning. The whole monastery courtyard was pretty quiet. Morning prayers and pujas had not yet begun. I was huffing and puffing, bowing up and down, sweating and chanting aloud to my heart's content in a singsong manner—bowing again at the feet of all the buddhas and bodhisattvas, dakas and dakinis and dharma protectors, sangha and lineage masters... all the entire Golden Rosary of Kagyu Gurus which were part of the visualized refuge tree I held in my mind for reverence and refuge purposes. I was outstretched totally on the floor; face down, mini-mala in hand, with my hands above my head in lotus mudra position, at the feet of the entire gloriously shining refuge tree... when I suddenly felt something sprinkling on my head.

Opening my eyes, I peered upwards, still lying flat—and who but His Holiness the Buddha Karmapa himself was standing there, alone, tossing blessed rice grains on me as a blessing, like a rain of flowers from the Pure Lands and Buddha-fields. He just smiled, walked around me clockwise, and continued on his morning round, mala in hand, intoning OM MANI PADME HUNG.

Since that day long ago, I cannot bow without being there and feeling those blessings raining down. Silly me! I still feel it now.

Karmapa Chastises Some Bigshots

I still remember how often my Tibetan friends used to marvel at how large and strong we were. Once some little Tibetan nuns took my American size 12 EEE boots from outside my door and weighed them on the handheld metal scale they used to weight milk, butter, meat almost every day for market and kitchen purposes. They reported with awe and delight that "the giant's shoes weigh four pounds!"

One day in the early Seventies, Massachusetts-born and bred Bryan Miller and I were spending some weeks at Rumtek Monastery. He, like myself, was known by our diminutive Tibetan friends as one of the tall "Injies" (Westerners), as we are both about six feet, two inches.

We were in His Holiness' room upstairs, sitting on the floor at the Master's feet, when some very well-dressed, high class Indian officials came in along with their sari-clad, jewel-adorned wives. One bigwig was a minister and the other a chief of police. They seemed like devotees of a sort; His Holiness had many such upper-class Brahmin visitors, supporters, friends, and followers on the Indian subcontinent. The monk attendants hustled up some nice chairs for them to sit in, and made them comfortable.

I couldn't follow all the proceedings. But it soon became clear that the visitors looked down on us, and must have asked His Holiness what we were doing there. I heard the derisive word "hippies" mixed in with the foreign tongue—Hindi, Nepali, Sikkhimese— I couldn't tell which languages exactly were being spoken.

His Holiness heard them out, as he always did, patiently, graciously. He was quiet for a moment. The he asked Bryan if he could touch the bare light bulb on the ceiling. Bryan said yes, and His Holiness suggested he show us that he actually could, which obviously seemed amazing to the much shorter Asians present. Bryan grinned, slowly unwound his long crossed legs and stood up from the floor; reached up; and twisted the bulb and removed it. His Holiness looked at me. I stood up, reached up, and proudly put it back in. Then we both sat down. The twin towers.

His Holiness said to the Brahmin big shots: "Do you see how much merit and good karma they have? They are so tall because of their good deeds and practice in previous lives." Those nonplussed Brahmins were a lot less haughty toward us after that!

Bryan and I joked together long and hard in the following days, amusing ourselves by wondering what the visitors must have made of all that. We were the teacher's pets.

Over the years, I heard many stories about the Buddha Karmapa from his colleague-lamas, including the four Kagyu regents. He was among the most legendary and talked about lamas of Tibet, the pre-eminent lama of Kham—Eastern Tibet: an enlightened master, and a genuine miracle worker who appeared to different people in various guises, images, dreams, visions, and apparitions, sometimes even simultaneously in different places.

Here are some of these stories.

Consciousness Transference

It was customary in Tibet to summon a lama when a family member passed away, which usually took place at home. Priestly rites would then be performed, and—if possible—the consciousness of the recently deceased would be transferred to one of the buddhafields, transcendent paradises. A powerful practitioner can instantaneously deliver his own consciousness, or that of the deceased, to such an enlightened realm—through the secret yogic practice known as phowa, consciousness transference.

One day the head of a nomadic household in desolate, windswept northern Tibet passed away. In such a sparsely inhabited region it was rare to find monasteries and lamas, so the family members wondered what to do.

They happened to spot a ragged individual travelling on foot, who appeared as if he could be either an itinerant yogi or a beggar; therefore they went to inquire. The mendicant turned out to be, in fact, a lama. The grieving family requested his ministrations for the deceased, and he complied. When he reached the man's deathbed and began his incantations, the family respectfully requested the lama to perform phowa, or consciousness transference, in order to deliver the deceased to superior rebirth in the Western buddhafield of Dewachen, the sphere of sublime delight.

The lama, however, said: "I am just a poor, unlettered practitioner of the Buddha's teachings; I have not mastered that esoteric practice. But I do have one positive quality, infinite faith in the living Buddha named Lama Karmapa; he is like the great gate to Dewachen."

Then he began reciting again and again the famous name-mantra of the Karmapa, "Karmapa Khyenno!" "Karmapa Khyenno, Karmapa Khyenno." After each and every rosary of fervent recitation, he would hit the corpse with his prayer beads, commanding that in the name of the Buddha Karmapa the spirit of the deceased be reborn in Dewachen, that paradise beyond the setting sun.

After some time, everyone noticed that the signs of successful consciousness transference began to appear. Hair fell from the top of the corpse's head, there was a pleasant fragrance in the air, and a large bump appeared at the crown aperture where the spirit of the deceased had departed for the other world. Everyone present rejoiced, and gratefully thanked the mendicant lama. Moreover, all began to faithfully practice the mantra of the Karmapa, praying to realize the great freedom and bliss of Dewachen in this very lifetime.

The traveling lama soon continued on his journey. One day he heard that the omniscient 16th Karmapa was visiting south Tibet; he travelled there to meet him. The first thing the clairvoyant Karmapa said to him was: "That was a difficult phowa we performed up there in the north, wasn't it?" Then Karmapa laughed aloud, hitting the other lama with his rosary. And the mendicant knew with unshakable certainty that the Karmapa is an omniscient living Buddha, truly a master of liberating buddha-activity, who always keeps his disciples, wherever they are, in his heart and mind.

Karmapa's Blue Sheep

The late 16th Karmapa, head of the Kagyu Order, was an animal lover, and an avid collector of exotic birds. He was always accompanied by various pets, including parrots which he trained to recite "Karmapa Khyenno," his own name-mantra and invocation. He had an aviary atop Rumetk Monastery in Sikkim, which he visited early each morning. But, he especially loved his faithful blue sheep.

As a youngster in Tsurphu Monastery, His Holiness Karmapa had a pet Himalayan blue sheep, which followed him around. Everyone said the sheep was the reincarnation of a former servant who had suddenly abandoned the Karmapa's employ. The servant's name was Yonga. He left mysteriously in the middle of the night, and never returned. The Buddha Karmapa divined that no harm had befallen Yonga, and simply let the matter rest.

Several years later, news of Yonga's death reached Karmapa's retinue. Appropriate prayers and benedictions were made in his memory. Time passed. One day while travelling with his followers in the sparsely inhabited northern plains of east Tibet, the young Karmapa hierarch, Rangjung Rigpe Dorje, wandered off after his party had stopped to rest. An elderly attendant who followed him suddenly heard the Karmapa call, "Yonga, Yonga," just as he used to do when hailing his late servant. The elderly attendant-monk wondered what was going on, but kept his own counsel. "After all," he thought, "what harm can possibly come to His Holiness here? The enlightened guardians and dharma protectors are always watching over the Action Master, a living buddha."

For a time the Karmapa wandered through that lonely, deserted grassland, gently calling his former servant's name: "Yonga, Yonga." Suddenly there appeared, mewling, a little blue sheep. Fearlessly, the sheep approached and licked the kneeling Karmapa's outstretched hand.

The Karmapa turned to his faithful old attendant, smiling sweetly. "Now Yonga has come back to me," he said.

From that time on, they were inseparable. Old lamas from Tsurphu Monastery say that, near where Karmapa left hand and footprints embedded in a boulder, the sheep's hoof prints in rock can also be seen.

Five Rupees' Worth of Prayers

Once Ringul Tulku's mother was in the Gangtok, Sikkim, hospital with a serious illness. Ringul and his uncle, who was also his dharma teacher, went to Rumtek Monastery early one morning to ask His Holiness the Gyalwang Karmapa what could be done to help her, for the Buddha Karmapa was universally renowned for his powers of prognostication.

Resorting to his unimpeded clairvoyance (rather than to formal divination through the use of beads and other devices), His Holiness advised that she ought to receive the Thousand Buddhas Empowerment rite as soon as possible, if she would be cured. Otherwise, the outcome seemed bleak.

Tulku and uncle went immediately to Dilgo Khyentse Rinpoche, who was there in Sikkim at the time, to request the empowerment for Amala. They offered the Grand Lama five rupees and a white silk scarf, symbolic of purity of heart, and sought his help.

The compassionate Khyentse Rinpoche was famous for having time for whoever was in need. He immediately accompanied the pair to Gangtok hospital, and performed the all-day rite at the woman's bedside—much to the delight of everyone present. Rinpoche's prayers and pujas continued on long after dark.

When Amala awoke the following day, she was cured, and left the hospital. She lived long afterwards, and often mentioned the great blessings and kindness of her lamas, and remains alive today.

(This was true when I heard the story in the late 1980s.)

Karmapa Speaks English

Once Khyentse Khandro Tsering Chodron[2] and her sister, Sogyal Rinpoche's mother, were enjoying the Karmapa's company at Rumtek Monastery. Suddenly a group of foreign visitors came through and formed a long line to see him.

---

2 (1929–2011), the spiritual wife of Jamyang Khyentse Chökyi Lodrö, was universally acknowledged as one of the foremost female practitioners of Tibetan Buddhism of recent times and was considered to be an emanation of Shelkar Dorje Tso. (Rigpa Wiki)

One after another the "Injies" knelt to put their heads down before His Holiness, making offerings and prayers. He blessed them each by placing his right hand atop their head, saying, "Very good!" For those were actually the only English words the Omniscient One seemed to know.

After the crowd left, Tsering Chodron ragged the awesome enlightened master, whom no one ever dared criticize. "I learned some English today. You really do have a way with Injies!" the insouciant Khandrol-la teased him, adding: "Don't you know any other words in foreign language?!"

Karmapa Blesses a Bird

Dewachen is the Western Buddhafield or blissful paradise of Infinite Light of Amitabha Buddha, located just beyond the setting sun—that is, everywhere—where Chenrezig lives on Mount Potala. Karmapa is one of Chenrezig's emanation/pseudopods on earth. To

HH Karmapa with white cockatoo, KTD Woodstock NY, 1980.
(Courtesy of Dale Brozosky)

be transported to Dewachen is one of the greatest aspirations of many Mahayana Buddhists—such as the large Pure Land School in East Asia—for once there, liberation and ultimate enlightenment are assured.

The late 16th Karmapa was an avid bird lover and collector. He had countless rare birds at his aviary upstairs at Rumtek monastery in Sikkim, many of which he had taught to intone his own name mantra, Karmapa Khyenno! Action Master, please heed me.

His Holiness used to jokingly tell visitors: "Those birds are some of my late monks reborn." At other times he would say,

Chenrezig. (Painting by Diane Barker)

"Those birds seem to stay in their cages and chant better than many of my monastery's monks!"

One day Karmapa, the living buddha, entered the aviary. A large, gorgeously multicolored tropical parrot was chattering, "Karmapa Khyenno! Karmapa Khyenno!" (Karmapa, heed me, bless me!) His Holiness stood directly before the meditating parrot, and pointed his finger right at the bird in an act of instantaneous phowa. The bird immediately dropped dead. "He is in Dewachen (the Pure Land) now," the Karmapa said.

Trulshik Rinpoche's Dream

Venerable Trulshik Rinpoche is the august abbot of one of the world's loftiest monasteries, Thubten Choling, not far from the Mount Everest base camp eighteen-thousand feet above sea level. For years he rarely left his Himalayan retreat. In recent years he has built a gompa on Amitabha Mountain behind Swayambhu Hill in Kathmandu Valley. This venerable master passed away in 2011.

Decades ago, the abbot Trulshik Rinpoche aspired to receive the esoteric Mahakala empowerment from His Holiness the 16th Gyalwang Karmapa, the Kagyu hierarch. However, no matter how often Trulshik tried to meet the Living Buddha, his plans were thwarted. When he tried to travel to the Karmapa's monastery in Sikkim, it was for various reasons impossible. Whenever he tried to meet His Holiness in India, unexpected events unfailingly intervened. The abbot wondered, "Is there a negative force or inner obstacle hindering me?" Therefore, Trulshik performed the appropriate purification rites, prayers and offerings, and chanted continuously in an effort to dispel karmic obstacles, accumulate karmic merits and favourable conditions, and purify himself. How disappointed he was, then, when His Holiness passed away in 1981 without conferring upon him the desired initiatory empowerment.

One night, however—as if in answer to his wholehearted prayers—the late great Buddha Karmapa himself appeared in the clear light of Trulshik's dreams. Karmapa, the Action Master, bestowed completely the elaborate Mahakala Dharma Protector empowerment upon him. For him there was no difference between dream experience and everyday reality, life and death. Near the end of this blessed transmission dream, the abbot Trulshik asked: "What is real?" "Everything is equally real and unreal," Karmapa replied. "Nothing is real. In the absolute, everything is equally empty, transparent; nothing happens. In the relative, each karmic act counts."

Trulshik Rinpoche later acknowledged His Holiness' unique power and benediction. "Innate wisdom is the ultimate dharma protector," he said. "The Karmapa genuinely embodies all the buddhas and bodhisattvas. He completely initiated and empowered me."

THE WONDROUS ACTIVITIES
OF HIS HOLINESS
THE 16th GYALWANG KARMAPA
by Zhanag Dzogpa Tenzin Namgyal

*Zhanag Dzogpa Tenzin Namgyal (1933–2005) served as the
General Secretary to both His Holiness the 16th Karmapa, as
well as the 17th Karmapa, Ogyen Trinley Dorje. This account comes
from a talk Tenzin Namgyal gave at the request of some devotees at
Thrangu Tashi Chöling in Bodhnath, Nepal, in 1989. Peter Roberts
translated from Tibetan.*

Until 1981 I was the personal secretary of His Holiness the 16th
Gyalwang Karmapa. For the last thirty years of my life, I was next
to the Karmapa most of the time and wrote down almost every
word that he said, teachings that he gave, and letters that he wrote,
including the recognition letters of the various *tulkus*. I have wanted to write an official biography of the Gyalwang Karmapa and to
speak about another side of the Karmapa, which I will do now.

The subject of my talk is about the activities of the Buddha
Karmapa, the ocean of unlimited activities of the Karmapa's three
secrets of body, speech, and mind. It is something really indescrib-
able. The Karmapa appeared in this world as a human being, and

HH 16th Karmapa wearing the Black Crown, Rumtek. (Copyright Lars Gammeltoft)

I had the good fortune of being his attendant for thirty years. So, what I will describe is what I witnessed. In fact, it is impossible to convey everything, so all I can do is share the main things I experienced by presenting a brief account.

One of the main activities of the Karmapa is to wear the Black Crown in order to benefit many beings. I will give a brief history of the Black Crown.

The Black Crown

Many eons ago, a prince went into the mountains and meditated. He remained in *samadhi* for hundreds of thousands of years and became known as the "Sage Who Gave Rise to Realization." The *dakinis* had great faith in him and assembled before him. Each dakini pulled a strand of hair from her head as an offering to him. The hair was woven into a crown. As they all had black hair, the crown became known as "The Black Crown"; and because they were all wisdom dakinis, it was seen as a manifestation of ultimate, self-arisen wisdom. They crowned the Sage with this very crown of empowerment that is adorned with symbols of the sun and moon.

The Origin of the Inner and Outer Crown

Eventually "The Sage Who Gave Rise to Realization" became the great Brahmin tantric master, Saraha who was reborn in Tibet as Düsum Khyenpa, the first Glorious Karmapa.

All Karmapas manifest the Inner Black Crown throughout their lifetimes; it is ever-present in its subtle form as the spontaneous manifestation of ultimate wisdom and is not something that can be obtained. Having realization of ultimate wisdom, this subtle crown is naturally present. Therefore, all Karmapas have had the inner form of the Crown continuously, up to the 16th Gyalwang Karmapa. If someone has clear awareness and very pure karma, they can see it and I have heard accounts of people having seen it.

The 5th Karmapa, Deshin Shegpa was invited to China. The Emperor of the Ming Dynasty during those times was an emanation of Manjushri, so he had very pure karma. He saw the Crown on the Karmapa's head and said to him, "You are wearing a wonderful and excellent crown. If it were possible to have people see it, if I could have one made that looks the same, you could wear it so that others could see it. Would that bring great benefit to beings?" Karmapa Deshin Shegpa replied, "It is all right for you to make one. It will be of great benefit to beings." So the Emperor had a replica of the Crown made, which is the outer Crown that the Karmapa puts on during a grand ceremony for people to see—they see the outer Crown, which is a replica of the inner wisdom Crown. That was a description of the origin of the inner and outer Black Crown, which is a manifestation of wisdom and is always inseparably present with all Karmapas.

Question: Did anyone see the inner Crown during the life of the 16th Karmapa?
Tenzin Namgyal: Yes, there were people who saw it. I will describe this.

The tradition says that it is necessary for the Karmapa to visit and pay respect to the Dalai Lama. All Karmapas would go to see him; they would take off their hat and prostrate to him. When the 16th Karmapa was in his 8th year, together with his father, he went to the Dalai Lama, the 13th at that time. The Dalai Lama and his minister entered the audience room and the Karmapa performed prostrations. The Dalai Lama and his minister noticed that the Karmapa was wearing a hat, so the minister said, "Why are you prostrating with your hat on? That will not do!" He asked the father, "Where do you come from, a remote valley? Don't you know that it is not allowed to wear a hat when you prostrate? That is a big mistake." The father responded, "He is not wearing a hat. He hasn't even brought a hat along. The Karmapas always have a Wis-

dom Hat on, so probably this is the hat that you see him wearing."
Having heard this, the Dalai Lama and his minister were amazed
and felt great faith in the Karmapa. Then the Dalai Lama wrote
a long-life prayer for him. This was the first occasion in which the
secret hat was seen in the life of the 16th Karmapa, so it is quite an
extraordinary incident.

Later, when the 16th Karmapa was staying at Palpung Monastery to receive teachings from the previous Tai Situ Rinpoche, he
travelled to a monastery in Litang. On the way he and his escorts
passed Dsongsar Monastery, the monastery of Jamyang Khyentse
Rinpoche. The first and previous Jamyang Khyentse Rinpoche
was there. At that time, Jamyang Khyentse saw the Karmapa as
Düsum Khyenpa, the first Karmapa, and saw the Black Crown
floating in space above his head while he was prostrating to him.
So, he saw this and they heard Jamyang Khyentse describe what
he had seen.

In 1944, when the Karmapa was going on pilgrimage through
the south of Tibet, the 2nd King of Bhutan, Jigme Wangchuk, invited him to Bhutan. When the king met the Karmapa, he saw the
Karmapa's Crown and felt very great devotion for him from the
depths of his heart.

When the Karmapa left, the king cried like a little child—he
cried because of his great devotion and perfect faith after having
met the Gyalwang Karmapa.

In 1967, the Karmapa was invited to Ladakh. At that time a girl
from Kashmir without any faith came to see him. As the Karmapa
performed the Black Crown Ceremony, the girl saw the inner wisdom Hat inseparably on his head; when he placed the fabricated
outer Crown on his head, she saw the inner one inside the outer
Crown. This happened in Ladakh at that time.

Tashi Lada, who was responsible for looking after the college in
Rumtek, once lived near Tsurphu. When he was eleven years old,
he escorted his father to pay respects to the Karmapa. Next to the
Karmapa's seat in his room was a statue of the Karmapa. When

Tashi Lada entered the room he saw two statues and saw one moving about. He told his father, "There are two statues of the Karmapa. One is motionless and the other one is moving about. Which is the real one?" He had seen the statue with the Black Crown and he could see the real Karmapa with the inner Crown; they were identical, while one was moving about. He was very young when this happened and did not know anything about the Black Crown at that time. There are many other accounts about people actually seeing the inner Black Crown.

Wonders so True

When the 16th Karmapa was twelve years old and travelling from Tsurphu to Kham in East Tibet, he came to a village called Drome that is situated in an area called Tsumbu. At that time the river was frozen and he went to play on the ice. Later when the ice melted his footprints could be seen on the water and they remained there. Apart from Padmasambhava, the Karmapa is the only great master known to have left his footprints on water.

When the Karmapa was travelling in Kham, he reached a place called Chang Tang, the location of the monastery of Dechen Rinpoche. The Karmapa had a young antelope that had been given to him and also had his tiny pet puppy, called Yidrug, along with him. When they arrived at the monastery with his dog and antelope, both animals left footprints on a stone, which can still be seen.

When the Karmapa went to a nunnery to bless the site, he threw kernels of grain into the room; they usually do not roll under objects. But when the Karmapa threw the grains there, they rolled underneath all the objects in the room—they rolled under the feet of the statues and many lay in the hands of the statues. Half of some and the whole of other kernels transformed into *ringsel* ("precious white relics"). Some have been preserved from that consecration and are now in Rumtek.

HH 16th Karmapa in the meditation pose of Karma Pakshi, the 2nd Karmapa. (Courtesy of Norma Levine)

One time the Karmapa went to Phayul Monastery. The abbot there was a famous and great *siddha*. When the Karmapa arrived, he tied the sword he had into a knot. He gave it to the siddha and told him, "I am a siddha, too."

When the Karmapa went to a Bonpo Monastery in Nitang

with Tai Situ Rinpoche, they both left footprints in the stone; their horses did too.

How the 16th Karmapa Recognized Reincarnations

After he returned from a visit to China, the Karmapa recognized the 12th Tai Situ Rinpoche. He did not perform a divination with a *mala* or throw dice, as is sometimes the case. The same morning the child was born, the Karmapa chanted, rested in meditation, and immediately described where the Tai Situpa could be found. I was the secretary and had to write it all down—where he was born, what his name was, his father's name, his mother's name, what direction his house faced, and how far away they were, what year, whether the family was noble, poor, or wealthy. He described everything in meditation, and I wrote it all down. He saw everything very clearly, like looking into a mirror.

It is quite marvellous how the Karmapa recognized the Rinpoches Tai Situ, Jamgön Kongtrul, and the Sharmapa. For example, after recognizing Tai Situ Rinpoche and Shamarpa, the Karmapa found Jamgön Kongtrul in the same way. He specified all the details of where he was born. He said that there were seven people in the family of Jamgön Kongtrul, so a search team was sent to find the family according to these instructions. However, they found the family, but there were only six members. The search party returned to the Karmapa and told him that everything accorded with his description, the position of the house in relation to the Jowo Temple in Lhasa, and so on. They told him that there were only six instead of seven family members, though. The Karmapa answered, "One is inside the mother." He was Jamgön Kongtrul Rinpoche's younger brother.

Then there was the recognition of Gyaltsab Rinpoche. In his letter, the Karmapa described everything, and even gave the

HH 16th Karmapa and 12th Tai Situ Rinpoche. (Courtesy of Norma Levine)

name of the father, Tutob Lodrö. The search party found the house and the mother living with the baby, however the father's name was Tenzin Chögye. They discovered that Tenzin Chögye was Tutob Lodrö's brother. Tutob Lodrö had left to live somewhere else, so people had assumed that Tenzin Chögye was the baby's father. The Karmapa identified the real father. Not only was he able to recognize the birth of a tulku, he also recognized the father.

When seeing the rebirth of Sangye Nyenpa Rinpoche, in his letter the Karmapa said that his father's name was Sangye Legpa, the Tibetan name for the Buddha. The party with the letter in their hand went to Bhutan; they looked all around the area for someone with that name, but they could not find him. In fact, the father was the steward of the Guru Rinpoche Temple, and everyone called him Kungnyo ("Steward"); nobody called him by his real name. The search party gave up and reported back that they could not find anybody with the name Sangye Legpa; only a steward looking after the Guru Rinpoche Temple lived there. The Karmapa replied, "It is the steward. Go back and ask him his name." They did and found out that his name was Sangye Legpa.

The Karmapa recognized Sönam Garwang when his father visited him. He told his father that the baby his wife was carrying in her body was Tulku Sönam Garwang. In this way, he recognized Pawo Rinpoche and many other tulkus, too. ... The Karmapa recognizes them directly through his clairvoyance. This is truly amazing.

The monasteries of the Karmapa and Traleg Kyabgon Rinpoche in Tibet are very far apart. One time someone came to the Karmapa to find the incarnation of Traleg Rinpoche. At that time, the Chinese were always in the country, so the search party asked the Karmapa to please give them a direct answer due to all the difficult circumstances in those times. The Karmapa did this; he wrote that Traleg Rinpoche was still in the body of his mother and that they may only open the letter on the 12th day of the 1st month of the following year. They did as told and on that particular day they opened the letter stating where he had been born. In fact, Traleg Rinpoche was born on the 8th day of that month, exactly 4 days before they opened the letter.

There are many throne-holders and great masters of the teachings, but the Karmapa is the most significant when it comes to recognizing tulkus. When the 1st Karmapa, Düsum Khyenpa lived, there was no tradition or institution of tulkus. The rebirth of the 1st Karmapa as the 2nd Karmapa, marks the beginning of the institution of tulkus, reincarnate lamas. The recognition of rebirths and enthronements developed and spread in Tibet after the succession of the glorious Karmapas.

Question: What do the footprints in the water look like? Are they made of ice or something?
Tenzin Namgyal: At the time the Karmapa was 12. I wasn't there, but people witnessed this and described them as whole footprints on the water. First they were ice. They were made on the ice and when it melted the footprints remained on the water. For as long as he was in Tibet, the footprints remained in Drome, which is situated in the area of Tsumbu. However, I don't know whether they are still there now.

Question: Would you say something about the birth of the Karmapa himself?
Tenzin Namgyal: About the 16th Karmapa and the 17th? I can tell you about what has happened in the past but not about what is going to happen in the future. Regarding the Karmapa's prophecy letter, a letter for the birth of the 17th Karmapa, as seen by the tulkus, has to be written by himself. If someone else wrote it, people might doubt that it is genuine.

The Karmapa recognizes and identifies his own rebirth. It should be interesting for scientists to discover evidence for a future and past life and to explain how the Karmapa identifies his next birth. Wouldn't that astound scientists?

I have a copy of the letter written by the 15th Karmapa to identify the 16th, so I know what was written. In the letter, the 15th Karmapa stated that he would be born east of Tsurphu, near the shore of the Golden River (the shore at which he was born), at the glorious mountain (the mountain behind which he was born), Atup (the family name), the ox (the astrological month in which he was born), the mouse (the year he was born). The 15th Karmapa wrote the letter like that and this accorded with his next birth. The 16th Karmapa also wrote and left a letter to identify the 17th Karmapa.

Question: Did the 1st Karmapa see how many incarnations of Karmapas there would be?
Tenzin Namgyal: This is an important subject, which you find in the Buddha's teachings, who spoke of the Karmapa's coming. Guru Rinpoche also prophesied the coming of the Karmapa in hidden texts; in the *termas* it is stated that there will be 21 Karmapas in all.

Question: I heard that the 17th Karmapa is going to be the most powerful of all. Is that true?
Tenzin Namgyal: It is said that the sacred power of the Karmapa will depend upon living beings and disciples. There is no difference in the power and blessings of the Karmapas, but it just depends upon the followers. Just like the moon in the sky, its reflection depends upon the water on which it is reflected. If you have pure and undisturbed water, the reflection is perfect, otherwise not, but the moon stays the same. This is the same with the Karmapas—their blessings and sacred power are the same, but it all depends upon the recipients.

Question: What will happen when the 21st Karmapa dies? What is the reason?
Tenzin Namgyal: We see only one Karmapa—that is our way of seeing things. In fact, there are hundreds of millions of Karmapas emanating wherever help is needed. We hear that the 21st Karmapa will pass away and that there will not be any more. The reason for this is that he works to help all beings in this world. When this

world is finished, he will have finished too, and will then move to another realm.

Question: What was the main practice of the Karmapa?
Tenzin Namgyal: The main practice of the 16th Karmapa was Tara, a practice he always did.
Every morning of every day, he would do the Vajradhara, Manjushri, and Tara sadhana, and in the evenings he always did the

A drawing of Tara by the 17th Karmapa.

Mahakala sadhana, the protector practice. However, you could say that his main practice was the great non-meditation practice. There are different levels in Mahamudra practice: lesser, middle, and great one-taste, the last level being non-meditation, which also consists of lesser, middle, and great. The Karmapa's practice was great non-meditation. We know this, because once he was talking to the 2nd Jamgön Kongtrul Rinpoche, Khyentse Öser, and they discussed this practice. Khyentse Öser told him, "Your realization is right at the state of great non-meditation. That is your practice." He wrote that down in the account of his life, so it is definitely true. So, his real practice was great non-meditation.

Question: Why did only one Karmapa marry?

Tenzin Namgyal: The reason why only one Karmapa married, while the others didn't, was that he was practicing Nyingma teachings as well as Kagyu teachings; following the Nyingma tradition he married. However, it really makes no difference whether he married or not; it is not the same as thinking, "It's better to be married" or "It's worth being married"—it really makes no difference.

Question: There's a photo of the 16th Karmapa—he is sitting on his throne and his body is translucent (p. 143). Can you explain this?

Tenzin Namgyal: Yes, I have seen the picture. If one has faith and devotion in the Karmapa, then seeing this picture will really increase one's conviction in him. The photograph was taken while he was in meditative *shunyata*—then his body became translucent and you can see through it.

Question: Do beings such as the Karmapa always appear as lamas? Do they appear as other beings, perhaps even as women?

Tenzin Namgyal: Many beings become manifestations of lamas— high people, low people, and animals. Buddhas also take birth as animals, or as parks, bridges, and so on. They manifest in all sorts of ways. The dakinis who offered their hair for the Black Crown were also emanations, so there are lots of female beings.

In the Tibetan tradition, there are great female masters, such as Machig Labdrön and the consort of the XVth Karmapa; her name was Khandro Chenmo ("Great Dakini"). If you look at the history of India, there was Gelongma Palmo, who benefited beings immensely. In terms of emanations, there is no distinction between male and female—whatever benefits beings.

Wondrous Activities

The Karmapa left Palpung Monastery for Tsurmang Monastery of Garwang Rinpoche in 1940. Since it was very cold, he stayed there that winter. During that time there was a special day for Jetsun Milarepa. On this day the Karmapa did Milarepa Guru Yoga and had a vision of him in a great sphere of light. The Karmapa wrote a prayer to Milarepa that reads: "Milarepa appeared in the midst of all this light, like the bright sunlight." This prayer still exists in his own handwriting, and we can see it.

Many miracles happened while the Karmapa was staying at Tsurmang. When the Karmapa was in his own room and looking out the window onto the courtyard, he saw two horses, one called Zhutrul ("Miracle"), which belonged to Situ Rinpoche, and the other called Tamug ("Brown Horse"), which belonged to Beru Rinpoche. In fact, the miracles I mentioned about the horses leaving footprints on stones were by these horses. This time they were being groomed and fed to become even more beautiful so that they could be presented as a gift. These horses were very renowned for having left their footprints in many places. In a text, Chökyi Dekyi Lingpa Rinpoche wrote about what these horses with great power would become and this happened. Not only one or two people witnessed the footprints these horses left in stone, but also everybody saw them.

At that time the Karmapa told the previous Tsurmang Garwang Tulku that he was going to give him a very big present. Tsurmang Tulku pondered, "Oh, I wonder what that is." The Karmapa
brought a crystal about the size of a hand, and Tsurmang Garwang
wondered, "Why is he giving me a crystal that's not very valuable?
But he gave it to me, so it's an important present." He then went
to the window and threw the crystal onto the stone pavement
of the courtyard. The crystal cut into the stone and stuck there,
not broken or split. Garwang ran downstairs and thought, "He is
a great siddha, and he gave me such a fabulous present." He called
everyone to come and see how the crystal stuck in the stone. He
kept this crystal as a great blessing, and this was something everyone could witness. I wasn't there at the time, but all of the Karmapa's attendants told me about this event. I have seen the crystal,
because Tsurmang Garwang Rinpoche kept it.

A new temple was being built next to the older temple at Tsurphu, so there were lots of monks as well as older people working
there. One night when the Karmapa was there in 1944, he told
one of the treasurers at Tsurphu to go and check that area. He
told him that there would be a sign there. The treasurer went at
night with the secretary of Tsurphu and someone called Norbu.
They searched for a sign, but the only thing they saw was a stone
that looked like the surface of water—it had the colour of water
and the designs on it were like ripples on water—it was the only
interesting thing they could see. They returned to the Karmapa
and told him. He replied to them, "Yes, that is it, so everything is
fine. The signs are there, so tomorrow something will happen."
The next day the workers dug about 5 ft. under the stone and
found a treasure of gold, the amount a coolie could carry in a bag.
They laid a *khatag* on the stone and told the Karmapa what had
happened. He reacted in a way that showed that he already knew
and told them, "So, you have found the gold." He asked them,
"How did you find it?" They told him the story, and he remained

as calm as someone who knows. Then he told them, "You must look after this gold very well and not let anyone else get their hands on it, because it is a gift from Karma Dorje Gyalpo, one of the guardian deities of the Karmapas, also one of the water deities. He continued, "Nobody else should use it, because it is a gift for the monastery." So they used the gold for the Tara statues, for the *gyanjara* on the top of the roof of the temple, and for all the sacred things in the temple. Everybody saw the gold that was found.

After the 21 Tara statues at Tsurphu were completed and the mantras and all the things necessary to fill the inside of the statues had been done by Yeunzin Rinpoche, the Karmapa performed the ceremony of blessing the statues. When he did this and threw the grains, everyone saw that the main Tara not only moved but also grew in size. The Tara statues had been placed in boxes designed specifically for them, but the main Tara was now 5-finger widths too big for the box after the blessing ceremony, because the wisdom deity who had been invited merged into her. When the 16th Karmapa blessed this statue, the Great Buddha Statue at Tsurphu moved. This also happened when the 2nd Karmapa blessed a statue there.

One time when the Karmapa and his escorts were travelling from Tsurmang to Tsurphu, they were going through the area of Ani Öd. Ani Pen-kye is the local deity of that area, who had made offerings to previous Karmapas. The deity had offered a huge *phurba* to the 16th Karmapa, Tegchog Dorje, for the practice of Dorje Phurba, Vajrakilaya. This deity gave the 15th Karmapa a sword. When the 16th Karmapa was travelling through the area, the deity came to greet him. The Karmapa was sitting at the table with his escorts and they saw a big *zhee* (a black and white onyx stone) on the table. Nobody saw where it had come from. The monks looked around but didn't see anybody, just the precious stone, which was called Ma-me ("Precious Stone without a Cord"). As they continued along their journey and reached a mountain, the

HH 16th Karmapa in Beijing in 1954 during a trip with HH Dalai Lama.
(Photographer unknown)

Karmapa blessed and offered a white yak to Ninchen Tangla, the local mountain deity; then they set the yak free. The yak went straight ahead as though it was being led, but it was on its own. The Karmapa explained that Ninchen Tangla had actually arrived to greet him and that the deity was there to accept the yak and lead it away. It is said that Ninchen Tangla is a Bodhisattva on the 8th *bhumi*, and the Karmapa told us, "Having met him, this is true, and he looked very majestic. These deities are on the side of goodness, on the white side, and he is one of the most powerful ones."

In 1947 the Karmapa was twenty-four years old and went to West Tibet. At one point the group had to cross the Upper Tsangpo River, which isn't deep in the morning but becomes a torrent when the snow melts during the course of the day. The group told the Karmapa, "We have to leave very early in order to cross the river, otherwise we can't." The Karmapa seemed annoyed about leaving so early. A few in the group left on their own at dawn, but the Karmapa didn't leave until 10:00 or 11:00 a.m., and by then the river was very deep. Those who stayed behind with him thought, "Now it is too deep." The Karmapa was travelling in a palanquin given to the 5th Karmapa by the Ming Emperor; it was attached to two strong poles, and eight people who had specific uniforms and wore special hats had to carry it. The Karmapa insisted that they cross the river and that two mules pull the palanquin. The mules could not reach the ground when they were in the middle of the river, so they swam while the palanquin rose higher and higher. The carriers held it firmly, hoping it would not tip over. Two carriers, Chig Tarche and Rinchen Puntsok were shorter than the other six and were holding on for their lives when they both lost their grip, fell into the river, and were swept away by the current. Thousands of people who lined the shores to see the Karmapa saw Chig Tarche and Rinchen Puntsok sitting on the bank of the other side of the river with their clothes and hats on, as though they had stepped off a boat. Everyone was astounded about their ease; this is another miracle witnessed by many people. Actually, they had assembled along the shores to witness the Karmapa and now they saw that even his carriers have miraculous powers. But it wasn't their doing, rather that of the Karmapa.

The Karmapa continued the pilgrimage to Bodhgaya, India,

from West Tibet. There is a mountain near Bodhgaya, which is the base of the six-armed Mahakala, and this is the location of the Jetavana Charnel Ground. When there, he actually saw the six-armed Mahakala, who told him that he would protect his teachings. Ever since then, this has been true.

The Karmapa loved birds and had many that he fed every day. Birds usually fall over when they die, but when the Karmapa's birds died, they sat upright for three or four days, like advanced meditators.

The Karmapa's dog, called Yidruk, who left footprints in rocks, always sat on the Karmapa's lap. While in West Tibet, many worms crawled around a wound that Yidruk had; the wound became bigger and bigger and more worms crawled over the dog's entire body as a result. People who saw this felt so sorry for Yidruk and asked the Karmapa to please do something about it. He didn't seem to respond, though, and the people begged, "We must use medicine against these worms." The Karmapa told them, "No, there is no need, because this dog is Bodhisattva Maitreya." You know the story about Maitreya appearing to Asanga as a dog? Therefore the Karmapa told them, "This is Maitreya." There is a cemetery called "The Cemetery of the 500 Arhats' in West Tibet. When Yidruk died, the Karmapa took his remains there personally.

Question: I heard that when the 16th Karmapa was cremated, his heart came out.

Tenzin Namgyal: When he passed away in 1981, he was cremated. There are four portals in the *stupa*, one in each cardinal direction, and Tai Situ Rinpoche was standing at the side from which it came out. This is something that happens when exceptional teachers like Gampopa and the 16th Karmapa are cremated: their eyes, tongue, and heart gather into a lump. This exceptional relic of the 16th Karmapa is inside the Great Stupa in his room at Rumtek Monastery. One must see it when one goes to Rumtek and do wishing-prayers there. Whatever you wish for there will come true.

When we fled Tibet in 1959, I was asked to be one of the Karmapa's attendants. I was all alone, without my family, and the Karmapa's driver could not take the car, because the Chinese had destroyed it. They fled on horseback and reached Drongsa in Bhutan; I was young, so I walked. I was very tired when we reached the refugee camp and ate the joints of animals that the Bhutanese generously cooked for us. Exhausted from all the duties that needed to be done, one day I leaned against a tent while chewing on a cooked bone. I accidentally breathed in the bone when I slipped and fell and woke up choking. I tried everything to get it out, coughed and drank so that it would come out, but the bone was stuck in my lungs; blood and pus came gushing out of my mouth when I coughed for six whole months. When I arrived at Rumtek, everyone thought I had tuberculosis. People always received medicine from the Karmapa when they were sick and they recovered quickly—not me. He told me, "It looks like your illness is due to past karma. The best treatment is to drink my urine. Maybe this will help." I did so every day from them on. A few weeks later we were climbing up and down the steep gorge that separates Rumtek from Gangtok. When we arrived at Gangtok, I spat out a glass-full of pus every time I coughed every night. The Karmapa told me that he could smell the pus on my breath when I opened the door to his room. The Karmapa and his escorts then returned to Rumtek on horseback; he told me to stay behind another day. I was very upset and thought, "I have been working for the Karmapa all these years and this is how he treats me." That night I thought, "The Karmapa is behaving very badly towards me. All the others are healthy and may ride on horses, but poor me, I have to walk." I was very annoyed all night, because I couldn't say anything to the Karmapa but simply had to wait.

The next day I had to scramble down the slope to return to Rumtek and didn't cough. When I climbed the steep slope to reach the Monastery, I could only take ten steps and then had to sit

HH 16th Karmapa. (Courtesy of Norma Levine)

down and rest. I coughed pus and blood again and again. Then I felt a huge lump in my throat and thought a neck bone had broken from coughing so much. I was terribly frightened; something came out of my mouth and it looked like my whole neck. Then I recognized that I was holding the bone that I had swallowed months earlier in my hand and was very happy—I felt the same joy it is said that practitioners experience when they attain the first bodhisattva bhumi. Now I know what that joy is like and felt inconceivable conviction in the Gyalwa Karmapa. Had I left a day earlier and gone by horseback, the bone would never have come out and I would have died. I was already as thin as Milarepa probably was—just skin and bones. People were already whispering to each other, "He will die soon." Having spit out the bone, I was able to reach the top of the hill in one go. Ever since then, I have total certainty and pure devotion in the Karmapa, not just faith, but changeless and unshakeable conviction, and I do whatever he says. The Karmapa saw what was taking place and saved my life. This is truly amazing.

Thank you very much.

May virtue increase!

Transcribed and edited by Gaby Hollmann (1992/2007), responsible for all errors in this account.

MEMORIES FROM TSURPHU MONASTERY
by Lama Khanchuk

L ama Khanchuk first met the 16th Karmapa at the age of three when he went from Derge with his family to Lhasa on pilgrimage. The Karmapa was then 20 years old.

At the age of seven, he became a monk at Tsurphu monastery. There he heard stories about the young 16th Karmapa's education and how even he was punished for not studying. One of his tutors was dismissed by his parents because of his harsh punishments. Another, who was more lenient, came to take his place but still the young Karmapa was naughty. Before this tutor administered corporal punishment, he made prostrations to the Karmapa, weeping all the while.

Lama Khanchuk told these stories to Jingliu Jiang

Karmapa and the Bonpo Pilgrim

A few months after I became a monk, the Karmapa went on pilgrimage to Mt. Kailash where he met a young Bonpo pilgrim. The young man was walking around the mountain anticlockwise following the tradition of the Bon, which is contrary to the clockwise tradition of Tibetan Buddhism. Karmapa tried to persuade the young man to walk clockwise. They continued walking while they argued. Not knowing his fellow pilgrim was the Karmapa, the young man was about to unsheathe his sword to resist, when he was stopped by the Karmapa's attendants. They all completed one clockwise circumambulation of the mountain with the Karmapa, when just as suddenly the impetuous young man declared he was now abandoning his deep rooted religious belief to become a Karma Kagyu follower.

Devotees link this story to a similar conversion which had occurred at Mount Kailash when the twelfth-century yogi, Milarepa, defeated a Bonpo priest. The extraordinary coincidence made people have all the more faith in the Karmapa.

A Brocade Terma Treasure

In the 1940s, the Karmapa made certain demands on the Kashag—the Tibetan Government in Lhasa. Government officials proposed that the Karmapa offer a lustrous, precious silk fabric in return for fulfilling his wishes. On the way back to Tsurphu Monastery with his attendant, the Karmapa passed a mountain cave. According to the attendant's description afterwards, at first sight this cave was no different to other forbidding, cold, dark caves. However, after Karmapa stepped into it, the attendant who was waiting outside, suddenly saw the cave glittering, ablaze with light from magnificent Tibetan silks and brocades, the most beautiful he had ever seen. Some time elapsed before the Karmapa walked out, holding a very delicate, brilliant brocade square in his hands, of incomparable beauty. The attendant was greatly surprised to see this. When he returned later to the cave, it was as forbidding, cold and dark as the first time he saw it, exactly as if nothing had ever happened! This brocade square brought out as a terma treasure by the Karmapa is enshrined on the ceiling of Byams-pa Hall at Drepung Monastery near Lhasa.

HE WAS ALWAYS IN SAMADHI
by Gyaltsab Rinpoche

Gyaltsab Rinpoche is a leading incarnate lama (tulku) in the Karma Kagyu lineage of Tibetan Buddhism. He is believed by his followers to embody the activity of Vajrapani.

The first Gyaltsab Rinpoche (1427–1489) received the title Goshir (literally: "state teacher") from the Emperor of China. In Tibet, Gyaltsab Rinpoche is known as Tsurphu Goshir Gyaltsab Rinpoche. He is the regent looking after Tsurphu monastery and the interests of the Karmapas in between two Karmapas. In Tsurphu, Gyaltsab Rinpoche's monastery Chogar Gong lies directly behind Karmapa's monastery. In Sikkim his monastery is at Ralang in South Sikkim.

Gyaltsab Rinpoche was recognized by His Holiness the 16th Karmapa. After the official enthronement by the 16th Karmapa in 1959, Gyaltsab Rinpoche made the journey to Sikkim together with His Holiness.

The activities of His Holiness the 16th Karmapa are all about benefiting sentient beings. We can see that His Holiness benefits *human* beings by giving teachings and empowerments, but at the same time he is also benefiting animals, insects, fish, birds. There are many stories about His Holiness Karmapa benefiting non-humans, or invisible beings by giving them blessing, teachings, empowerments. But these are stories that we cannot say much about.

One of the amazing qualities of His Holiness the Karmapa is that he is clairvoyant, and has the ability to read other's minds. There are many stories about the Karmapa talking to some people by reading their minds. He would talk with them and give them guidance. He was always in samadhi, always in meditation, like Lord Buddha, like the 7th Karmapa, and Lord Gampopa. This is one of his wonderful qualities.

There were many situations when His Holiness Karmapa didn't have a translator and he didn't speak English or Hindi. But when he met with Westerners or Indians, he could read their minds, understand what they wanted and gave them teachings and guidance without a translator. This is the essence of his activity. I saw it many times.

KARMAPA PLAYS IN THE SAND
by Kalsang Rinpoche

The Venerable K.C. Lama Kalsang Rinpoche was born in Tibet ninety-five years ago, and came to India in 1961. He is an accomplished Vajrayana master who has been a source of inspiration and healing to the people of Bylakuppe for fifty years. He first visited the West in 1996, and continued to travel internationally offering insightful teachings and compassionate guidance. Over the years, Rinpoche's powerful spiritual teachings have helped people where other methods have failed. He is a holder of the Gesar of Ling mo or divination lineage and a chöd practitioner.

Kalsang Rinpoche entered parinirvana in May, 2013.

I was about thirteen years old when Jamgön Kongtrul, the son of the 15th Karmapa, came officially to visit Eastern Tibet and inspected all the temples. When I was eighteen, I went on pilgrimage to the Lhasa area. The 16th Karmapa was already enthroned but he wasn't in the central Tibet region. He had gone back to East Tibet, to the area of his birth place.

One master who is a few years elder to me, told me the following story. This master saw it and he shared his experience. His name is Lama Tipa Pema, from the Riwoche area of Kham. He has now passed away.

HH 16th Karmapa in Tsurphu Summer Lingka. (Photographer unknown)

Shortly after His Holiness the 16th Karmapa was enthroned, there was a very big flood in Lhasa from two rivers. When that happened it was a huge threat to the Jowo and the Jokhang. It was of tremendous concern to the Tibetan government who thought that the Jokhang could be destroyed by flood.

There is a prophecy that people believed in, that the Nagas would invite Lhasa. This means that the Jokhang temple may be taken away by the Nagas. This is why the Tibetan Government finally decided to invite the Karmapa to help, although His Holiness the Dalai Lama was there. Nonetheless, the government invited Karmapa to come to the riverside. They arranged a tent and reception area to welcome him. His Holiness the Karmapa was extremely young at the time.

When the Karmapa got out from his palanquin, he started playing with the sand, making different shapes. He played there for two days, quite casually. Within those two days the water level receded. That is one miracle many people believe.

Then the Government was concerned that the Karmapa would become too powerful. So they requested him to go back to his temple at Tsurphu, urgently.

As I was returning back from Lhasa to my temple in East Tibet, I heard that His Holiness Karmapa was returning to Tsurphu. His mother was with him and he was seeing her off in a public ceremony. Thus I had the opportunity to attend a reception at Tsurmang Monastery where Karmapa would be passing on his way back to Tsurphu. I came on horseback to attend the reception.

At Tsurmang there are three temples. There were so many people you could hardly walk on the ground. The Karmapa was in a palanquin carried by sixteen people, and thus his horse was riderless at that time. His Holiness' horse left an imprint of its hoof on the stone floor outside the monastery. I saw this myself.

THE LIGHT OF THE WORLD
by Ayang Rinpoche

*H*is Eminence K.C. Ayang Rinpoche was born into a nomad-*ic family in eastern Tibet after numerous auspicious signs appeared. He was recognised to be a reincarnate Drikung Kagyu lama by a delegation of high lamas including the 16th Gyalwang Karmapa.*

After finishing his studies and receiving many teachings, he went on pilgrimage in Tibet to many of the holy places of Guru Rinpoche, doing a lengthy retreat at Phulung, where Guru Rinpoche practiced phowa *for a long time. At the end of the retreat, he performed an offering puja which was attended by many naga, who came with offerings and circumambulated his retreat while performing mantras of Guru Rinpoche. Ayang Rinpoche felt that this was a great sign and it might mean that in the future he would be teaching phowa in foreign countries.*

After leaving Tibet, he received the Kalachakra initiation from HH the Dalai Lama in Lhasa, and in Rumtek, HH the 16th Gyalwang Karmapa gave him the initiations and oral transmissions of Chagchen Kundzod Chigshe Kundrol and a special Maha-mudra introduction. He is a lineage-holder of both the Nyingma phowa and Drikung phowa, and has done extensive retreat on the practice.

HH 14th Dalai Lama and HH 16th
Karmapa. (Courtesy of Ward Holmes)

In East Tibet they have independent small kingdoms; they accept the Dalai Lama as just a Lama. They don't accept him as king for all of Tibet because they have many separate kingdoms. For example my parents are not Karma Kagyu followers but belong to another lineage, the Drigung Kagyu, but I remember when I was a child they were always praying to the Karmapa. Similarly, all over Tibet, Karmapa is like the Buddha.

We came to India in 1959, the same year that the Dalai Lama came out. I was around seventeen years old when Tibet was taken over by the communists. Then I met His Holiness Karmapa and received many teachings and empowerments at Rumtek Monastery. The Karmapa was the most important root master of my life.

One story I heard of miracles is from his closest attendant, an old monk called Dronyi Gyaltsen. He told me that when Karmapa was aged ten, he left his footprint in the water. Generally other lamas in history make footprints in the rock; but they can't make that in water. Then his devotees thought, if we drink this water Karmapa's footprint will be in my body and it will make a great blessing. So they took some water and drank it many times but the footprint was still visible in the water. Karmapa showed many kinds of miracles, but not only miracles. His realization is very extraordinary.

For example, it is most important to recognize the true nature of mind. I received that teaching from many different masters. Finally I had clear recognition from the 16th Karmapa. Those great masters who have high realization give empowerments: among these empowerments are body, speech, wisdom. The fourth empowerment is the word empowerment. This is to introduce your true nature of mind through a symbol. That is the word empowerment. I had heard some disciples could recognize the true nature of mind through the word empowerment.

I heard it but I never went to any other master than the 16th Karmapa. He was giving many empowerments, particularly the Vajrasattva empowerment. During the fourth empowerment, the word empowerment, he said, "You have to keep the natural state of mind; be free from all the different kinds of distracting thoughts at this moment." He himself kept to that state. In that moment I had a clear recognition of the true nature of mind. For this reason I say the 16th Karmapa is my special root master. When I say "root master" I can see his picture. Other masters don't have this level.

If one doesn't break samaya with the master, when the master and disciple come together, the true nature of mind will be recognised through the word empowerment. I am keeping samaya with the 17th Karmapa, Ogyen Trinley Dorje, same as with the 16th.

HH Karmapa mandala body.
(Courtesy of Goodie Oberoi)

I have a picture. There is a history regarding this photo: Sikkim is on the border of India and Tibet. One time India and China were about to go to war. Then the Indian army chief came to Karmapa and talked about the war. "It will be very soon. Then there will be a big problem. Please do prayers," he requested Karmapa. Then Karmapa said, "Ok, go down, face the temple and also make prayers. I will look down

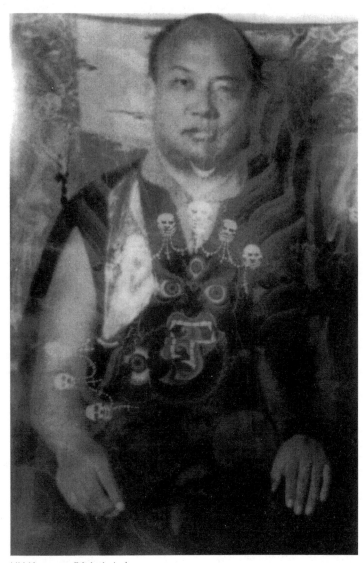

HH Karmapa/Mahakala.[1]
(Courtesy of Ayang Rinpoche)

above the temple and I will do prayers as well."

After his prayer, there was no war between India and China.

I saw another picture like this. His Holiness was standing in Delhi at the Bhutanese Embassy. That moment some Westerner met him and took a photo. They took a picture of Karmapa but he wasn't there. It showed a complete very clear mandala.

In Rumtek one summer time he gave empowerments and teachings for many months. I was in South India and he sent me a message, "I am giving an empowerment; you must come." I had to get a special permit from Delhi. I didn't know what time he was starting the empowerment. He called me many times. Have you got the permit or not? Finally I reached Gangtok. Then his attendants called me. They sent me their car from the monastery.

When I reached the monastery, everybody was inside the temple. His attendants told me to go quickly to the temple, that everybody was waiting. I am not an important person, just his disciple. Those people told me His Holiness had already decided to start at a particular time, but he was waiting and told everyone to recite the Vajrasattva mantra. They thought some king or minister was coming. I sat down and then he started. I'm just an ordinary disciple. But his loving kindness was great for his disciples. His nature was very kind, and he never showed his greatness. I had many meetings alone with him. He was very natural, very kind, always.

The Karmapas had a long connection with the Chinese emperors. One day I was alone with the Karmapa sitting outside on the balcony when he talked about the Chinese Emperor. The Chinese Emperors gave positions to different masters. Sometimes they would say, "You belong to the earth; or to the sky." He showed me a letter written in golden ink on special brocade in which it

---

1 Editor's note: It would seem that in the instant the photograph was taken, the Karmapa's protectors, Mahakala and Mahakali in union manifested on the film, making it look like a coincidental superimposition (see the photograph on the preceeding page).

HH 17th Karmapa performing Black Hat Dance, Bodh Gaya 2012.
(Copyright Filip Wolak)

was said both the earth and sky belong to you. There was a big red stamp on this letter. This level is extraordinary. He's the emanation of all the past, present, and future of the buddhas' activities. His blessing power is great kindness. Many Tibetans experienced

HH 17th Karmapa at Woodstock, 2012.
(Photographer unknown)

HH 17th Karmapa, Losar 2012.
(Photo by Norma Levine)

this with him.

What I described just now are my own experiences with him, not reported from another person. Many Westerners told me just seeing his Crown Ceremony—only that, not even any teaching or empowerment—completely changed their mind, and their lives. Many people just looked at him and their mind completely changed.

I can see the 17th Karmapa Ogyen Trinley Dorge is the same as the 16th Karmapa Rigpe Dorje. Just to look at him, people feel confidence that this is the Karmapa. This natural feeling is very important. Just to look, then we feel confidence. We can only have this experience with very few reincarnate Lamas. Usually Lamas have more attainment as they get older. But this 17th Karmapa was not like a small child from an early age. We can see how he's grown up, every year, every month. His knowledge, his morality, his behaviour, his kindness, whenever he gives teaching or even in his ordinary speech—everything is perfect.

I haven't any doubt that he is the real Karmapa. I don't have any special power, but I follow my feeling. I will continue with him. I can't see any difference between him and 16th Karmapa. I think it is very lucky that he came into this world during the kali yuga time, like the sun shining. He may be the last chance for light in this world.

I never saw any master like the 16th Karmapa, and this one, the 17th. A master like this, is very rare.

THE MAN WHO TURNED
ON THE WORLD
by Michael Hollingshead

British born Michael Hollingshead researched psychedelic drugs and hallucinogens at Harvard University, together with Timothy Leary and Richard Alpert (aka Ram Dass) during the mid-twentieth century. He is said to have introduced a number of famous people to LSD among them Paul McCartney, Keith Richards, Timothy Leary, Richard Burroughs, Alan Ginsberg, John Lennon, George Harrison. He is the author of several books including The Man Who Turned on the World *(1973) in which he describes a meeting with the 16th Karmapa in Nepal.*

It was shortly after the Ambassador's session that Rama Prasad came round to see me about arranging a meeting with the celebrated Buddhist monk saint, His Holiness the Gyalwang Karmapa, who was visiting Kathmandu and staying with the monks at Swayambhunath. Rama knew Karmapa quite well, and had even entertained him once at a reception in his town house. I was naturally very interested in having an audience with Karmapa, for I had heard and read much about him. He was the head of the Kagyudpa order of Tibetan Mahayana Buddhism, and recognised as the 16th Karmapa incarnation.

The audience was arranged for dawn on the following morning, and Rama Prasad said he'd pick me up at my house in his car. I stayed up all that night, preparing myself for the temple meeting, and performing chillum and acid Sadhana. When Rama Prasad collected me, I was very stoned indeed, and could hardly find my way out of the garden into the Mercedes. Then we sped off into the blackness and reached the top of Swayambhu just as the first light of dawn appeared through the gaps between the surrounding mountains. It was a glorious sight. And I felt a very special sense of reverence; there was a holiness about the place, more intense than I had ever experienced there before; my head and heart were open to anything.

We were taken up some stairs to the top floor and shown into an antechamber where a monk tied a piece of orange cloth around my neck. He then indicated that I should follow him, and he led me from the chamber into a huge sal[1] brilliant with tankas, and murals, and statues. At the far end, seated on a throne, sat Karmapa; and next to him, seated on a cushion in the full lotus position, was Rama Prasad.

I approached Karmapa slowly, my eyes to the floor, with short bows every few steps. When I reached the throne, I looked up and saw a beam of bright light issuing from the centre of his silver crown or it may have been a beam of sunlight catching a reflection through the lattice-work windows. But the effect was quite startling. It really could seem that he was emitting light from his "third eye" in the centre of his forehead. I recovered from this startling hallucination, sufficiently anyhow to hand him the white silk scarf I had brought as a present. Karmapa then spoke to me through an interpreter: "According to the tradition since the Buddha, it has been customary to preserve the record of gifts, as a token of one's inner sense of benevolence. This is so

---

1 Editor's note: The word is difficult to source but it can be inferred from the context that it means 'temple' (in Tibetan *lhakhang*).

King of Nepal greeting Karmapa with traditional offering scarf.
(Photographer unknown)

that it may serve as a historical record of the dharma too. Your name will therefore be added to the names of people contributing to this tradition."

I was then asked to say anything I wished to Karmapa. What I wished to say was for the future: to see many of the Lamas and families of the esoteric dharma move to the West. And, how this work could be furthered by the lamas opening a dialogue with the Chiefs and Elders of the North American Indian Tribe called the *Hopi* whose villages I had once visited in Arizona. The lands of the North American Indians stretch from parts of Canada down to the Mexican border and comprise some of the most beautiful countryside in the world, parts of which are remarkably similar to Tibet, particularly in Colorado and New Mexico. But these lands are now under siege again, for, as the indigenous Indian population is encouraged to leave the reservations and accept an alien white culture—which is happening in the case of the young Indians at a truly frightening rate—these holy lands will be taken over in a few years by the US Government, and then by the builders. Yet potentially they could provide a sort of "spiritual backbone" for a future, more spiritualized America.

Karmapa remained silent throughout all this. When I had finished, he beckoned me closer and, as I bent my head, his hands touched the centre of my head, and suddenly, unaccountably, like a bolt, I experienced *Samadhi:* one of the most extraordinary moments of consciousness of which man is capable. And I felt utterly and completely cleansed, as though the divine thunderbolt had gone through me like a million volt charge. It was a feeling that was to remain with me for quite some days.

The memory of this great Initiation persists. I believe that on that special morning when I met Karmapa my life was changed and in ways that I am only now beginning to understand, which I have yet to assimilate, and, in time, express outwardly and through my being. For if ever there were a living god, Karmapa is it: of this I am utterly convinced.

Like all the other Karmapa incarnations, His Holiness[2] is famous for his erudite scholarship, integrity of character, and excellence in yogic practices.

The embodiment of compassion, in human form, Karmapa cares for and loves all human beings, and takes pains for their spiritual salvation. He is equally well-honoured and followed by Kings, Lamas, and laymen, in Tibet, China, Mongolia, India, Nepal, Sikkim, Bhutan, as also throughout south-east Asia, Japan, Ceylon, Burma, Thailand, Canada, Great Britain, USA., Sweden, Denmark, Spain, etc. And daily now Karmapa prays for the world … "May all spiritual leaders enjoy long lives and prosperity. May the Sangha multiply and fulfill their duties. May the blessings of the Dharma liberate all departed souls. In the world may sickness, poverty, wars and all evil influences be cut at the root and destroyed. May all things of the Kali Yuga (Black Age) be dispersed."

---

2 Editor's note: This passage was written in 1973 about the 16th Karmapa.

KARMAPA AND THE GELONGMA
by Kabir Bedi

Kabir Bedi is one of India's most famous international actors, the villain who battled James Bond in "Octopussy," star of the Euro-Italian "Sandokan" series, a voting member of the Oscars Academy, a Knight of the Italian Republic.

His Holiness the 16th Gyalwang Karmapa was a large man with a big laugh. Whenever I think of him, he's sitting cross-legged in maroon robes, hints of yellow beneath, head thrown back, laughing from the belly. But I knew, even when I first met him in the 1960s as a college student in Delhi, that the power of his position, and extent of his religious responsibilities, were no laughing matter. As head of the Kagyupa order in Tibetan Buddhism, he was widely considered second only to the Dalai Lama in worldwide importance. If the Dalai Lama was the Pope, the Karmapa was the Archbishop of Canterbury.

My respect for the Karmapa stemmed from a far more personal reason: he was the guru of my mother, Freda Bedi. He first ordained her as a nun in 1963, and five years later sent her to Hong Kong to receive full ordination as a Gelongma, the highest rank for women in Tibetan Buddhism. Under the Karmapa's tutelage, "Mummy" officially was transformed into "Gelongma Palmo."

She lived at his iconic Rumtek Monastey, high in the Indian Himalayas of Sikkim, for the last decade of her life. It was the fulfilment of her life's religious journey.

Most foreign visitors to Rumtek, in the late 1960s and 1970s, were taken aback when introduced, often by His Holiness, to a fair-skinned, blue-eyed Buddhist nun, who looked and sounded completely English (though she proudly held an Indian passport). Naturally, they wanted to know her story. My mother would tell them, if they insisted, only after their meeting with the Karmapa.

English by birth, Freda Bedi had been one of Mahatma Gandhi's handpicked "satyagrahis," non-violent resisters, and was jailed for leading demonstrations during India's struggle or freedom from the British. In 1953, six years after India's independence, my mother discovered Theravada Buddhism on a United Nations mission in Burma. When the 1959 Tibetan uprising against the Chinese led to over 100,000 refugees following the Dalai Lama into exile in India, my mother was sent by Prime Minister Nehru to oversee the main camp, Misamari in Assam. She was like a mother figure to them. Attending to their problems, she discovered Tibetan Buddhism. Then she met His Holiness Karmapa and that changed the course of her life.

With His Holiness' blessings, she founded the Young Lamas Home School, with small donations doggedly raised, to teach English to incarnated rinpoches and tulkus, from all the Tibetan orders. Unlike other refugees, my mother reasoned, high lamas did not need to be given "a vocation." They already had one. Knowing English was all they needed to preach anywhere.

In 1963, a few years before setting up the Young Lamas Home School, my mother brought home two Kagyupa lamas, who lived with us in Delhi, for about a year, while she taught them English: Trungpa Rinpoche, who went on to found the biggest network of Buddhist centres in America, the Dharmadhatus and Vajradhatus; and Akong Rinpoche, who has built Samyeling, the most beautiful Tibetan monastery in Europe in the wilds of Scotland. Many other "students" of the Young Lamas Home School, heads of important monasteries, also founded major Buddhist centres abroad.

In her final decade, Gelongma Palmo based herself in Rumtek. There she could assist His Holiness as well as receive teachings from him and go into meditation retreats. She always had far-seeing projects, like the meeting she set up with Chief Ned, the American Indian Chief of the Hopis on the Karmapa's first trip to America. Many photographs taken at that time show her at his side. She spent a lot of time lecturing abroad, setting up Kagyu centres from Singapore to South Africa to England and America. His Holiness often expressed in many ways how much he cherished and trusted her.

There was a palpable spiritual power that radiated from the Karmapa. I sensed it whenever I saw him, felt it when he blessed me. At times I didn't see him for many years. Being a well-known international actor, I lived abroad for over two decades, in Hollywood, London and Rome. But some great memories of the Karmapa will always remain. Once I visited His Holiness in Rumtek and, learning of cash flow problems, I offered a small donation. Accepting it gracefully, he instructed that the money be used for the translation of texts. I was dumb-struck he'd chosen to spend it on spreading the dharma, rather than needed running costs. He was that kind of being.

I remember seeing him once in Woodstock, his biggest centre on the East coast, above New York. He'd come to lay the foundation stone of their new Buddhist temple. The day of the ceremony was a morning of sunshine filering through the green pines which covered the hillside. A well decorated spot on the lawns had been pre-determined for the stone to be laid. His Holiness stepped out of the centre's wooded office cabins and looked at the people gathered around, Tibetans and Americans, maybe fifty. Then he looked at the hill above, and briefly at the sun. He strode forward to another spot far removed to the right, pointed to it, talking in Tibetan. That place became the cornerstone of the imposing Bud-

HH 16th Karmapa in Woodstock.
(Courtesy of Dorothea Fischer)

dhist temple that is now a Woodstock landmark, a far cry from the seminal 1960s rockfest that first made the town so famous.

The Karmapa was the only Tibetan religious leader who left Tibet, to base himself in India months before the uprising of 1959. Had he foreseen the calamity that would come upon Tibet? Whatever one believes, he was undoubtedly a man of great vision, and compassion. The extraordinary spread of Kagyupa centres round the world is the 16th Karmapa's greatest legacy. He lived for spreading Buddhist dharma.

In 1977 my mother passed away while attending the World Buddhist conference in Delhi. So, as if blessed even in death, Buddhists from around the world attended her cremation. Four years later, I heard of His Holiness' death in Chicago. His doctors had been amazed by what they experienced with him in his final days. Once again, I felt deep sorrow. It was as if a great link to my past had been lost. But I counted my blessings too. A great man had died, and I'd been part of his incredible life. I'd been blessed by him. And Gelongma Palmo, my mother, had been a significant part of the Karmapa's path-breaking journey to the West.

DUSUM KHYENPA
by Goodie Oberoi

Mrs Goodie Oberoi is the daughter of the late Sardar Bahadur, Rajinder Singh Sahol, one of the wealthiest landlords of the Punjab prior to partition. She was married to Biki Oberoi of the Oberoi Group of Hotels, in November 1959 and had two children with him. She hosted the 16th Karmapa and his heart sons on many occasions at Oberoi hotels around the world. She now lives in New Delhi where she remains steadfast in her spiritual practice and in her devotion to the Karmapa lineage.

During the course of my life, in my mid-thirties, I had an intense longing to know a Tibetan guru and thus started my journey. During this time, I met a lot of spiritual people including the Dalai Lama. In the course of our conversation, he mentioned, that I would be meeting my guru very soon.

When I first heard it, the name "Karmapa" gave me a tingling feeling. Then I met His Holiness, the 16th Karmapa, Rangjung Rigpe Dorje, for the first time in the mid-1970s when he came to Delhi. When I saw him, I touched his feet. He held my hands and asked me to recite OM TARE TUTARE TURE SOHA and joined his forehead to mine. These gestures

HH 16th Karmapa going into his summer house at Rumtek, 1980.
(Copyright Katia Holmes)

made both of us laugh. He held my hands for a long time; we did not speak but I felt I had known him all my life.

After we met, His Holiness had a vision and the following morning, Sister Palmo (Freda Bedi) telephoned me and said, "His Holiness has had a vision and wants to initiate you." When I heard this, I was astounded and felt I was soaring high into the sky. I went there and was initiated into Tibetan Buddhism. I closed my eyes and repeatedly recited OM TARE TUTARE TURE SOHA and took refuge in this. I felt that I had known His Holiness all his life and therefore requested Sister Palmo to ask His Holiness if I had known him before—to which he answered "Yes."

In all his visits to Delhi he always requested me to come to Rumtek. I finally went for three days duration. His Holiness gave up his bedroom for me and moved out of his summer house to the monastery.

I was unaware of the significance of this gesture. In the morning when I awoke, it was cold. I would look at the sunrise through the window and always saw round diamonds—sparkles streaming through the sunlight—this amazed me. However, if I left my room and went into the garden, I was unable to see any sparkles in the sunrise. I remember asking him why I was unable to see the same thing when I walked in the garden. He laughed and said, "You figure that one out."

As mentioned before, I was unaware that I was using his bedroom. One day on our walk, I suggested we go back together to the house. That was when he mentioned that I was staying in his bedroom. This embarrassed me and later I shifted to the study and His Holiness re-occupied his room.

One morning during the Black Crown Ceremony whilst sitting next to Sister Palmo and praying, I looked at him and instead of the 16th Karmapa, I saw a hunched man with almond shaped eyes and elongated ears. In my disbelief, I began pinching myself. Sister Palmo was watching me and nudged me and asked why I was pinching myself. Time stood still— it could have been a minute or a century; I felt hypnotized. I looked at the Karmapa again. He was not wearing his own hat but another one. I really did not know who this was.

Whilst walking back to the house I mentioned to His Holiness what I had seen during the Black Crown Ceremony and described the vision I had of the hunched Lama with almond shaped eyes and elongated ears. He looked at me and then clapped his hands. His attendant came and the Karmapa said something to him. When he returned, the monk was holding a thangka in his hand.

When I looked at it I saw the same person that I had seen in my vision. To my amazement I realized I had seen the first Karmapa, Dusum Khyenpa.

His Holiness went on to say I had first become involved in Buddhism with Dusum Khyenpa. On departing Rumtek he gifted me a thangka for which I was very grateful. His Holiness asked me if I would like to see it; he mentioned that it was over 700 years old. I opened it and to my delight realized that it was a thangka

Dusum Khyenpa tankha presented by HH Karmapa to Mrs Goodie
Oberoi. (Copyright Norma Levine)

of Dusum Khyenpa. He then told Sister Palmo that he had realized my connection with the first Karmapa at our first meeting in
Delhi, well before my vision. I had intended to stay for only three
days but instead of leaving I stayed there for three more weeks and
took initiations.

While I was at Rumtek I noticed white peacocks in the garden. Whenever His Holiness entered the garden, these peacocks would all start dancing and showing off their finery in front of him. It is nature's great spectacle, strutting around with their fans displayed—a live performance. However, when I went out alone, none of them danced.

One evening during his teachings a big beautiful butterfly came and sat on his knee. He knew that the butterfly was dying. He closed his eyes and started reciting. It was a beautiful feeling to see that butterfly die in so much peace and tranquility. He later asked one of his monks to bury the butterfly in the rose garden.

His Holiness knew I had gone through a huge transformation from the life I led to this present being. There was a dramatic change in me. He asked his attendant when I was going back to Delhi. I burst into tears and said that I was not going back and that I wanted to become a nun. I told him that I had a very difficult marriage which was impossible to continue with. Before marriage I was brought up in a traditional, disciplined family with strong values. However, I married into a very worldly family, far from the way I was raised. I was not able to live with the lies and deceit of this new life.

His Holiness asked me, "You want to become a nun? That is the easy way out; you will not be a nun." He then went on to predict my life thereafter. He said, "Your life will become so unhappy, there will be much turmoil, you will make attempts to end your life." At that time all this did not make sense and I questioned him as to whom would do all this to me. He said, "those who are very close to you." He meant my husband and his father. He also went on to say that I would have no one to talk to during this period of my life and would undergo tremendous suffering.

All that he predicted came to pass. He also mentioned that "during this time you will not have a guru after me but I will always be there with you every step of the way guiding you. You will have no guru but you will discover your own spirituality just like

Buddha." His Holiness then made me read Milarepa's life story three times. He said to me, "Do you see what he went through? You will experience the same." I took his predictions in my stride though, because I did not actually believe it—I thought he was only preparing me for the worst.

His Holiness also predicted that there would be a lot of trouble for the new Karmapa and that eventually he would come from Tibet. He said that the 17th Karmapa would be very spiritual and finally all difficulties would be resolved. At that point in time, we were looking for land in Delhi to build a new Institute. I assisted in getting land allotted to them in Mehrauli. When His Holiness went to lay the foundation stone for the building, I accompanied him and I realized he was not well—and that he was suffering with cancer.

His Holiness asked me to accompany him on his trip to the United States for treatment, but being an Indian housewife I had to listen to my husband who did not want me to go. During that time, I always kept abreast with what was happening to His Holiness through his Lamas and understood that he was dying. When his body was brought back in a coffin to Rumtek to be cremated, I was devastated and crying inconsolably.

It was incredible; on the day of the cremation, from nowhere it began drizzling even though there were no signs of rain before. Right after the rain there appeared a double rainbow in which I saw His Holiness being cradled by the rainbow—he was no longer lying on the floor but sitting on the rainbow.

It became very difficult to live without him to guide me through my life. I could, however, feel his presence and started talking to him. Even though he was not physically there, he was always there spiritually, and is still. Certain thoughts would come to mind showing me the right path to follow.

Life was extremely difficult and one could not imagine what I was going through. I was virtually thrown out of my own home but having read Milarepa's life story, I was able to practice patience and tolerance without malice. I thought that His Holiness was speaking about the misery of losing a Guru, but he was not.

All that I was going through brought about physical manifestations in the form of a nervous breakdown. The doctors said that it was all stress related. Twice in my life I almost died and during this time I always found myself bathed in white light in a monastery in Tibet. I saw the 1st Karmapa as a baby and I was holding him. He had almond shaped eyes and big feet. When I did come back to life, I remembered holding the Karmapa like a baby on my hips. I described this to the 17th Karmapa and he said, "Yes," that this was the first Karmapa I had envisioned. I was indeed happy to be in this spiritual world even in my unconscious state of mind.

However, the greatest thing that happened during this time was that I found the Oneness of God. It came to me all on its own. With my new discovery of oneness, I stopped socializing and going to parties. Instead I became totally spiritual. All this started in March 1990, and finally I became a total recluse. Negativity was now a word that did not apply to me; everything changed to being positive. I enjoy what I am doing and it is all with His Holiness' blessings.

One day I was sitting in my garden, looking around. I quietly asked His Holiness to give me a sign that he was with me. A beautiful butterfly came and sat on me, and it was sick. I picked it up, put it in a small dish and took it upstairs to my room where I started reciting mantras keeping the butterfly on my lap. It died and I buried it in the garden. I then knew that His Holiness was always with me. I went up to my room and started dancing.

When the 17th Karmapa, Ogyen Trinley Dorje, escaped from Tibet and came to Dharamsala at the beginning of 2000, I wanted to see him and asked if I could come for an audience when he visited Delhi. However, instead of me going to see him, he came to visit me in my house. When he walked in, I immediately saw the 16th Karmapa in my mind. I kept picturing him. The spiritual aura was the same; a very intense feeling. I felt the 16th Karmapa was everywhere. He came in front of my eyes.

16th and 17th Karmapas. (Photographer unknown)

The 17th also loved sitting in this room, the same as the 16th Karmapa. Then he came to my prayer room and mentioned certain things that were said between the 16th Karmapa, an old Lama who passed away, and me. He picked up something that was a continuation of that moment. Their soul is the same.

My daughter Natasha telephoned me and asked my permission to get married. Without thinking I told her that His Holiness the 17th Karmapa will solemnize the wedding. She could not believe that it was possible. I asked His Holiness and he straight away agreed.

The wedding was held in Jaipur and the climate was hot and dry. All of us were sitting on the floor, waiting for the ceremony to begin. There were both Indian and international guests present for this wedding; When the Karmapa walked in, a quiet cool breeze walked with him. Everyone noticed the sudden change in temperature. To our utter surprise, there were a number of colorful birds of Jaipur who formed a canopy above his head.

In the evening at the reception a lot of the guests wanted to meet him and shake hands with him. He had only one request and that was all who wanted to meet him could come but they should not be holding a glass of liquor in their hands. There were about eighty to one hundred people and he patiently shook every guest's hand in that room. In fact, one of the guests mentioned that he did not want to wash his hands after shaking hands with His Holiness.

There was always a family feeling with both the 16th and 17th Karmapas. The 16th was like my father; the 17th could be my son. It's a mutual feeling but we have not spoken about it. The 16th Karmapa used to play with my children. They treated him like a grandfather, with complete relaxation. It's a miracle to me that now the 17th is playing with my grandchildren, just like the 16th did.

The 16th Karmapa has been my Guru throughout and continues to be my Guru in the form of the 17th Karmapa.

THE MEETING OF MAHASIDDHAS
by Didi Contractor

Delia Contractor (nicknamed Didi by her parents) was born in 1929 to professional artists. She grew up in Germany, Texas and New Mexico and trained in art. In 1951 she married an Indian and moved to India. She had four children. In 1977 she moved to the Himalayan foot hills where she continues to pursue an interest in sustainable building.

We used to live near the ocean in the Bombay suburb of Juhu, just down the beach from Kabir Bedi, who later became known internationally as a film star. When I met Kabir through mutual friends in the late 1960s, he said, "You must meet my mother." His English mother, Freda, had also been, as I still was at that time, a foreign wife in India interested in spiritual matters, so he thought we would get along. And we did. We got along famously.

Freda was secretary to His Holiness the 16th Karmapa who used to call her "Mummy-la." She was a marvelous character, a little formal as the British often are. She still seemed, in spite of her carefully worn robes and her shaved head, very British with her crisp enunciation and her brisk no nonsense manner. Tibetan nuns' shaved heads are supposed to make them less noticeable; this didn't work with Freda. The large pale pink head of this striding English woman made her more rather than less noticeable.

During one of her visits with Kabir I took her out to the ashram in Ganeshpuri to meet my own guru, Swami Muktananda. He was so impressed by her deep devotion to the Karmapa, that he told her, "You are so devoted to your guru that I would like to meet him. If he ever comes to India you must bring him here to meet me."

"Didi, we will create history," Mummy-la declared to me on our long way back in the car. "We will reunite the branches of the siddha tradition." After it was taken to Tibet, the siddha traditions had grown apart. Both the Hindu siddha and Buddhist vajrayana traditions stem from roots in the same historical lineage of the earlier Tantric tradition. We both thought such a meeting would be seen as a land mark in the history of comparative religion and the new spiritual movement.

Sometime in the fall of—was it 1971 or 1972, those heady years get muddled in my memory—I got a letter from Freda saying the Karmapa was planning to come out of Sikkim on pilgrimage and would also tour around India. If I announced this to Muktananda at the ashram, and if he repeated and confirmed the invitation in a letter, she could have Ganeshpuri added to the official itinerary. I was thrilled. We were organizing something truly meaningful in the religious traditions! So out I went to the ashram.

Babaji, as we called Muktananda, would come out of his rooms onto a high marble-coated platform in the corner of the shaded courtyard to sit cross-legged giving darshan. As the devotees in the darshan queue with their offerings and garlands of flowers moved slowly forwards to reach him, he would lean down to talk to each in turn. I stood in the line feeling, for once, full of importance. When my turn came and I told him what Freda had written to me about the Karmapa's coming, Muktananda started to shout at me.

"Your friend's guru is a very high Tibetan Lama. Tibetans take rank and ceremony very seriously. Do you know the proper protocol for receiving him? How many cushions higher does he have to sit? What is the correct height of the cushions? You got me into all this trouble." His compelling glance blazed into my eyes, "You got us into this and you had better not let us disgrace this ashram. You have to find out everything and arrange it all. It's up to you."

I turned away in a state of bliss: nothing like the blast of energy you get from the Guru shouting your ego down. I felt that he wasn't really angry with me; it was just: "stop feeling so important. Just go out and do it." The person behind me, one of the many non-Hindi speaking foreigners who had followed Babaji back from his trips to the West, said, "Well, I bet that whatever you did, you won't do *that* again!"

"No way," I replied, as I bustled off to organize the letter to Rumtek, "would *anyone* ever get that chance again!"

The Karmapa was scheduled to arrive in Bombay in the early morning on New Year's Day. It was decided that before they embarked on the long drive out to the Ganeshpuri ashram, I could give him and his party breakfast at my home. By then Juhu was becoming built up and our cottage was surrounded by tall newly constructed hotels. On New Year's Eve, each hotel had its own set of rock music blasting. In that noise, no one could sleep.

My friends from the ashram included a master chef; we were inspired, and cooked throughout the night. I had a small oven so we had to bake in successive batches and in the intervals each batch of the many breads and cakes got varied in flavor and garnished differently. I had bought some yellow and maroon cloth and we rearranged the living room, which was still decked out for the festive season. We piled up mattresses to make a high throne that would command both wings of the spacious L-shaped living area, which extended from the large north window of my studio to a deep veranda that opened out towards the west into a tropical garden. Two beds piled to make a high throne stood in front of the decorated palm leaf that had served as a Christmas tree.

It was chilly and still dark when I drove down to the railway station carrying fragrant flower garlands to welcome the Karmapa in the Hindu tradition. For the tour, the Karmapa had been assigned a special coach. It was fitted up with elaborate amenities and could be attached to the tail end of the regular trains. During their stay at any place, this detached bogie could be left at a siding. They could then come back to their own things in the state rooms of their own carriage. My heart thumped with excitement as I waited, watched as the train roared in, then rushed down the whole length of the platform to arrive, breathless, at the end of the train.

His Holiness the Karmapa was a large man, quite plump, with an immense presence that recorded in one's mind as even larger, like when children draw important things in a huge disproportionate scale. He seemed to be simply immense, 7 feet high, dwarfing everyone in the group around him. Everyone else was dashing about arranging luggage while he seemed to be in calm slow motion. Shamar was with him, his main Tibetan secretary with his two little boys, Ponlop and Drupon Rinpoches and a crowd of other impressive Lamas and friendly Tibetan lay people.

I got them into taxis and cars and took them through the awakening city to Juhu where they all had breakfast. The lavish spread, so lovingly made, looked magnificent. We had prepared white and yellow butter, laid out sweet and salty spreads and served endless rounds of tea and coffee. The brilliant light of the rising winter sun poured directly into the room illuminating the special occasion with a magical light. Some of the party settled down at the Karmapa's feet sitting on the cushions and durries spread across the living room floor; others found their way to spill out into the garden. Freda was there of course, as were other friends of hers and of mine who were spiritually inclined. The Karmapa and his entourage had been eating train food so they were absolutely delighted with the breakfast feast. To this day, everyone who was there remembers that occasion.

After eating, we took the Karmapa to the ocean, aware that he was probably the first Karmapa to arrive at the sea. He came to the top of the steps leading down to the beach where, before walking down to the shore, he stopped and stood poised looking out over the expanse of the ocean. He seemed an oceanic sort of person; and indeed the ocean seemed to swell as a symbol of the ancientness of the world.

Gradually I got everybody off on the long drive to the ashram, leaving last to make sure that no one had left anything and everyone had a ride. The younger translator who rode with me said it was a real bodhisattva act, to see that everyone was sent off first and not to seek the limelight. He proceeded to explain bodhisattva vows to me. I liked the idea of vowing to see to the welfare of others, and took consolation for not being there to take part in the spectacle planned for the ceremonial arrival. So I missed my share of the fame for that moment, of the introduction between the two ends of the separated siddha lineage. Freda was of course there, having ridden if not in the actual car with His Holiness, at least in the long cavalcade of accompanying vehicles.

When we finally arrived, the Karmapa's party were busy setting themselves up in one of the buildings in the ashram garden, where they promptly got out their tea churns to make their butter tea, but no one at the ashram had thought to provide butter. I should have warned them! Kirin, my daughter, who was then about thirteen, rushed off to the village with Judith, one of our close ashram friends. They came back breathless carrying heaps of butter. This offering of butter was considered greatly auspicious.

I heard about how the Karmapa had been garlanded outside of the ashram gates by Muktananda's elephant and ceremonially greeted by a bevy of pretty foreign women in rich brocade saris swirling trays full of lights.

Muktananda and the Karmapa gave a brief darshan together
and then they ducked into Muktananda's rooms with their translators for a private confab. According to the younger Tibetan
translator, whom I had made friends with in the car on our way
out, they had a very interesting talk. They did not discuss the distinction between the Hindu and Buddhist aims of practice but
one of the topics that he said they did talk about was secrecy at the
different stages of sadhana. They discussed what was kept hidden
at each stage of practice in their different traditions and found that
in each tradition different bits were kept secret. So, I wondered, if
you could study both and put the two traditions together would
the whole thing come out in the open and become completely accessible?

Muktananda had already been on a tour of the West so there
was also talk about what the West was like, what sort of disciplines
Westerners were capable of, and was it worth taking teachings to
them? At that time Karmapa seemed quite disturbed about the
way in which Chögyam Trungpa Rinpoche was modifying the traditional teachings to fit into the West and about the effect that the
West was having on him. [I later heard that as a result the Karmapa
was quite strict with the young Shamar and Situ Rinpoches, hoping to protect them from the corrupting influence of the West.]

After lunch, we were all assembled in the main *darshan* and
meditation hall to see the Black Hat ceremony. A huge black
statue of Nityananda, the guru's guru, sat enshrined at one end
of the hall, and the Karmapa's high throne draped with brocades
was placed facing this at the other end of the hall. They had traveled with all the musical instruments and opulent ritual objects for
the ceremony and with the precious Hat carried in a tall brocade
covered box shaped like a regular Hat Box! In the already charged
sanctified setting of this cool marble hall, where we all meditated
and chanted daily, the whole dramatic ceremony with the high
sustained notes of the Tibetan horns and the deep rumble of the
chanting and the drums was very impressive. Everyone in the ash-

ram was completely blown away. A lot of devotees were affected by *kryias*, involuntary movements during meditation. Some people were thrown into exotic forms of whirling trance. Some devotees were still whirling in various forms of trance while the Karmapa gave out blessing threads and even while his procession filed out.

Along with the thread, I was blessed by a disturbingly deep penetrating glance from the Karmapa's seemingly fathomless eyes.

After that, the turmoil began. The intense energy that had been generated by that ceremony and by His Holiness' presence threw many of the more literal minded followers at the ashram into a state of great confusion. They had all been convinced that their own guru was the one and only source of such charismatic spiritual power. Then here came this person, this Karmapa, from a different tradition radiating another powerful source of this same intense energy. Here were two very different individuals from two different, if equally exotic, traditions displaying the same form of compelling greatness. How could there be two gurus?

We had all been taught that to find and realize the Self we were each to look inwards, beyond the individual ego, towards the inner "Self" but in the practice observed on the external plane, we were only supposed to bow to our own one and only outer guru. Since most of the foreign followers had strong monotheistic backgrounds they were well prepared for single minded prophets and solitary jealous deities. But since I had already encountered and embraced Hindu polytheism, this dichotomy between what was taught and what was practiced had always struck me as being a little strange.

The Tibetans were not all that comfortable either. The long historic rivalry backed by the intricate philosophical debate between the Hindu and the Buddhist faiths is very strong. The entire party consisted of people closely attached to the Karmapa. They didn't want to be caught in the disciplined schedule of this sanctimonious ashram. Also the various lay people wanted to be sightseeing. They wanted to be in Bombay; there was, after all, the

HH 16th Karmapa and Swami Muktananda, 1974. (Courtesy of Dale Brozosky)

lure of Bollywood. The very vegetarian ashram food didn't make much impression on the meat-eating Tibetans. So the next day they all packed up and went back to Bombay, several days earlier than planned. There was no further meeting between Muktananda and Karmapa in India[1]. Neither sought it.

The confusion in Ganeshpuri continued. I thought that Baba Muktananda's first statement after the Karmapa's departure was great: "if you see a difference between us, it is in you not in us." And indeed the photos of them together showed a very deep personal connection and love.

But that tune was quickly changed. The authorities in the ashram felt threatened by the foreign seeker's enthusiasm. The photographers who regularly fulfilled our desires for a pictorial record had taken some wonderful images of Karmapa and Muktananda which

---

1 Editor's footnote: The 16th Karmapa and Swami Muktananda met again in Ann Arbor, Michigan in 1974. In 1977 during the Karmapa's second tour to the US, he is reported to have said that Muktananda was an emanation of Tilopa; while Muktananda considered Karmapa to be "a great mahasiddha."

HH 16th Karmapa and Swami Muktananda, 1974.
(Courtesy of Dale Brozosky)

were eagerly bought up as quickly as they could be printed.

Suddenly the photographers were ordered not to sell anymore and Babaji made declarations about the importance of single minded faith. As a result very few of the seekers, only about ten to fifteen, out of the few hundred living in the ashram at that time, actually visited Rumtek, and if they attempted to return to the Ganeshpuri fold they were made unwelcome. Only a few people actually defected to Karmapa.

Since I was still an independent householder, not yet at that time bound to the Ganeshpuri ashram in any formal way, I gathered my family during the next school vacation and, acting on a personal invitation from the Karmapa set out for Rumtek without advertising out destination. My daughter Kirin describes our adventure in her book[2].

So those two lines of the Siddhas came together to meet and then, unchanged, both blew apart again.

When Time and Eternity Met

My memory of the Black Hat ceremony[3], sponsored by the Ambedkar Buddhist community[4] during the Karmapa's visit to Bombay, seems to have expanded over time to encompass the emotional essence of all those glorious sunsets that consistently moved my heart, throughout the years when my home was on the shore of the Arabian Sea. The grounds on which the ceremony was to take place adjoined the burning ghats at Worli, a seaside suburb of the city.

Astrologically it was a dark night, one of the times of extremely

2 *My Family and Other Saints*, Kirin Narayan, University of Chicago Press, 2007.

3 This story describes the second Black Hat ceremony which the author witnessed after the ceremony at Swami Muktananda's Ashram at Ganeshpuri.

4 The Buddhist community in Bombay is mostly made up of the thousands who had converted to Buddhism under the inspired leadership of Dr Ambedkar during the period when India was striving towards Independence. Under colonial rule Indians had often escaped social evils, such as the caste system, through conversion to the foreign faiths of their rulers: first to Islam and then to Christianity. Dr Ambedkar saw an indigenous patriotic alternative in the conversion to Buddhism, which had been virtually extinct in India for many centuries, as means for the oppressed to redefine themselves and attain an acceptable social category in the new independent India. This new congregation, open and eager to connect with all the various forms that Buddhism had developed in other cultures, had welcomed the arrival of the intricate ritual forms of Tibetan Buddhism.

low tide which left a huge expanse of polished sand that reflected the sunset. You could see in every direction. I remember the Karmapa's back was to the sea, as he faced us from his throne. In the background, the huge expanse of shining beach water. To one side corpses burned on funeral pyres, each arising from a luminous reflection of its consuming fire. People filed in with the funeral processions to the sound of conches, and calling out "Hai Ram." From the windows of the city's tall buildings to the south, the reflection of the setting sun blazed, as though the buildings were filled with destructive fire. Water and fire, the edge of the day and the edge of the sea, the conjunction of moon and sun near the solstice, which divides the halves of the year—it could not have been more propitious.

The Black Hat ceremony is an epic drama. One understood the depths to which drama could go and the extent to which ritual can dramatize the divine. In Ganeshpuri, in the smaller but very charged sacred setting where we all chanted daily, the Black Hat ceremony had suddenly filled with explosively strong energy. Here on the seaside, that energy seemed to extend, boundless beyond the ocean's vast horizon, into infinite space.

Time seemed to stop as His Holiness lifted the Black Hat aloft, poised it above his head and then placed it crowning his head, holding it there while the horns maintained a clear, high, piercing crescendo.

To feel universal love and compassion in the midst of the mourning of the figures coming into the burning ghats, you knew: This is It. You could not get more than that. It seemed to reveal what the burning ghats were about: mortality as a moment in eternity, a moment of utter transformation. The sun slipped into the glowing sea. As dusk descended, the first stars came out.

In that huge crowd of maybe thousands, many people must have been as moved by that transfixing moment, as I was. Some people from the Ganeshpuri ashram also came and caught the colour and drama, with this huge orange background of the sunset.

It was a transcendent moment, the depths of which could only be experienced.

One perceived the immensity of the Karmapas, touching the deepest core of the identity one was striving to reach: the spiritual understanding in which all things outside of "me," what we call reality, the sort of history that comes and goes, becomes a play. When you experience that immense sense of play, everything else becomes a little trivial.

As a teaching of what stands above the different hells and realms, given in the midst of a scene when this was actually embodied, it became a moment of live drama; a moment in which reality and myth come together. In Christian theology, it's the crossing of time and eternity.

I think of the Karmapas as producers of such moments. I sense the 17th Karmapa as bursting with the capacity, although he's not allowed to go and visit anyone or just hang out as a person; whereas the previous Karmapa could move freely and come, as he had, to my house, and offer all these gifts. He could take personal care, and he did. He was a very motherly man. The Karmapa gave me a way to see greatness.

When His Holiness was leaving Bombay, we visited him in his railway car to see him off. I was standing at the back of the group that was crowding in for blessing. He called me to come forward and motioned me to sit at his feet. He put his foot, shod in heavy black leather, onto my lap and rested it there for the whole darshan, as though I had become his living footstool. Feeling an immense space opening within my being, I drifted into an extraordinary state. This experience was a powerful blessing, much more than one deserved for having had the privilege of taking part in the meeting of the siddhas. I stumbled out, as though drunk on champagne, onto the railway platform and watched the departing train gain speed, and rattle away beyond sight.

Karmapa in his Rumtek room.
(Courtesy of Lama Surya Das)

THE LION'S ROAR
by Ngodrup Burkhar

I came to Rumtek at the age of twenty in June, 1973. My family were all Karma Kagyu lineage followers, simple nomads from Western Tibet, close to Mt Kailash. I had barely finished high school in Dehradun in India and knew only basic English and basic Tibetan.

In 1973, during the three-month break before going to university, I went to Bodhgaya for the Kalachakra Empowerment. There I met a lama from Western Tibet whom I knew already, who said it would be very good if I could work for His Holiness Karmapa; that now his Buddha activity was so great he was even attracting foreigners. I told him that I had no qualifications to serve His Holiness. Nevertheless he mentioned me to His Holiness at Rumtek and about a month later, I received a signed letter from His Holiness on an inland letter form. It said, "Lama Dubsing told me about you and I pondered upon it. You might be of some assistance. So you can come." I was getting closer to the hot seat and I got really nervous.

Since then I served His Holiness the 16th Karmapa as one of his translators in India and on his tours abroad and have continued to serve the 17th Karmapa.

It is said that the great masters bestow the seed of liberation through the four doors: hearing, touching, tasting, seeing. Some great masters are able to inspire us with their presence alone rather than through words. Of all the great masters whom I've met, the presence of His Holiness the 16th Karmapa was incomparably awe-inspiring. I can express this only as a conflict—I didn't want to be there, it was too overwhelming. At the same time I didn't want to leave. I felt like I was frozen to the spot. It was a beautifully frustrating dilemma.

I was not alone in feeling overpowered by his presence. Nor was the effect limited to Buddhist devotees. At that time Rumtek was a tourist hotspot in Sikkim and I soon found myself assuming the role of tourist guide as well. In 1974, a group of about twenty elderly Mexicans visited Rumtek. I think they were mainly Christians; certainly none of them were Buddhist, so they had no idea who the Karmapa was.

I was showing them around Rumtek on a day that happened to coincide with a Crown ceremony upstairs in the Crown ceremony shrine room. The Crown ceremony is a very rich ceremonial ritual during which the Buddha of Compassion becomes manifest. No description can do justice to it. You have to be there. It's a ritual, a spectacle, and a blessing, depending on how you view it. I thought to myself, why not bring these tourists in? It was an interesting and colourful ritual and I thought they would find it at the very least, entertaining and informative. At the same time, as a Buddhist, I believed it would also sow the seed of liberation. I expected them all to enjoy watching the Crown ceremony, nothing more; but while the ceremony was happening and His Holiness was in deep meditation, I looked around. They were standing there with tears flowing down their faces. This is the kind of teaching the Karmapa gave. The effect of his presence on people was palpable.

On another occasion, I found myself in a very distressing situation as translator at Harvard University. The occasion had been advertised as a unique teaching organised by Dharmadhatu and other Buddhist study groups, including the well-known Associate Professor at Harvard Medical School, Dr Herbert Benson. They had advertised the event with an elegant banner: The Dharma King His Holiness the Gyalwang Karmapa will Teach on Compassion. The auditorium looked like the court of a spiritual king, all decked up with Buddhist symbols on the finest silk brocade. Rows of impeccably dressed academics and professionals were waiting expectantly. I was wearing my best suit and felt proud to be the translator. "Now these people will know what a real teacher is like," I thought.

His Holiness talked for only about twenty minutes in a event scheduled to last an hour. If he had talked longer I would have collapsed because, to my horror, I didn't understand what he was saying. It didn't make sense. People were looking at me as if to say, "What a jerk this guy is!" I was thrown completely out of my comfort zone. After the teaching, there was a question and answer session. People were coming up to the microphone to ask questions. I translated the questions, but again, to my bewilderment, the answers bore no relationship to the questions. After this had happened a few times, I could see that people were thinking I was totally incompetent. At one point it went so far that I couldn't handle it anymore. I decided His Holiness hadn't understood the question. I repeated it. His answer still didn't have anything to do with the question. I began to repeat it for the third time. "Your Holiness..." He looked straight at me and replied forcefully but with great equanimity: *You just translate what I said.*

A couple of years later at Karma Triyana Dharmachakra when I was translating for Khenpo Khartar Rinpoche, one lady in the audience referred back to that time. She asked, "When your great master came and performed this ornate ceremony with the Hat, I was there. It's been some years ago and I can't get that Hat out of my mind. So I guess I'm supposed to do something with the Hat. What shall I do with the Hat?" Khenpo Khartar Rinpoche explained nicely that she had made a connection with the Buddha.

Karmapa at Rumtek.
(Courtesy of Dorothea Fischer)

On another occasion at KTD, someone remarked, "Two or three years ago I asked the Karmapa a question and the answer at that time didn't make any sense. But now I can see it was the best possible answer." Both times I felt a tremendous surge of relief.

In contrast, His Holiness offered a Crown ceremony in San Francisco. The event was not as formal as it had been at Harvard. Although only the Crown ceremony was scheduled, His Holiness gave a beautiful spontaneous teaching after the ceremony. At the same time he was scheduled to meet Richard Blum, the husband of Diane Feinstein, mayor of San Francisco. One of the main organisers was looking at me and at his watch as if to say, time is up, next on the agenda is Richard Blum. When the Karmapa was on tour like this, it was impossible to keep to tight schedules. I sat there wondering why he hadn't given that teaching at Harvard? The answer was clear: his teachings had to arise spontaneously.

That incredible awesome presence shook the ground beneath

my feet. I was also young, and somewhat afraid of him, so I wasn't seeking to be alone with him. There were only a couple of times when the opportunity to be alone came anyway. When he called, I would just jump.

One time he called me into his room. He was sitting there alone and began to sing spontaneously his song of prophecy about leaving Tibet. The spontaneity was somewhat akin to the Gesar of Ling tradition when the singer becomes suddenly inspired. It was one of his special melodies that could vibrate, sung with a voice and presence that sent shivers down one's spine, like the lion's roar. It was so beautiful, but it was impossible for me to relax in his presence. More contradiction. I was alone there with him and he was singing a song with a celestial melody. Yet even in his most relaxed state, with his beautiful voice, I still couldn't relax. I had to be constantly alert.

Another time he called me and again I was alone with him. In Tibetan there are almost three languages: colloquial, honorific and dharmic. There are different words for everything. And there are many levels of honorific. But because of all the disruption to our culture, it can be difficult for Tibetans in exile to know some of the finer points of the language. The language has become mixed up. One day I failed to come up with the correct honorific words. As it would not be good for this to happen in public, His Holiness called me and said very lovingly, like a father, "When you address me you have to say it this way." He didn't want me to make a fool of myself. He was kind like that. He was also very generous and caring.

Sometimes he could be very wrathful. But for me his presence was enough to feel like I was being pushed down anyway. It's as if you are afraid of the person you love the most. The experience is so real. I would never call it a bad experience but it was certainly never comfortable.

I never felt relaxed near him, which was good because then I was always alert and respectful. If one remains around great teachers without practice, there is the danger that one will get numbed, calloused, habituated. If one practices, everything remains fresh. In those days I felt awesome freshness. Vigilant freshness.

It is somewhat similar with the 17th Karmapa. However, one thing is now reversed—age. Now I feel more relaxed. And he's gentler in his demeanour. I have the chance to be around him a lot. But still his presence is the same as the 16th. He's younger, less traditional, more reachable. But the amazing thing about the 17th is he's doing his best to hide his qualities, to be as unassuming as possible. It's like covering the sun with your hand, but it comes through anyway. He often says "I don't know, I have no experience." But the depth of his knowledge on anything is extremely profound. Kyabje Bokar Rinpoche remarked that even if you were incredibly intelligent and studied diligently for fifty years continuously you couldn't attain that depth of wisdom. It's obviously not coming from now; so it must come from past lifetimes. He has so many extraordinary qualities but for me the most impressive is his utter humility.

When it comes to his activity, he does not have the opportunity to extend his reach as fully as he would like. But he is certainly the greatest example of how to be down to earth. Stay on the ground, be realistic, be practical. In his instructions on practising the dharma, he makes it plain there is no option. He says it has to be part of your life. If it is not, you haven't got it. It's very sane. He teaches in a different way to the 16th Karmapa. But still it pushes you to the edge because there is no escape. No exit. His skilful means is so penetrating, it cuts right to the bone.

This recall came out spontaneously from my mind.

THE PICNIC
by MJ Bennett (Jangchub Zangmo)

I met His Holiness the 16th Gyalwang Karmapa in 1974 on his first world tour at the dharma centre of Canada near Kinmount, Ontario. Some of us from the Yukon in the north of Canada had gone to the centre to help prepare for his visit. In 1977, on his second world tour, His Holiness visited the Yukon Territory. At that time, he invited my husband, Bob and me to work for him at Woodstock, New York which would become his North American seat. In 1980, on his third and last world tour, he invited Bob and me to Rumtek Monastery in Sikkim, his main seat outside Tibet. We stayed there for six months. My assignment was to establish the Kagyu International Office; Bob's was to prepare for the construction of His Holiness' monastery in Delhi. We arrived in Calcutta, India in January 1981. At the time of this story, we had been living in Rumtek village for about one month.

It was a beautifully warm sunny day, perfect weather for a picnic. We were told His Holiness was going on an outing the next day and Bob and I were to be the drivers. The journey was to a botanical garden somewhere in south Sikkim. That's all we were told. I still have only a vague idea where we went that day. I assume it was southeastern Sikkim, an area out of bounds for foreigners.

It was customary to turn up at the appointed departure time, and not really know the plan. We knew that His Holiness wanted to bring back more plants for the gardens around his aviary which was just behind his private residence above the main monastery.

It was 1981, but from the moment I arrived at Rumtek, I felt as if I'd stepped back in time to a medieval age in ancient Tibet. Had time stopped there, as with Shangri-La? I seemed to have entered an alternate realm that had not changed since the beginning of Tibetan culture. The six months I lived there altered forever my perception of "reality."

We arrived outside the monastery gates at the top of the town in the early morning. A square ringed by the monastery store rooms, the Kunga Deleg Hotel (the only hotel in town) and a small shop selling soft drinks, cookies, and souvenirs, allowed just enough space for cars to turn around. Above the store was the Kagyu International Office. Day buses of Indian tourists and taxis coming from the capital of Gangtok would park in this open area. The gates on the right led into the courtyard of the main Rumtek monastery. At this early hour, the usually busy square was deserted.

The cars were already assembled. First there was His Holiness' car, a glossy maroon Mercedes Benz, with his driver standing beside it. The second car, a shiny blue Ambassador coupe belonging to the General Secretary, was parked just behind, attended by his driver. Two more cars—an older grey Ambassador coupe and behind it, an old Indian army Jeep—both looked rather the worse for wear.

We were dressed in our finest. The only dress I owned that swept to the ground was a Bhutanese plaid woolen tunic made in Tibetan style. As personal secretary and assistant to His Holiness, I learned that I was not supposed to wear a traditional dress that did not sweep the ground. Only coolies and labourers did that. The ground was dirt mixed with cow dung, spittle perhaps infected with tuberculosis, and remnants of feces.

Suddenly, His Holiness emerged from the monastery gates, followed by the General Secretary and the highest ranking Rinpoche and Tulkus of Rumtek Monastery. His driver jumped into action opening the door of the dazzling Mercedes Benz. The General Secretary's driver opened the door of the shiny blue Ambassador for him and his two sons. His Holiness strode purposefully towards the little grey Ambassador and Jeep and began assigning their drivers. He chose me to drive the grey Ambassador that was to carry several of the younger tulkus. Bob was assigned the Jeep with the two Tibetan monk servants. The young Lamas were terrified that they were going to be driven by a woman.

But there was no time to complain. Quickly His Holiness got into his vehicle followed by his heart-son, Jamgön Kongtrul Rinpoche. The General Secretary got into his car followed by his sons, Dzogchen Ponlop Rinpoche and Drupon Rinpoche. The younger Lamas, in order of rank, Sangye Nyempa Rinpoche, Garwang Rinpoche, and Yongdzin Rinpoche, got into the grey Ambassador and I took my place at the wheel. The servants rushed into the Jeep with baskets of picnic food and supplies. Bob got in and we were off.

The young Lamas particularly loved Bob. He was likeable, loved to teach them English, and answered their questions about the magical West. In clandestine moments he let them listen to Western music on his Sony Walkman—His Holiness would not have approved—but they were teenagers as well as reincarnate Lamas.

They were sad that he would not be driving them. But worse, they were horrified they were going to be driven by a woman. Surely they would not be safe! I was only the second woman ever to drive in Sikkim. The other was a Bhutanese princess, who drove only once for a day. Women just did not drive in Sikkim at that time. Since the Lamas knew little of the West, they did not know of my backwoods driving skills, or how many large American cities I'd crossed at rush hour. One never knew why His Holiness arranged things as he did. He loved to shock, to scramble people's relative views of reality.

But, no time to wonder why, we were off...

It was no secret that His Holiness the 16th Karmapa loved a fast drive when he could get it. So it wasn't long before we'd reached the bottom of the mountain. At the fork in the road, there was a filling station, the road to Gangtok and another road I'd never been on. That's the road we took after the cars were filled with petrol.

In the hierarchy of our caravan, His Holiness' car was filled first, followed by the General Secretary's car, my grey Ambassador, and finally Bob's Jeep. But, before the attendant had finished filling up the Jeep, His Holiness' car took off up the mountain at great speed, with the General Secretary right behind. For a split second I wondered what to do. Then I took off in pursuit. Up and up we went; faster and faster following the new Mercedes and the shiny blue Ambassador. We were on one of those single lane mountain roads with no guard rails, just the occasional stone marker and widened grassy area for passing.

They were losing me. The precipice loomed just off to the side of our car. My grey Ambassador had a slipping clutch. Trying to catch up, I sped even faster. My hands were clutching the wheel. I was sweating in that prickly Bhutanese wool dress. The Lamas were also sweating, reciting mantras at top speed. Thirteen-year-old Garwang Rinpoche in the front seat was trying to keep his composure. All the young Lamas looked terrified as they clutched at the sides of the car. Those in the back were also holding each other. They must have thought any minute they'd be plunging to their deaths. OM MANI PEME HUNG. Once in a while one of them would look back longingly for Bob and the Jeep, but he was not yet in sight.

Finally we arrived at the summit of the pass, a flat area where the cars of His Holiness and the General Secretary were just pulling to a stop. As my dusty little grey Ambassador approached, His Holiness got out of the big Mercedes Benz and walked over towards us with his majestic swaying walk. Patting our car on the hood he boomed, "Very good car!" Then he looked far into the

Cosmic laughter of HH Karmapa.
(Photographer unknown)

distance, down the road behind us and scanned below. "Where's Bob?" he asked, and broke into gales of laughter. He enjoyed himself so much his belly shook.

He threw his head back and laughed again.

Then he turned around towards his car and went to the side of the road for a break. Everyone got out of their cars stretched, rested, and waited. His Holiness walked towards his car, the driver opened the door, and he got in. Once again everyone scrambled into their respective cars and we were off in a shot without a single warning; and without Bob.

Down, down the winding narrow single lane road. As we descended towards the plains it became much warmer. By now I was unbearably hot in the woolen Tibetan dress. The clutch slipped and slipped. The Lamas chattered nervously in Tibetan. All of a sudden we arrived at the botanical gardens and parked the cars. The manager came out to greet us. All the drivers, including me, waited by the cars as the manager gave His Holiness, the

Rinpoches and Lamas a tour. His Holiness selected a few plants to take back. Jamgön Kongtrul Rinpoche was beginning to be concerned. It was almost time for lunch, but lunch and servants were not there. No Bob and no Jeep.

Whenever it was time for His Holiness to eat, food was to be ready on the spot as if it could materialize out of the air. I knew this; I'd cooked for him in New York. You could wait and wait, but once it was time, that was it.... the meal had to be served. Jamgön Kongtrul Rinpoche came over to me, concerned: "Where's Bob?"

As His Holiness rounded the corner of the gardens, in rolled Bob with the Jeep just in time. The servants came rushing out the back even before the Jeep had rolled to a complete stop inside the gates. They brought out blankets to sit on and Bhutanese straw baskets filled with food, thermoses, everything that had been prepared for the mid-day feast. Once the Karmapa and his party were happily settled, I went over to the Jeep.

Bob emerged enraged, cursing about the condition of the Jeep, the clutch, the poor brakes, what a piece of junk it was. "Piss poor brakes," he said. "The clutch would barely disengage at all, then completely failed, on the trip."

So, he had to shift without the clutch, at just the right speed. "If it was in gear, you could not stop," he said, "since pressing the clutch did nothing." So, he managed the trip, "being an all around genius," without a clutch, noting to park on a downhill so it could get going again!

By the time he finished talking it was time to go. No way to repair the Jeep now! When the Karmapa got up, everyone jumped to their feet and quickly took their places. Off we went again for the journey home. Fortunately, the journey was now relaxed and pleasant, just driving at a leisurely pace.

Halfway home on a flat, remote stretch of road, the cars stopped. Now the Karmapa decided it was playtime, here in the privacy of nowhere. With a new video camera he'd been given on the last world tour, he wanted to film the young Rinpoches in pretend wrestling matches. I wandered off to leave them alone. Finally, Bob and the Lamas got to play, talk, and relax together.

We all got back into the cars and headed down the mountain-side, past the filling station at the bottom of the road along the river towards Rumtek. We drove towards the ford, crossed the river and drove along the straight stretch of road beside the river, and then began the long climb up the mountain to Rumtek. I hadn't noticed Bob and the Jeep, but I wasn't worried.

All of a sudden, when we were about a third of the way up the mountainside, we heard shouts coming from the road by the stream below. It was Bob and the servants with the Jeep. They had broken down. Past the ford, the river had a rocky bottom where the water came up almost above the wheels of the vehicle. You had to drive slowly there, or the motor could splutter and leave you stranded. But, Bob was at the bottom of the valley well past the ford, and on the only long straight stretch of road in the entire journey. It was there that their brakes had completely failed.

The procession on the mountain stopped. The Karmapa got out of his car, walked towards my Ambassador, past the General Secretary's car. He instructed the young Lamas inside to get out. Then he positioned himself at the edge of the road. There were no guard rails. The road was narrow; the grassy shoulder only about a foot wide. There the Karmapa stood making himself a road-block, his maroon robes and large frame outlined against the late afternoon sun.

He was strong and majestic, as if there was nothing to be concerned about. He began the motions of a traffic officer as I turned the car around to rescue the Jeep. Back and forth, back and forth with the Karmapa standing there directing each turn, totally confident he could stop the car from going over the cliff. Sweating profusely, I managed to turn the car around. The clutch did not give out. I did not send Karmapa plunging over the cliff. After several short turns, and what seemed like an eternity, the car faced down the road. His Holiness motioned me to get out. After discussion between His Holiness, His Eminence, the General Secretary and the Rinpoches, they decided that the General Secretary's driver would drive down to rescue them.

We all squeezed into the two remaining cars, and made the short drive up the mountain, returning to Rumtek just as the sun was setting. One man would spend the night with the Jeep to protect it, after bringing Bob and the servants back to the monastery.

Once we arrived back in Rumtek, I left the party at the monastery gates and returned to the little house in the village where Bob and I lived. It had been a long day. Finally I was able to take off that hot, prickly woollen dress, get into something comfortable, make a cup of tea, and rest. But Bob did not return home for quite a few more hours, well after dark.

He walked into our little home with a look of complete shock on his face, holding a beautiful carnelian rosary given to him by Karmapa. He told me the whole story of the Jeep and how he had nearly dropped over the edge.

Along the straight, flat road beside the river, on the Gangtok side, and after so many high speed turns all day, suddenly the Jeep headed for the 100 ft drop to the river! "The wheel spun freely in my hands" he said. "The tie rod end that hooks steering to wheels, and wheels to each other, completely let go. Everyone started shouting. Both brakes and clutch were barely working, So, I turned off the key, stood on the brakes, and held my breath. We stopped two feet from a dizzying 100 foot drop!"

After being rescued, Bob was called up into His Holiness' private quarters. His Holiness told him: "You had just enough good karma that the Jeep's brakes did not fail on the mountain road plunging everyone to their deaths. Instead, it broke down close to the monastery and on a flat stretch of road and no one was hurt. But," His Holiness told Bob: "You did not have enough good karma to prevent it from breaking down."

He instructed Bob to do 100,000 Vajrasattva purification mantras on the rosary that he gave him. As a further purification practice, he instructed Bob to repair the Jeep himself in the square in front of the monastery gates. It was a dirty job, demeaning and greasy. His Holiness would watch him work from his chambers above.

The 16th Karmapa gave few formal teachings. He bestowed blessing either by being in his presence (darshan), by the Ceremony of the Vajra Crown, or by wongkur (empowerment). This is how he taught—in the tradition of the Indian Mahasiddhas. The teachings would manifest on a seemingly ordinary day, a day just like this picnic.

This was how life unfolded during our six months with His Holiness the 16th Gyalwang Karmapa in Rumtek. There are many stories that illustrate these two views of reality, when the old masters from Tibet began to embrace their first Western disciples. Mr. Damchoe Yongdu, the General Secretary who had come out of Tibet with His Holiness, told me that we had been invited to Rumtek to teach them modern ways. I think Bob and I learned more about theirs.

Taking What Hasn't been Given

During the six months that I lived in Rumtek and worked for His Holiness, often in the early morning hours I would arrive before His Holiness at his summer palace just above the monastery where he had his main chambers.

I would enter the room where the cages of Gouldian finches and the most delicate of the canaries were housed. On the altar that was on one side of the room, there were often trays of fruit—a real luxury in Rumtek at that time. These had been offered by the wealthy devotees who would visit His Holiness from Gangtok, the capital of Sikkim across the valley. Then, he would offer them to feed his birds.

As I was existing on the extremely basic rice and lentils diet of the Administration workers, with a tablespoon daily of white radish—we did get a vegetable once a week—I often looked forward to helping myself to some of the bananas for breakfast before beginning to check on the birds.

One morning, when His Holiness and I were alone in that room together, he said very kindly to me; "You know, if I arrived early and ate some of those bananas and fruit, that would be stealing!" I was shocked and embarrassed. How did he know? He'd never seen me eat one! That was His Holiness' way of teaching. Ashamed, I never ate one again.

"Now You Can Never Be Selfish Again"
by Dechen Cronin

Dechen Cronin completed two three-year retreats under the previous Kalu Rinpoche and now divides her time between Kathmandu and Sweden where she continues to practice the dharma.

April 1972, Rumtek

My husband Nick and I were music students playing music in Bangalore. We heard about His Holiness the Karmapa from Ole and Hannah Nydahl, a Danish couple on the hippie/guru trail; so we packed up our house in Bangalore, and made a Buddhist pilgrimage all the way up to Sikkim. When we got there, His Holiness invited us to tea. It was a very happy occasion. Perhaps we were one of the first Westerners to visit Rumtek after Ole and Hannah. His Holiness handed me his tea to drink out of his nice big silver cup. I drank the buttery salt tea, thought it was disgusting, and gave it to Nick. Karmapa laughed and said, "You're going to drink a lot of this tea in your lifetime." He laughed a lot and said, "You're going to see Kalu Rinpche."

We took refuge with Karmapa at that time. He said, "Now you should remember this day for the rest of your life." It was April 9th, 1972 at 10:25 a.m. I wrote it down.

We went back a second time after a few months, with offerings such as white scarves, tea, money, and a beautiful plant with large red flowers and green leaves. Sitting in the back of the Jeep going to Sikkim from Darjeeling, I was holding the flower to protect it from the goats and chickens travelling with us. It was such a hassle in that old Jeep with canvas windows on the sides and I had to protect the plant the whole journey, which took nearly eight hours.

We gave the offerings to His Holiness and the only thing he looked at was the flower which was by now just a brown stick. He said he loved it and would find a place for it in his garden. For me it was a very profound moment because there was also a big piece of Kalimpong cheese and the finest white silk offering scarves, yet all he saw was the brown stick. I think he liked it because it was brought with the utmost care. I believe he saw us coming.

His Holiness said, "Now you should take the bodhisattva vow." When we took the vow he looked at Nick and he said, "You have to stop taking bad medicines." Nick stopped taking drugs just like that and never took them again.

Then he turned to me and said, "Now you can never be selfish again."

HH 16th Karmapa.
(Courtesy of Dorothea Fischer)

WAKE UP!
by Erika Belair

My mother died when I was three years old ; later in life my father disinherited me. I was disillusioned, uprooted and hopeless when I had a dream, and took Refuge soon afterwards. Then I met His Holiness the 16th Gyalwang Karmapa for the first time.

Since then I have tried to "wake up" by studying and practising the dharma under such teachers as Situ Rinpoche, Kalu Rinpoche, and others. My efforts culminated in a solitary three-year retreat at Kagyu Ling, France from November 1988 to March 1992.

After twelve years of upheaval while I attempted to re-establish my life, I met His Holiness the 17th Karmapa in Bodhgaya. He was like the rising sun.

Now I am living in southern Portugal making and selling jewellery to tourists in the summer season. My sincere wish is that anyone who sees, touches, or buys my jewellery will meet with the teachings of the Buddha and ultimately be liberated from suffering.

His Holiness the 16th Gyalwang Karmapa was staying at the Oberoi Hotel in Calcutta for a few days upon his return from his first visit to the USA. I heard about it in Bodhgaya and was encouraged to go and see him as I had only recently taken refuge. Upon arrival in Calcutta I phoned Achi, the translator, to ask if it was possible to come for a blessing from His Holiness. He asked me to be there the next day at seven o'clock in the morning. Not yet quite awake at such an early hour, I managed to arrive at the appointed time.

His Holiness was royally seated in a beautifully decorated reception room, talking to two wealthy Bhutanese sponsors seated at his feet. He radiated a soft golden light and such compassionate warmth that I felt right at home and settled somewhere in the back. As I was gazing at him, mesmerized by the sound of his voice, I understood that he was talking about his experiences in the USA. He described everything in that land as huge and said that the earth was rich and the fields really big and well-organized in big parcels tended by amazing machinery.

Suddenly I realized that he was speaking Tibetan, a language I did not understand. As I perked up in surprise, he looked at me directly and waved to ask me to come close. I sat at his feet and looked up still totally surprised. Then he made this huge gesture with his hand, almost frightening, so I ducked a little bit. But he only put his hand very gently to my ear and said—this time in perfect English—"Wake up!" Maybe he had a little gadget in his hand like an alarm clock.

I just looked at him smiling somewhat mischievously and I had to giggle. He also started to laugh and we spent a few blissful moments just laughing.

I felt there was nothing to be added. I got up, bowed and left.

A House on Wheels at Rumtek
by Jim Ince

Jim Ince, (Karma Mingyur Trinley) received teachings and traveled throughout the 1970s with both His Holiness and the late Kalu Rinpoche. During this period, Jim also founded a small charitable medical clinic serving Tibetan refugees on the outskirts of Kathmandu, Nepal. Jim now works with non-profit organizations on environmental and climate change issues and lives on the family ranch/part-time retreat centre in Oregon, known as Kagyu Yonten Gyatso. Both the former and present Kalu Rinpoches have enjoyed spending time there.

To the best of my recollection, it was in May of 1971 when Dominique and I made the arduous road trip across southern Nepal eastward and then, fording the river on the border into India, continued north up into the Himalayan foothills and British tea plantations around the hill station of Darjeeling. The monsoon had not yet begun. We were travelling in a Mercedes-Benz van converted into a rustic but comfortable camper.

Near Darjeeling, we stayed a few weeks at the monastery of our primary meditation teacher, Kalu Rinpoche, whom I had previously met in Vancouver, Canada. I had been wondrously drawn to the person and teachings of this great lama, whose lineage and life very much embodied the tradition of Milarepa.

Kalu Rinpoche suggested that we travel to Rumtek Monastery, above Gangtok in Sikkim, where we could hopefully gain an audience with His Holiness the 16th Gyalwang Karmapa. Accordingly, we were granted permission from the Indian Government, which administers Sikkim, to visit Rumtek and remain there for one week.

Upon our arrival outside the gates of Rumtek, hundreds of monks greeted us. Clearly they had rarely seen Western visitors and we were quite a spectacle, especially in our own "house on wheels." We were quickly escorted a short distance above the monastery to His Holiness' residence. We politely declined the sincere offers of accommodation, since we were completely at home in our camper. What followed in the days and weeks ahead was the most profound, inspiring, and spiritually invigorating experience of my life.

One evening in our candlelit camper just as we were thinking that our wondrous time at Rumtek could not get any more sublime, we heard another sound above the roar of the torrential monsoon on the metal roof. At first we thought it was thunder, but then we heard more clearly a loud pounding along the side of the truck, moving from front to rear where the entry door was located. I peered through the curtains to see what the commotion was, and saw the beam of a flashlight in the rain and perhaps 6 or 8 monks using the spare folds of their robes as umbrellas. I quickly opened the door to their excited exclamations in Tibetan, "Yishin Norbu pheb gi re!" (Yishin Norbu is coming.) "Yishin Norbu pheb song!" (Yishin Norbu has come.) Yishin Norbu wants to see your "house on wheels!" (Yishin Norbu, or "wish fulfilling gem" is a respectful term of endearment identifying His Holiness the Gyalwang Karmapa as well as His Holiness the Dalai Lama.)

A few seconds later, His Holiness, a handsome, portly and very unpretentious man, appeared with the grandest smile I have ever seen. With his robe tails gathered together in one hand, he stepped up into the camper. One of his attendants followed as I closed the door to the wind and elements. Taken aback, I quickly gestured at a place on the only seat we had to offer, our bed, bidding him to sit down with an attempted honorific in Tibetan, "Kale Shu den Jag," and, awkwardly resorting to slightly less honorific, "Shu Ah," "Shu Ahhh!" This all seemed to be very fine with him as his face took on an intent look of highly focused attention. He gazed silently around at the unfamiliar furnishings and Spartan amenities of the humble camper for what seemed like an eternity, and finally he said, "Pe Yakpo du," very good! To which I replied, "Lasso, Yishin Norbu La, sheta kibu du. Tujeche," or Yes, Your Holiness, it's very comfortable, thank you. After a short chat, and almost as quickly as he arrived, he departed with his characteristic imperative that we come to see him the following day.

The Contest of the Beards

One sunny day while touring his magnificent aviary, His Holiness seemed to be pondering my beard, which, at that time, was very full, auburn red, and almost down to my belt. Smiling somewhat craftily as he stroked it and with a twinkle in his eye, he exclaimed something in Tibetan that I didn't understand. One of his attendants turned on his heels and disappeared down the path to the monastery below.

I soon found out that he had called for an immediate "contest of the beards." Indeed, my much fuller and longer beard at the time was to be pitted in contest against the somewhat shorter and thinner beard of Rumtek's elderly Chant Master, Omdze La. I asked myself, what is the contest, since my beard is so clearly larger and longer?

His Holiness gave the rules and instructions to me through hand gestures. Wide eyed, with animated face and pursed lips, he pantomimed gathering his non-existent beard and slowly wrapping it around his ear, around and around, counting in Tibetan as he went. "Chik, nyi, sum, zhi, nga." Okay, I got it. The winner was the one who could wrap his beard around his ear the most times. Omdze La would go first. As he started wrapping his long, though somewhat spindly beard around his ear, once, twice, thrice, I realized I had a problem. I don't remember how many times he managed to string it around his ear. I lost count.

My turn. Anticipating the emerging problem, I tightly gathered up my abundant mane in an effort to compress it, since being as thick as it was, the diameter of the roll around my ear was growing by a few inches with each turn, so fast in fact that I ran out of beard after only three or four (thick) wraps!

As news of the contest got out, quite a few monks had gathered around. So when I got to the end of my "rope," which was way short of the Omdze's count, the monks joined His Holiness as he roared with laughter. The happy Omdze had won, fairly and squarely, because of the peculiarly Tibetan method of measuring beards!

THE INCONCEIVABLE ACTIVITY OF THE KARMAPAS
by Hella Lohmann

Hella Lohmann was a devoted disciple of Jamgön Kongtrul Rinpoche and the 17th Karmapa. Sadly, she passed away in 2011 after being in a coma for many months; and therefore her biographical details are incomplete.

Unfortunately, I did not have the karma to meet the 16th Gyalwang Karmapa personally. But something incredible and very special happened in 1990 during my very first visit to Rumtek Monastery. I immediately felt close to His Eminence Jamgön Kongtrul Rinpoche at Rumtek, one of the four lineage holders and heart sons of the Gyalwang Karmapa. In fact, I saw him almost every day. During one meeting, I confessed candidly that I did not feel any connection or devotion to the Karmapa as I had never met him. At the same time, I expressed how much devotion I felt for the Dalai Lama whom I had met several times in Europe and India. Jamgön Rinpoche listened attentively and nodded his satisfaction.

During that time, I used to walk the long circumambulation path around the monastery every morning before sunrise and sit in meditation while the sun was rising. I would take some incense

HH 16th Karmapa and Jamgön Kongtrul Rinpoche.
(Photographer unknown)

with me to stimulate my meditation practice. The morning following my confession to Rinpoche, I walked up the hill to sit under the trees where thousands of prayer flags were gently blowing in the wind far above Rumtek. Halfway up, I realized that I had left the incense on my table but I did not feel inclined to walk all the way back to my cabin. I decided to meditate without it.

The moment I closed my eyes—at that time I would meditate with eyes closed—there was suddenly a beautiful fragrance in the air. I opened my eyes and discovered right in front of me a single stick of incense stuck in the grass. It had just started burning—the ashes hadn't even dropped yet. I stood up and glanced across the valley to the hills. To my great surprise, there wasn't a single person to be seen. So, where did the incense come from?

I felt confused and puzzled—and excited. As I wasn't able to continue my meditation after what had happened, I walked slowly down to the monastery to see Jamgön Rinpoche. I described the experience and asked whether the Karmapa could perform this kind of miracle. Jamgön Rinpoche listened very carefully and, as in the past, nodded his satisfaction.

From that moment onwards, I felt a very strong and unwavering connection to the Karmapa and the Kagyu lineage. In July 1992, three months after the untimely death of Jamgön Rinpoche, I was fortunate enough to meet the reincarnation of the 16th Karmapa at his monastery in Tsurphu, Tibet; and with gratitude, I have been meeting with the 17th Karmapa almost every year ever since then.

EMPEROR OF LOVE
by Lama Palden

*L ama Palden Drolma (Caroline Alioto) met her root teacher
Kalu Rinpoche in 1977 in San Francisco, after studying and
practicing in various traditions. Following that, she had the great
good fortune to study with him and other great masters, including
the 16th Karmapa. She moved to Bhutan in 1979 until her three-
year retreat in 1982. In 1997 she founded Sukhasiddhi Foundation,
a Buddhist center in the Shangpa and Kagyu lineages in Marin
County, California. Lama Palden is also a licensed psychotherapist
in California and combines psychological and spiritual work in her
Stream of Being work.*

I met the 16th Karmapa in Rumtek in 1978. In 1979 I moved to
Bhutan, and for the next few years I spent a lot of time with His
Holiness Karmapa and even travelled with him from Calcutta, to
Athens, and then to New York in 1980. I was married to a Kagyu
tulku who is Bhutanese, Benchen Khenpo Rinpoche. He was
raised from the age of nine by the 16th Karmapa and escaped from
Tsurphu with His Holiness to India.

Blessing the Universe

It was 1978 when I first went to Rumtek. My immediate impression of the Karmapa was his incredible love. Karmapa embodied pure spiritual power. I never met anyone who had so much power, infused with compassion and love. He would walk around his room and talk about his different activities. It was like being in the presence of a spiritual emperor—the embodiment of compassion and love, power and wisdom.

He invited me to a private empowerment he was giving for a few members of the Bhutanese royal family, a private Vajrapani initiation. The members of the royal family of Bhutan who were taking the empowerment turned out to be his relatives by marriage; and were also his sponsors throughout the years.

When I was leaving a few days later, I went in to say goodbye. He put his hand on my head and started chanting for what seemed a long time. My body opened into the universe with his blessing pouring into the central channel. It was an extraordinary, unforgettable, and unique experience. As I was leaving, he gave me some presents. Once outside, I saw his monks following me. They told me there was another present. Just then His Holiness came towards me and gave me a small Buddha statue.

I was shy, respectful, and devoted but I thought, now he's outside here... so I went ahead and asked him, "May I take a photo?" I got a beautiful picture of him that day.

The most precious thing he told me was that I was part of his family.

The main thing I remember from the Black Crown ceremony was the incredibly powerful transmission of Chenrezig where His Holiness would really become Chenrezig and transmit the blessing of this bodhisattva of compassion.

He would fully embody Chenrezig during the Black Crown ceremony. I'd see him go through the changes. He would put on the Crown and his face and body would transform, open into

Chenrezig. (Painting by Marianna Rydvald)

and fully embody the presence of Chenrezig. He was still visually Karmapa but in the inner sense of my direct experience I could feel and see Chenrezig. There was an amazing amount of love and compassion coming from him.

In those days it was possible to have great intimacy with

His Holiness. He made himself available to all those who came to Rumtek. Often lamas and tulkus came to see him and it was clear they were not always behaving properly. They would go astray sometimes. He was like a father trying to help them. They would come out of his room and say, "Karmapa knew everything I was doing yesterday." He would have seen something that they shouldn't have been doing and they would be astonished that he could see it.

Whenever I went into His Holiness' room to visit with him, my mind became like a movie screen. Just walking into his presence any ego thought I had was instantly recognizable. I could see each thought completely clearly and if it was an ego thought, I let go of it. When I saw my thoughts to be ego thoughts, there was no point in sharing them with him. At that point I didn't understand Mahamudra but the experience of seeing one's mind revealed clearly seemed to be part of the blessing of His Holiness' realization. It enhanced the clarity and awareness of my own mind.

His Holiness would give gifts to everybody. With some people he would extend himself and invite them to stay with him. But sometimes they didn't really understand what a rare opportunity they were being offered. For me there wasn't any point in going anywhere; to sit at the feet of Karmapa—or my guru Kalu Rinpoche. There was nowhere else to go.

Medicine for the Sick

I went back a year later when I was about twenty-eight and spent some time with His Holiness. I became really ill in the early part of my month there, with pneumonia and pleurisy. After lying in bed for weeks, one day I walked up the hill to the house inside the monastery grounds where the two Bhutanese royal grandmothers were living. One had been very ill and the other was taking care of her. I knew Ashi Pema Dechen, the younger one who was healthy, from Bhutan. She had done a three-year retreat when her children were very little. She and her sister were both married to the second king. I got to their house, knocked and Ashi Pema Dechen opened the door herself. She was such an embodiment of compassion that I immediately burst into tears. One of the princesses was also there. They were so concerned at my tears they called my husband and told him to come as soon as possible. He drove straight through from Bhutan. As soon as he arrived he told His Holiness that I was ill. Karmapa sent his own medicine to me that he kept on his body and by the next day I was much better. Just taking that medicine from him turned the pneumonia and pleurisy right around.

The two Bhutanese royal grandmothers stayed there for several years. One day Karmapa told me one of them had a dream the previous night and said that whenever they had a dream or a vision he would listen to what they had to say because they were wisdom dakinis. They were both extremely humble.

A Pair of African Birds

One time when I was at Rumtek, two guys showed up. One was from East Germany, the other from the deserts of Morocco and America. His father was a Berber chieftain, his mother was American. They had met while travelling around India and were both magicians and musicians, doing magic tricks and playing music.

Karmapa became extremely excited when they arrived in Rumtek to see him for an audience and asked "Where did you two find each other? You were my pair of African birds in your last lifetime." He invited them to stay in the monastery and arranged a grand welcoming party for them during which he gave a Milarepa empowerment. He told them to stay together and keep performing their music and magic.

In 1980, when he travelled to the West he already had cancer but only a few people knew about it. When he gave an empowerment he was radiant and very much there; but when people left he looked exhausted.

We were a party of eleven flying with him on Air India from Calcutta to Greece and then to London. I was the only woman and the only Westerner. On the flight to Athens, the Indian flight attendants knew he was a Buddhist holy man. They came up to me and asked if he would read their fortune in their hands. I had never heard anyone ask a high Lama to do that and had never seen it done. But they kept pestering me so I asked His Holiness for them. He was so loving and kind he actually did read their hands and shared what he saw with them, while Jamgön Kongtrul translated.

In London we stayed in a very grand house with magnificent gardens. One day all the tulkus living in Europe came to see him, worried about his health. It was then I realized he was going to die in the near future. I went into the garden and sobbed, heartbroken.

HE WAS ALWAYS FREE
by Ringu Tulku

Ringu Tulku was recognised by HH 16th Karmapa as a reincar-nation of one of the tulkus of Ringu Monastery in East Tibet where he was born. He is one of the most prominent contemporary Rime, or non-sectarian masters. Since 1990, he has been travelling and teaching in Europe, the USA, Canada, Australia and Asia. He is the author of a number of books on Buddhism, as well as children's books in both Tibetan and European languages. He is the founder of Bodhicharya, an international organization that co-or-dinates his worldwide activities to preserve and transmit Buddhist teachings, to promote intercultural dialogues as well as educational and social projects.

I arrived in Sikkim in 1959 when I was almost seven and that's when I met His Holiness the 16th Karmapa. I remember going to old Rumtek Monastery which was mostly a wooden structure. There was no road to Rumtek, so everyone had to go by foot or mule. The Karmapa was on one part of the upper floor; the previous Dzogchen Ponlop Rinpoche, who was the younger brother of the 16th Karmapa, was also staying there, as was the former Sangye Nyenpa Rinpoche and Tenga Rinpoche. They all stayed in bamboo huts.

The Karmapa went to Bhutan from Tibet, then to Sikkim. He had been to Sikkim in 1956 when His Holiness the Dalai Lama was invited to the 2500th anniversary of Buddha's parinirvana. Nehru invited all the other Tibetan masters as well as the Dalai Lama.

When Karmapa was in Gangtok, Rumtek Monastery invited him to stay. He said, "I can't come now but I will come later on and I will stay a long time." So when he came out of Tibet as a refugee, the King of Sikkim, Chögyal Tashi Namgyal, who was a great devotee, asked him to come. He offered the Karmapa a lot of land where the new Rumtek Monastery was to be built, and invited him to stay in Sikkim and be his teacher.

We Tibetans see Karmapa as almost like a buddha, so everything is special in a way, and nothing is more special than anything else. I don't know if I had any special experience. I was very happy to see him and I always wanted to stay with him in a monastery. It didn't happen exactly that way because in 1960 or 61, he sent me to the Young Lamas Home School in Dalhousie.

He was always free, that was the impression I got. He was free in the sense of not busy. He used to sit, sometimes with a text in front of him. Anybody who wanted to see him could come in and sit down. We would talk, laugh, make jokes, and have a cup of tea. From 4:00 or 5:00 a.m. until the evening, he was always there ready to see people, ordinary people as well. He would just sit there. It was really very special, though we didn't think so at the time. Anybody, rich or poor, high or low, came. Everybody was very happy. He would tell them what to do or not to do. Even after he went to the West, it was the same. There were not so many translators at that time or I'm sure he would have taught much more, but that didn't hinder him. It's surprising. Everybody got something.

To genuine practitioners, he gave pointing out instructions. Those who were not, he just talked to them. They would go away so happy. Everybody wanted to help him.

I would go to see him very often. There was not much conver-

HH 16th Karmapa at Rumtek, 1980.
(Courtesy of Katia Holmes)

sation because your mind would go blank. Sometimes he would ask me what I was doing, what was going on in Sikkim. But he would guide people and say little things which would have a big effect. The main thing he told me was that when Tibet is open, go back to Tibet and rebuild your monastery. This was in 1979. I was surprised because to go back to Tibet and rebuild a monastery at that time would have been very unusual. Later I did go back and rebuild my monastery.

There was one Sikkimese, a mountaineer who went to see Karmapa. He was also a Buddhist. Mountaineers are not only mountaineers, they are also Intelligence people. He went there, sat down, and thought, "I need to eat lunch." His Holiness said, "Bring lunch, bring a good lunch for him." Then he thought it would be nice to have yoghurt. His Holiness said, "Bring yoghurt." So he had yoghurt. There was very little you could hide. It was very difficult to say anything. You just sat down and replied to what he asked.

He was greatly helped by the king of Bhutan, who offered a diplomatic passport for him to travel with. There was nobody obstructing him. Mrs Freda Bedi, his secretary, was close to the Nehru family. I used to go with her to visit Indira Gandhi after she became Prime Minister.

I was there at the end when His Holiness died. I came to Rumtek on the same day that the news broke that he had passed away. I stayed there for the forty-nine days.

The 17th Karmapa, Ogyen Trinley Dorje, must get that kind of freedom, of course. But the situation is a bit different now, so it is difficult but yes, he should be able to get that kind of freedom. Things can change.

I don't think there will be a political leadership role. His Holiness the Dalai Lama said there is no lama rule any more. He said it is out of date. He is adamant about it. So they cannot pass that onto Karmapa.

His Holiness has a big role to play anyway. He is very important for Tibetans and that will never change.

KARMAPA'S RAINBOW BODY
by Sue Campbell-Felgate

I started to go to Samye Ling in my late twenties and began to learn more about Tibetan Buddhism. I also met Peter Mannox whom I married. It was through Peter that I ended up going to India. He was asked by Akong Rinpoche to go to Sikkim to photograph sacred paintings for Samye Ling. That's how I ended up at Rumtek in 1980. I wasn't Buddhist at the time. It was an extraordinary experience.

I met His Holiness for the first time in the early months of 1980. I remember a lorry full of people from Gangtok disgorging outside the monastery. I looked at the entrance to the Monastery and it had a profound effect on me. The enormity of spiritual activity in the place was intimidating. For the first few days I didn't get further than that entrance. It felt too much to cross that space and go into the Monastery.

We arrived just before Losar. On New Year's Day, we all got up really early, about 4:00 a.m. to go into the monastery. There were crowds gathering. There was a great influx of Westerners who came for Losar and a core group would then remain. Devotees would turn up for a few days and disappear.

Then I saw His Holiness for the first time. He took his place on the throne and sat rearranging his robes. I looked at him and tears came into my eyes. I have no idea why. I had no connection with him or Buddhism, I thought. But just seeing him had a profound effect on me at a visceral level.

We stayed at Rumtek for about a month. I used to help carry Peter's photography equipment up to the balcony at the top of the monastery and then just hang around. All the Regents including Shamarpa were there. Peter was accepted by all the monks and Lamas, but I felt like I was in a man's world.

Throughout my time at Rumtek I felt like I was a hanger-on. Somehow my presence was not legitimate. All the people were Tibetan Buddhists who knew mantras and rituals. I felt quite alienated from it, because of the iconography. I knew it was very powerful but I felt outside of it all. However, I knew it was the real deal. I knew it would have a positive impact on me. So I would go up for the Black Hat ceremonies.

Over that period, Karmapa performed many Black Hat ceremonies. The ceremony would always be heralded by the sound of *jalings*. As soon as we heard the jalings, we would all rush up the hill and His Holiness would perform the Black Hat ceremony. At the end, everybody would go up and get a blessing.

I thought, here I am with a being whose love and compassion is all-embracing. I felt it was a privilege to be there to receive these blessings. I would normally follow Peter up there for the blessing. As Peter had already met His Holiness, when he gave Peter a blessing there was an exchange of looks between them. When I followed Peter, His Holiness went into his neutral gaze. I'd get a tap on the head and off I'd go.

Until one day. The jalings went off, we ran up, all the prayers were said. The attendants came in with a black box, wearing masks on their faces. They offered the Hat to His Holiness. With one hand he took out the Black Hat, with the other he held a crystal rosary. Everything was the same until he put on the Hat. Suddenly his face and hand which was holding the Hat dissolved in front of my eyes.

HH Karmapa «Rainbow Body», Rumtek, February 8th, 1978.
(Copyright Peter Mannox)

Nothing was different but everything was different. I looked around. Everybody else was just the same. I looked back and he had dissolved. All the exposed flesh of his body, his hand, his arm, his face and neck, all of it was transparent. I could see through his body. I was in a bit of a state wondering what had happened.

The ceremony ended and I went up for a blessing. He looked at me and gave me a huge, broad, beautiful smile as he blessed me. It was like saying, now do you begin to understand? I just thought yes, now I get it, now I can start. It was such a manifestation of his power to me. It was a transmission.

Looking back on it and how my life has evolved in terms of my meditation, it feels that there was so much going on for me at that time, to have a direct transmission from His Holiness was an extraordinary blessing. It felt like all encompassing love, a sense of oneness, totality. It had that quality to it—a hugely expansive quality. I've touched it again from time to time in my meditation practice.

Peter took that special photograph of His Holiness disappearing into rainbow light before I met him. He had a plate camera and I think he took it with his plate camera. He developed his own photos. When it was developed he showed it to Akong Rinpooche, who blinked a bit and said obviously it's a double exposure. Peter felt he knew exactly what it was but he didn't want to play it up. He never allowed the photograph to be reproduced for sale. Peter did not doctor that photo at all. He didn't see that with his own eyes. So it's strange that I saw with my own eyes the photograph he had taken five years before.

There were two other encounters. The first one was when we were leaving Rumtek. Because of Peter's connection with His Holiness, we went to see him personally to say goodbye. It was a very short meeting. He was in his rooms. I can't remember what was said, if anything at all. Peter presented his offering scarf and received his blessing. When I went up, His Holiness looked at me in a very particular way, with huge kindness and compassion, sadness almost. He took my head in both his hands and ruffled my hair like I was a small child. I was very moved at the time. I didn't quite understand it.

The whole time at Rumtek I had felt quite abandoned by Peter. I had to make my own way as much as I could. It also seemed to be prescient of what lay ahead. Peter and I were to go through some very painful times. It was as though His Holiness could see some of that. I felt very much held by him.

I only saw him once after that. We went from Rumtek to Nepal and spent some time trekking in Nepal. We arrived in London on the same day as His Holiness arrived in London in transit on his way to the US. That seemed like an extraordinary coincidence. We didn't know he was travelling to the US. We had purchased our tickets a long time before. We turned up at the same time as he was in the airport. We were somehow able to get into the transfer lounge where he was sitting. I saw him across the room and he looked at me once and seemed to be in great pain. He was clearly very ill. That was the last time I saw him.

The following autumn Peter and I were back in Scotland where we lived. We were driving back home on the edge of the river Tay which had the most extraordinary open skies. A rainbow coloured comet appeared in the sky for a few seconds. We both remarked how extraordinary it was. The next morning we got a call from Samye Ling saying His Holiness had died the night before. By that time we were thinking, yes, that's what the comet was.

That's how it was.

16 th Karmapa
in North America

1974 · 1977 · 1980

USA Introduction

Steve Roth and Norma Levine

THE COMING OF BUDDHISM to the West was predicted by
historian Arnold Toynbee to be one of the major events of
the twentieth century. At the end of the nineteenth century, Sir
Henry Olcott, a military officer, journalist and lawyer, became the
first American Buddhist of European ancestry. Olcott and Rus-
sian occultist, Helena Blavatsky, founded the Theosophical Society, whose motto was "There is no Religion Higher than Truth."
The major 20th century cultural figures who would prepare the
ground for the spirituality of the 1960s, were the writers Jack Ker-
ouac, whose most famous title *On the Road* became a handbook
for seekers everywhere; William Burroughs, a talented writer and
drug addict; and Beat poet, Allen Ginsberg. Suddenly, "there was
music in the cafes at night and revolution in the air" to quote Dylan.

The general cynicism and loss of heart in the American Dream
gave way to the counterculture of the 1960s and the subculture
of the hippie movement—experimenting with psychedelics, "free
love," communal lifestyles, the Women's Movement. The music
of Dylan, the Beatles and the Stones, amongst others, amplified

the feeling of freedom and alienation. In the mix of this backdrop was the Vietnam War and the Watergate scandal with Nixon's departure from office in disgrace. All this and more composed the tumultuous, unwieldy, and outrageous years which produced in so many a profound disappointment and disillusionment in life and society. This revulsion gave way to openness and an inherent inquisitiveness.

This was nowhere better illustrated than in the creation of Naropa Institute by the Vidyadhara Chögyam Trungpa Rinpoche in Boulder, Colorado in 1974, three months before the arrival of the 16th Gyalwang Karmapa. Naropa was to become the first accredited Buddhist university in America where Allen Ginsberg and Ann Waldman would eventually form the Naropa School of Disembodied Poetics. There were also intellectuals, such as Gregory Bateson, psychologists such as Stanislav Graf, the post-psychedelic guru, Ram Dass, and hippies in transition. These were the minds that in the late 1960s and early 1970s gathered around Trungpa Rinpoche and other Buddhist teachers—Suzuki Roshi, Tarthang Tulku, and Kalu Rinpoche. The times were indeed changing.

There were many major players in the transplantation of buddha-dharma to America. In 1971–1972, the great meditation master Kalu Rinpoche visited the West at the request of the 16th Karmapa. He created one of the first Tibetan Buddhist dharma centers in Vancouver, Canada with many more to follow during his second trip in 1974. Tarthang Tulku, the Tibetan Nyingma master, founder of Dharma Publishing and author of *Time, Space and Knowledge*, settled in Berkeley California in 1969 with his wife Nazil Noor, who was a disciple of the 16th Karmapa.

The visionary Chögyam Trungpa Rinpoche arrived in the United States in 1970 from Britain, after co-founding Samye Ling (Scotland) with Akong Rinpoche. Trungpa very quickly gathered a large group of sincere students and eventually formed Varjradhatu, an association of Buddhist meditation centres in Boulder, Colorado. Vajradhatu later became Shambhala International, in Nova Scotia.

HH 16th Karmapa and Chögyam Trungpa Rinpoche.
(Photographer unknown)

It was the winter of 1973 when Trungpa Rinpoche requested His Holiness Rangjung Rigpe Dorje, the 16th Gyalwang Karmapa to visit America. Sister Palmo, one of the Karmapa's personal secretaries, and the first Western Tibetan Buddhist nun, was sent as an emissary to interface with Vajradhatu and its centres. What followed were intense, uninterrupted preparations for "The Visit."

Trungpa Rinpoche became the living example of unbridled devotion by his level of hands-on engagement. He formed a variety of committees from administrators and master planners to carpenters and craftspeople who carved magnificent thrones, and talented seamstresses who worked late into the night with exquisite silk brocades imported from India and China. Later, the walls in the private quarters of His Holiness were covered in satin to complete an elegant environment befitting a Universal Monarch.

The jet plane carrying His Holiness and a travelling party of twelve including Vajra Master Tenga Rinpoche, Sister Palmo, and, Achi Tsepal, his main translator, arrived in New York on

September 18, 1974. They all stayed at Bodhi House, the lavish Long Island estate of C.T. Shen, the principal patron of Buddhism in America.

His Holiness presented the first Black Crown ceremony in New York on September 21st and despite the fact that Tibetan Buddhism was almost unknown in the US, about three thousand people gathered to see it in a gloriously transformed dockyard warehouse. He then travelled to Tail of the Tiger Center in Vermont, which he renamed Karme Choling, the Dharma Place of the Karma Kagyus. His Holiness bestowed the Vajra Crown ceremony, gave empowerments, teachings and refuge vows, everywhere he travelled during this and subsequent visits.

Then he traveled to Boston, Ann Arbor and Boulder. At the 600 acre Rocky Mt. Dharma Center at Red Feather Lakes in Northern Colorado (later renamed Shambhala Mt. Centre), he pointed to and blessed the spot that would become the future site of the Great Stupa of Dharmakaya.

From Colorado, His Holiness headed a large caravan on a pilgrimage to Hopiland, via the Great Kiva and Canyon de Chelly in New Mexico, and other sacred American Indian sites. To the wonderment of the Hopi, who had requested His Holiness to relieve their drought-stricken land, Karmapa conducted a ceremony and a deluge of rain fell for the first time in seventy-five days. In the evening, the Hopi and Navajo people gratefully received the Chenrezig empowerment from His Holiness. Next was the Grand Canyon and eventually Phoenix where he boarded a flight for San Francisco.

In San Francisco and the surrounding areas, His Holiness met with Tarthang Tulku and his sangha, Roshi Richard Baker, Suzuki Roshi's dharma heir, and then was the guest of honor at a Japanese Tea Ceremony hosted and conducted by Mrs. Shunryu Suzuki, Suzuki Roshi's recent widow. Just prior to his departure for Canada, His Holiness performed the Black Crown ceremony at San Francisco's Fort Mason by the Bay for over 2,500 people.

HH Karmapa with Jamgön Kongtrul, Khenpo Karthar, Tenzin Chönyi and Bardor Tulku at KTD, Woodstock, NY. (Photographer unknown)

During his first visit to the US, the Karmapa carefully planted "seeds," which would soon sprout into dharma centres. During the Karmapa's second visit in 1977, C.T. Shen donated 300 acres of land in Putnam County which was later sold to buy twenty-five acres of land and Meads Mountain Resort, an old hotel. This eventually became Karma Triyana Dharmachakra, KTD, the Karmapa's North American seat. KTD was eventually located at the heart of the new spiritual generation, in Woodstock, New York.

After the first tour His Holiness sketched a plan for the whole complex to include a courtyard for lama dance, living quarters for resident lamas and staff, and rooms for monks, nuns, and students. Tenzin Chönyi, the Karmapa's personal attendant, was appointed to oversee the administration; Bardor Tulku Rinpoche was mostly responsible for KTD's construction.

Sometime before the Karmapa's second visit to America in 1977, Werner Erhard, the Deepak Chopra of his time, made the long journey to Rumtek in Sikkim and made a strong connection

HH Karmapa and Werner Erhart, founder of EST, circa 1977.
(Photographer unknown)

with His Holiness. During His Holiness second visit, he bestowed
the Black Crown ceremony on five separate occasions in four US
cities—San Francisco, Los Angeles, New York and Boston—to
over 10,000 of Werner Erhard's Erhard Seminars Training (EST)
graduates and friends.

One of Erhard's many connections was with Hugh Heffner,
whom His Holiness visited in Beverley Hills. In one of the more
comic twists of fate, Hefner was not only a connoisseur of a particular species known as the Playboy bunny, but also had a vast
collection of exotic birds.

During His Holiness' Los Angeles visit, James Coburn, actor
and narrator of the documentary film, "The Lion's Roar," took
the Karmapa for a thrilling spin in his ultra-high-end sports road-
ster. In New York, His Holiness stayed for six weeks in the Fifth
Avenue apartment of Sai Baba devotees Phil and Diane Budin,
where he met geodesic dome architect-cum-guru, Buckminster

Fuller. In Woodstock, Albert Grossman, Bob Dylan's manager and one of the most influential names in the music business, was a frequent visitor. In Washington, His Holiness was an honoured guest at the mansion of Senator Charles Percy, a Tibet supporter. He was also received at a reception on Capitol Hill attended by ninety-two senators and congressmen. Another reception was hosted by the Director of the Smithsonian, Dillon Ripley, a friend of His Holiness.

The elegance and splendour so exquisitely created with loving devotion by Chögyam Trungpa and the Vajradhatu organisation, was carried throughout all three tours in 1974, 1977, and 1980. There were grand receptions with lavish displays, such as at the Park Plaza hotel in New York where the entire top floor was booked for the occasion; sumptuous and regal venues for the Black Crown, like the world-famous Lincoln Centre; palatial mansions where His Holiness was hosted by people who were rulers in their own realms. The 16th Karmapa was welcomed like a Universal Monarch at the centre of this magnificent mandala.

On July 27th, 1980 during his last visit to the USA, His Holiness consecrated the land for KTD, with a two-day Red Chenrezig puja. Both Buckminster Fuller and Senator Charles Percy were named as honorary members on the first Board of Advisers of KTD. Albert Grossman was on the original Board of Trustees.

The Karmapa also made an important visit to Southern Colorado to the Baca Grande Estate in the Sangre de Christo mountains, a spiritual power place sacred to the indigenous people of the area. Hanne and Maurice Strong,[1] who owned Baca Grande, offered the Karmapa 200 acres of the land to fulfill his vision,

---

[1] Maurice Strong was the Canadian Undersecretary General to the UN who organised the Rio Earth Summit of 1992. Hanne, his Danish born wife, was working with indigenous people of the US and Canada. They had both taken lay precepts with His Holiness Karmapa in Rumtek. Their wish was to establish a community to include Native American, spiritual, and environmental groups. They acquired the Baca Grande Estates in 1978.

which included a Tibetan medical centre, a retreat centre, a monastery and lay community. After seven years of intensive work, a forty-foot stupa containing many relics of His Holiness the 16th Karmapa was completed. Tashi Gomang Stupa was consecrated on July 6, 1996, sixteen years after His Holiness had passed away.

An estimated 30,000 or more people came to see His Holiness during the three US visits—the range included people from various Buddhist traditions to people with no particular affiliation. The great benefit of the Karmapa's visits is that His Holiness embraced everyone equally, acknowledging and affirming their basic goodness. He caused a virtual meltdown of the heart with his sphere of radiations as the thousand arms of Chenrezig, manifesting the energy of unconditional love and compassion. In his embrace everyone experienced their own finest qualities. Dignitaries, police, bird breeders, street cleaners, movie stars—all were included in his great, loving embrace.

Karmapa's parinirvana, or passing beyond, took place in a cancer clinic in Zion, Illinois, on November 5th, 1981. Here the Karmapa's unceasing compassion manifested for hospital staff and visitors as he demonstrated that awakened mind is beyond the body. He claimed to have no pain, took his last breath as the 16th Karmapa, and left his body. To the utter amazement of the doctors and staff, after his clinical death, he remained in the postdeath meditation state with his skin supple and with warmth at the heart area for a further three days.

Canada and the Three World Tours of His Holiness Karmapa

by MJ Bennett and Norma Levine

I N 1973, on the eve of the 16th Karmapa's first visit to the West, the political landscape was less distinctly drawn than it is to-day. The Karmapa was able to travel to the West five years before His Holiness the 14th Dalai Lama, due partly to the patronage of the Bhutanese Royal Family who issued diplomatic passports to His Holiness and Jamgön Rinpoche, and national passports to his Tibetan entourage. Due to these favourable circumstances, the Karmapa was one of the first of Tibet's great spiritual leaders to visit North America.

The 1970s in Canada under the charismatic Prime Minister Pierre Trudeau was a peaceful, vibrant period. The sleeping giant to the north of the US became a haven for Vietnam pacifists and an island of sanity in the Western world. Prime Minister Trudeau was convinced of the significance of meditation in a life well-lived. He was the first world leader to meet John Lennon and Yoko Ono on their "tour for world peace." James George, the distinguished

16th Karmapa and Namgyal Rinpoche at the Dharma Centre of Canada.
(Photographer unknown)

Canadian ambassador to India and Nepal, had also met many spiritual leaders. Because of his influence, Canada was among the first countries to open its doors to Tibetan refugees.

Canada is a land with a vast wilderness, very like Tibet. And in that vastness, peace. Much of the country is cut off from the rest of the world by lack of roads and eight to ten months of sub-zero temperature. Perhaps it was this solitude and its striking similarity to Tibet that created the favourable conditions for Canada to play a significant role in the 16th Karmapa's first visit to North America.

Namgyal Rinpoche[1] first visited Rumtek in 1968 with a group

---

1 Canadian-born George Leslie Dawson was later given the name Ananda Bodhi Bhikku after training in the Burmese tradition. In 1967, he requested the Mahabodhi Society of the UK to offer Johnstone House in Scotland to Chögyam Trungpa Rinpoche and Akong Rinpoche, who re-named it Samye Ling. He took full Gelong or monastic ordination with the 16th Karmapa at Rumtek Monastery, after which he became known as Namgyal Rinpoche.

of over one hundred students. It was his group, the Dharma Centre of Canada, that issued the invitation in November 1973 to His Holiness to visit Canada. The invitation requested His Holiness to "consecrate the land of the Dharma Centre of Canada in full Kagyu tradition," and offered to pay for round-the-world tickets for "His Holiness and a full complement of attendants." This invitation and His Holiness' subsequent reply sparked the beginnings of the first world tour.

Namgyal Rinpoche received a reply to the Dharma Centre's invitation in early 1974 in a letter written by Sister Palmo and signed by the Karmapa. In this letter, His Holiness suggested the countries that he would like to visit, beginning in North America and then travelling on to Europe before returning home. He also added a note to contact Chögyam Trungpa Rinpoche in America.

When the Vidyadhara Chögyam Trungpa Rinpoche was informed of the proposed tour, he contacted the Dharma Centre of Canada and with characteristic aplomb, offered to sponsor four first-class tickets, one for His Holiness and an attendant, one for Sister Palmo and one for the sacred Black Crown![2]

A flurry of letters and telegrams between Canada and the US followed. The number of attendants in the entourage increased together with the cities to be visited. With Chögyam Trungpa's enthusiasm, aided by the size of his organization, it soon became a very grand tour.

On the 400 acres of land belonging to the Dharma Centre of Canada, preparation for His Holiness' visit began. Several families travelled more than 5,000 kilometres from the Yukon Territory to help Namgyal Rinpoche's group build suitable accommodation. They lived in tents on plywood platforms and built an outdoor kitchen to feed everyone, while they worked on an extension to the main cabin. A stupa was started, the temple renovated, and

---

2 This was told to me by Bruce Cowen, Secretary-Treasurer for the Dharma Centre of Canada at the time of the Karmapa's world tours.

HH Karmapa arrives in the Yukon with the Black Hat.
(Courtesy of Cheryl Buchan)

electricity and a bathroom added to Hill House cabin for His Holiness' use. Even the rain of that memorable Canadian summer, the wet tents, the black flies, and mosquitoes could not dampen youthful optimism; the joy at the arrival in the West of Tibet's great spiritual king.

In October 1974, after travelling throughout the US, His Holiness and entourage arrived in Vancouver to a personal welcome at the airport by the Very Venerable Kalu Rinpoche. His Holiness was then received by the Lieutenant Governor of British Columbia at Government House in Victoria. They all enjoyed front row seats at the Vancouver Aquarium for a whale diving show; and Karmapa was delighted when the whales flapped their tails and sent a huge wave of water over him and his monks. He was flown without his full entourage, in a small floatplane and persuaded the pilot to allow him to take over the controls. It is said that before landing in Victoria, His Holiness turned the plane in a big circle over Mount Tuam on Salt Spring Island, circling land that

HH Karmapa relaxing in Yukon, 1977.
(Courtesy of Cheryl Buchan)

would later become the first three-year retreat centre in Canada. In the ballroom of the Bayshore Inn in downtown Vancouver he bestowed the Vajra Crown ceremony to a rapt gathering of an estimated 900 people[3].

His Holiness then spent three weeks in the Canadian countryside at the Dharma Centre of Canada near Toronto. During that time he conferred the Black Crown ceremony, gave refuge, bodhisattva vows, Kagyu Lineage empowerments and monastic ordination. He consecrated not only the temple and a stupa, but also a small Mahakala shrine in the forest, conferring the empowerment of the Kagyu Lineage protector at twilight, to a few select students who had prepared for the transmission in retreat.

In nearby Belleville and Lindsay, His Holiness visited the Tibetan communities, and again bestowed the ceremony of the Black Crown.

In 1977, on his second world tour, His Holiness travelled with

---

3 Lama Drubgyu Tony Chapman, organizer of HH 1974 tour to Vancouver.

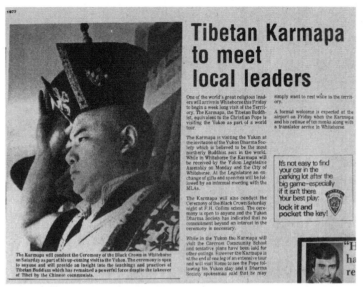

1977

Tibetan Karmapa to meet local leaders

One of the world's great religious leaders will arrive in Whitehorse this Friday to begin a week long visit of the Territory. The Karmapa, the Tibetan Buddhist, equivalent to the Christian Pope is visiting the Yukon as part of a world tour.

The Karmapa is visiting the Yukon at the invitation of the Yukon Dharma Society which is believed to be the most northerly Buddhist sect in the world. While in Whitehorse the Karmapa will be received by the Yukon Legislative Assembly on Monday and the City of Whitehorse. At the Legislature an exchange of gifts and speeches will be followed by an informal meeting with the MLAs.

The Karmapa will also conduct the Ceremony of the Black Crown Saturday night at F.H. Collins school. The ceremony is open to anyone and the Yukon Dharma Society has indicated that no commitment beyond an interest in the ceremony is necessary.

While in the Yukon the Karmapa will visit the Carcross Community School and tentative plans have been laid for other outings. However the Karmapa is at the end of one leg of an extensive tour and will visit Rome to see the Pope following his Yukon stay and a Dharma Society spokesman said that he may

simply want to rest while in the territory.

A formal welcome is expected at the airport on Friday when the Karmapa and his retinue of ten monks along with a translator arrive in Whitehorse.

It's not easy to find your car in the parking lot after the big game–especially if it isn't there. Your best play: lock it and pocket the key!

The Karmapa will conduct the Ceremony of the Black Crown in Whitehorse on Saturday as part of his up-coming visit to the Yukon. The ceremony is open to anyone and will provide an insight into the teachings and practices of Tibetan Buddhism which has remained a powerful force despite the takeover of Tibet by the Chinese communists.

Yukon News, 1977, March 16, p. A3.

Jamgön Kongtrul Rinpoche as his close companion rather than Sister Palmo.[4] They travelled to the far north of Canada, to experience the vast, empty land of northern lights and midnight sun—the Yukon Territory.

When the party of Tibetan travellers, complete with a radiant spiritual master, were officially honoured in the Yukon Legislative Assembly, the grand occasion made newspaper headlines. Dignitaries and local people packed into the largest venue in the area, the high school auditorium, to see the Black Crown ceremony.

A devotee, Robert McCallum, offered thirty-three acres of land on Montana mountain south of the Arctic circle, an area sacred to the indigenous people. There it was dark only a few hours at night in summer and light for a few hours in winter. Four feet of snow covered the ground as His Holiness and entourage landed in

---

4 It was on this Canadian tour that His Holiness received word that Sister Palmo had died in India.

HH Karmapa in the Yukon, 1977.
(Courtesy of Cheryl Buchan)

a helicopter. They waded through waist-deep snow, as His Holiness blessed the site. The local Tagish-Carcross chief welcomed them at the base of the mountain; and offered a ride in a sled pulled by high-spirited Husky dogs, who yelped with delight. Karmapa was still roaring with laughter when he returned.

From the Rocky Mountain Ranch of Maurice and Hanne Strong just outside Calgary, His Holiness attended pow-wows with the Native Blackfeet and Peigan tribes; and a dance in his honour at the Sarcee Reserve[5]. When His Holiness offered a Black Crown Ceremony in the city of Calgary, an observer said all was magical.

At Saskatoon, His Holiness met with Herbert Guenther, a well known academic and one of the first translators of Tibetan, and gave a talk at the University of Saskatchewan. After Ottawa, he went to Montreal where he was received with the highest protocol by Mayor Jean Drapeau.

5 Now the Tsuu T'ina Nation.

HH Karmapa at Whitehorse, Yukon 1977. (Copyright Dharam Singh Gongologist, www.gongsongs. com)

For recreation, the Karmapa went shopping, frequently for birds. He had unspoken communication with his ever-increasing bird entourage. When the birds had to travel in a separate vehicle than their master, they would become very upset and make a lot of noise. At the end of the journey when they were brought to him, still chattering nervously in their covered cages, he would point at them with his finger and they would immediately all

go silent, as though completely calmed by his presence[6].

In 1980 on the Karmapa's third and last world tour, his health was already failing; and he could not travel extensively. A request was sent to His Holiness at Karma Triyana Dharmachakra to send a lama to Canada. In response, Lama Namse Rinpoche became the Karmapa's first official representative in Canada.

HH Karmapa at Whitehorse, Yukon 1977. (Copyright Dharam Singh Gongologist, www.gongsongs. com)

6 Bruce Cowen, Secretary-Treasurer of the Dharma Centre of Canada in a recorded interview with Norma Levine.

HH Karmapa at Whitehorse, Yukon 1977.
(Copyright Dharam Singh Gongologist, www.
gongsongs.com)

That centre today is known as Karma Sonam Dhargay Ling, the Canadian seat of His Holiness the Gyalwang Karmapa. His Holiness and Jamgön Kongtrul Rinpoche made a brief one day visit to Montreal from Woodstock, NY. There he gave teachings and refuge at the Milarepa Centre. Later the Rigpe Dorje Centre was founded under the direction of Jamgön Kongtrul Rinpoche, one of Canada's flourishing Kagyu Centres today.

His Holiness covered the ground of this vast, unpopulated country, not literally, as Guru Rinpoche covered Tibet with his footsteps, but metaphorically with his blessing. In each of the major cities he visited, he bestowed the Vajra Crown and blessed all the established, as well as the fledgling dharma centres. He left indelible imprints on the hearts of the people he met, and on the frozen wilderness and open expanse, so like his native land, that he seemed to love.

Intimate Encounters with the Buddha Karmapa
by Trinley Gyatso

Trinley Gyatso was born in Hawaii and has served both the 16th and 17th Karmapas for the past 35 years. After he met the 16th Karmapa in his twenties, he dedicated his life to Buddhism, working at Karma Triyana Dharmachakra, completing the three-year meditation retreat in Canada and from 1986–2001 in Tibet, where he helped to raise funds for the reconstruction of Tsurphu Monastery. At present, he is a holistic health consultant and meditation teacher and currently lives in Thailand.

When I was with some sadhus in India in 1970, I had a very powerful introduction to communicating telepathically mind-to-mind without words. It's important to understand this way of communication or the rest of my story will not make much sense.

Within a year of my first trip to the Himalayas, I heard an inner voice telling me that one day I would go back there and meet God in the mountains. It was early 1971 and I was on the hippie trail.

Yogi Chen in Kalimpong was one of the first great bodhisattvas I met. He said there was a great Lama in Sikkim called Karmapa, and that I should try to go and meet him. He would give me a letter of introduction. I immediately applied for a visa to Sikkim.

Meeting the Karmapa, Rumtek, 1971

I obtained the required permit within the first year of meeting Yogi Chen. I went to Sikkim the day after a very special experience

Yogi Chen.
(Courtesy of Ward Holmes)

with him. I was carrying his letter of introduction to Karmapa and one acid (LSD) tab which I was saving to take before seeing Karmapa. I followed my inner voice and opened the letter. To my surprise it was in English. After reading it, I felt a powerful force like a psychic hand pulling my heart to get up now and go see Karmapa. It was as if Karmapa was talking to me very clearly: words like, you may never see the Western world again; you may become a monk. It felt like he was opening my heart and testing my ego.

After walking from the valley floor where the main road is, I reached Rumtek Monastery. When I arrived four little monks greeted me and in my mind I heard them say, "Welcome Home." They took me by the hand to first meet Sister Palmo, Karmapa's secretary. I said no, I just wanted to see Karmapa. But I felt Karmapa didn't want to see me that moment while I was on acid, so they showed me to the monastery guest house to stay overnight, with the assurance that I would have a chance to meet him the following morning.

The next day I was taken to meet the Karmapa. A few people were in front of me making offerings. When it came my turn to meet him, I was overwhelmed by his immense and compassionate

HH Karmapa.
(Courtesy of Lama Surya Das)

presence. I was then told to sit on the floor right in front of him. He asked me, "What do you want?" At first I was a little hesitant to say exactly what I wanted. I remembered the letter from Yogi Chen and pulled it out to give to him. He opened it, looked at it, and pretended to read it. "Yes, but what do *you* want?" I broke down in tears and said, "Please show me the right way to live." He said, "Oh-hh, okay." He said to come back in an hour or so.

When I came back, he gave me a Milarepa initiation, even before I had taken the basic Refuge ceremony to become a Buddhist. There were four or five other people there in a very small room. He arranged for me to stay for nine days by calling up the Chief Minister of Sikkim and requesting him to arrange the longest possible stay.

I was alone with His Holiness at Rumtek, April, 1971. When he clicked his fingers for the third time indicating transmission of the Buddha's blessing, that's when my life changed completely.

From being an aimless spiritual wanderer, I became totally dedicated and devoted to him. I felt like an empty vessel filled up with the elixir of wisdom and bliss. It felt like I knew a deeper truth that I had not known before. I was floating in a blissful state for the next two months after the most powerful blessing of my life. I saw His Holiness at least once a day privately and many times in public throughout this time.

Initiation in Benares

The next time I met the His Holiness was in Benares. He said he would make me like a monk or initiate me into a deeper level of Buddhism by taking certain precepts. There were three Rinpoches on either side of me, making a total of six in all including the Karmapa. They put me in the middle, three on one side and three on the other and did prayers and ceremonies for about half an hour.

He often invited me to stay beside him as much as possible. During my time there, I slept in the same rooms as his attendants.

Vancouver 1974

1974 was His Holiness' first trip to the US. I met him in San Francisco and he invited me to go with him to Vancouver. In the middle of the refuge ceremony in Vancouver, he pointed to me at the back of the room and motioned me to come up to him, *now*. He took out his vajra and bell and said, "You will never smoke hash, opium, or marijuana, or take LSD ever again." I was stunned as were others in the room and said, "Yes." That was the end of my career of floating in realms unseen, a wakeup call to come back and be mindfully present in the here and now of this world.

Hawaii 1976

When he asked me to be his driver on his second trip to the US in 1976, that's when the magic really started to happen.

A few days before the Karmapa arrived in Hawaii, it came to me very strongly to go to a friend's place high up the slopes of Mt. Haleakala in Maui. While meditating in the middle of the night, my inner voice was telling me to request Karmapa to do a Guru Rinpoche empowerment here on this land high in the mountains, in a place called Kanio. Karmapa was telling me tele-pathically to gather the owners of the land, give them a black pill, meditate together, and see who would offer a half-acre of land for a temple. We did exactly that and one of them promised to offer the land.

When Karmapa actually came to Honolulu, I said, "Your Ho-liness, you are invited to Maui and you are being offered a half acre of land in Kanio. You are requested to give a Guru Rinpoche empowerment on this land." He said, "No, not Guru Rinpoche. Karma Pakshi." I kept saying, "No, Guru Rinpoche," and he said, "No, Karma Pakshi." He then explained how Guru Rinpoche was in Karma Pakshi's heart and they were one and the same.

After the first Vajra Crown ceremony in Honolulu at Hawaii University, with about 3,000–4,000 people packed into it, we travelled on to Maui driving 5,000 feet up the mountain to do the Karma Pakshi initiation on the land offered to Karmapa. Getting to it was a miracle in itself. I could drive the Cadillac only halfway up and then we had to get into a four-wheel drive vehicle.

Sometime later, the donor of the half acre of land insisted that he offer it directly to Karmapa. So Karmapa got the half-acre and in 1976 we built a stupa there. It's one of the most amazing tem-ples in the world according to many Rinpoches who have visited it over the years.

At Heulo, the first Dharma center of Maui, in the jungle of the north shore, His Holiness performed the first Vajra Crown cer-

Kanio Stupa, Hawaii.
(Courtesy of Ward Holmes)

emony in Maui and gave a powerful phowa blessing afterwards. It was so strong that many people nearly passed out or were in a state of samadhi. When I asked His Holiness about it, he said he did that especially to wake them up from their stupor of ignorance as a result of taking too many drugs. Everyone seemed to be deeply affected, resting in meditation or blissful calm abiding.

"I am Karmapa. Remember?"

We were in Lahina in Maui, browsing around the shops right before a big Vajra Crown ceremony at a Japanese Buddhist temple. I mentioned that we were going to be late and I urged His Holiness to get going. As the driver I felt it was my duty to get to the next event on time. He just looked at me with astonishment and said, "I am Karmapa. Remember? I know when it's time to go."

He went on shopping, fascinated by all the red coral in Hawaii. Finally we got into the car near the Pioneer Inn. As I was turning the car around, a straggly old hippie came up to our brand new shiny Cadillac. It was the best car you could get in 1975, and this old hippie guy was knocking on my window. "Hey, I hear there's some dude up the road, giving some kind of religious ceremony. I'd like a ride."

I said, "Excuse me, sir" and motioned him to go away. As Karmapa's clean-shaven, short-haired driver wearing the new suit he had bought for me, I felt embarrassed by the incident. I rolled up the window and drove on. Karmapa asked me what the man wanted. I said he wanted a ride. Karmapa said, "Let's give him a ride, then."

Karmapa and Jamgön Kongtrul were in the back seat and Joel Wiley and I were in the front. I turned the Cadillac around and the hippie got in the front seat between Joel and I. As soon as he got in, he seemed a bit stunned perhaps from being in the same small space with Karmapa.

Then as we were starting to drive to the temple for the crown ceremony, Karmapa touched him on the shoulder and said, OM

Buddha at Japanese Temple, Lahina, Maui.
(Courtesy of Ward Holmes)

MANI PADME HUNG. Joel turned to him and said, "I think Karmapa wants you to say, OM MANI PADME HUNG." So he started to try to say it, but he could barely get it out. Karmapa asked him what he did for a living. I felt he was a little embarrassed to say he worked at MacDonald's or somewhere like that. Karmapa told him to go on saying OM MANI PADME HUNG.

By that time, we had almost reached the Japanese Buddhist temple where the Vajra Crown was to be held.

We arrived as the jalings were sounding. This was the biggest event the Karmapa ever did in Maui, the Vajra Crown ceremony by the ocean with hundreds of people present.

His Holiness Karmapa got out. Then the hitch-hiker got out. Karmapa turned to him and said, "As a result of getting into the car with us today, all your bad karma from your previous lives has been erased."

While the horns were blasting that deep eerie sound and throngs of people were bowing to Karmapa, he made his way through the masses. The hippie stood there completely awestruck by the entire experience, like someone experiencing a total mind transformation. I was also overwhelmed by the realization that Karmapa had the power to alter an individual's karma and assist them to wake up instantly to a higher purpose.

Master of Timing

The Karmapa was a master of timing, as he demonstrated again and again. There was a big Hawaiian festival and he didn't want to go. We went to a Chinese restaurant instead and he ate and talked, and ate again and sat, and kept on sitting, enjoying the view from this floating Chinese restaurant.

It seemed to me it was wasting precious time as his schedule was so packed. We finally decided to go. After we were quite far from the restaurant, he said he had forgotten his spittoon, so we had to go back and get the spittoon. On the way back, my new car broke down.

To this day, I am sure that Karmapa was instrumental in the breakdown of the car. When he finally got to the party, it was over and people were disappointed. I got all the blame, trying to explain what had happened while Karmapa was half-smiling at me. The Dharma event organizer didn't want to hear my excuses.

Another time, we were driving back from a ceremony on a road right beside the ocean near Makapu in Oahu, Hawaii. Suddenly His Holiness said, "Stop." I pulled over. We were in the middle of nowhere, no people anywhere. He got out of the car. We walked over to the edge of the road as if to look over the vast blue water of the Pacific Ocean. And there just below was a car on its side with a lady lying down next to it, blood coming out of her head. He made some prayers and said she would be all right. As we got back into the car and started to drive off, we saw an ambulance zooming along to find the place of the accident. There were no cars around when we had stopped. I felt it was quite amazing because I couldn't see any sign of an accident from the road, or anyone around who could have phoned for an ambulance.

A Dying Dove

One day we were sitting down in a house near the beach in Kailua on the island of Oahu where Karmapa was staying at the time, when there was a big crash at the window. I went outside to see what it was and found a dying dove. I brought it in to Karmapa and he said, "This dying bird was a disciple of mine and he wanted to die in my presence. He will have a human rebirth in his next life."

HH Karmapa and Trungpa Rinpoche, 1974.
(Photographer unknown)

Chögyam Trungpa

I accompanied His Holiness and entourage from Maui to Honolulu, San Francisco, and New York. When the plane landed at San Francisco airport, we were all told to stay in our seats. Nobody could move. The doors opened and Chögyam Trungpa appeared, walking down the aisle. He invited Karmapa and all of us out of the plane. We were led down a side set of steps, directly onto the red carpet where about nine black limousines were waiting to take us to the Sir Francis Drake Hotel. They had arranged a huge press conference for Karmapa, but he just looked at us as if to say, "What is this commotion?" He wasn't used to having the press people crowding around, trying to ask so many questions.

"Drive as Fast as You Can"

One time, we were driving along the empty NY thruway late at night back from New York City to Karma Triyana Dharmachakra. At one point the Karmapa said, "Drive fast, as fast as you can, as long as you feel comfortable." We drove on this wide, vast empty road until the speedometer was not registering anymore. Then he covered my eyes so I couldn't see anything. It was a little unsettling, to say the least, to be driving so fast and not see anything. Karmapa was laughing and joking with me. He knew when fear started to arise in me.

Once in Rumtek when we were together on one of the highest levels of the monastery building. Karmapa said, "Would you jump, if I asked you to jump? OK, GO AHEAD, JUMP!" My heart went upside down as I recalled the stories of Tilopa with Naropa and his fate. Would I jump and flatten my body because Karmapa told me to? Then he said he was just playing with me to test my faith as he put his arm around me.

Catching Birds

Almost every day we went for a drive around the lake in the Catskills or to pet shops. Once we went into a pet shop in upstate New York. There were lots of birds in a cage. The lady was having trouble catching the bird Karmapa wanted, so Karmapa asked to go inside the cage and get the bird he wanted himself. Karmapa went in and stood very still alone with all the birds inside the cage and in one moment grabbed the birds he wanted with his bare hands while the lady could hardly catch one bird with a big net!

Another time we went on a journey from Karma Triyana Dharmachakra to Connecticut in search of some special peacocks. Out of hundreds of birds, he chose the best ones to take back to

HH Karmapa, Jamgön Kongtrul Rinpoche, Barbara Pettee, Utta
Marstrand, Ward Holmes in the new suit bought for him by HH, and
Umdze-la. (Courtesy of Ward Holmes)

Rumtek. They were placed in small cages for the journey in the
van back to Karma Triyana Dharmachakra before they were eventually shipped off to India. He later decided he wanted two more.
He sent Lama Yeshe and I back there to get them. The task was to
find the right one. Neither of us was sure exactly which ones to
choose. The selection was huge and Karmapa had spent so much
time picking the right ones on the previous trip. Eventually we
chose two at random.

Upon arriving back, Karmapa was furious. Lama Yeshe got
hammered but I quickly slipped away. It was terrifying to witness
Karmapa's display of vajra-like anger.

*It came time to go to New York, once again under the auspices of
Chögyam Trungpa Rinpoche. He was offered a driver from Vajradhatu but Karmapa said he wanted me to be his personal driver.
We sometimes had police escorts or the Vajradhatu people would
often open up roads that were closed to be used as shortcuts. Because
we had diplomatic license plates, we could go anywhere and park
almost anywhere.*

Karmapa's Escape

Sometimes after a big event, His Holiness wanted to break from the large entourage of cars so he directed me at the right moment to drive off. At times he would actually instruct me to lose the entourage. Nobody knew where we went, and in those days cell phones were not readily available, so we just drove off to look for a place to eat, shop, or look at animals in various pet stores. No other cars were in front of or behind us. Everything was always planned in such a formal way, but this was not scheduled. After a while, they got used to it, and understood that Karmapa just wanted free time after a big event to explore and be without all the formality that normally surrounded him.

He loved to shop and to bargain with the salespeople. One time he went into a fancy watch shop and the salesperson was showing him watches. He said, "I want to see that watch." The salesman said pointedly that that watch was very valuable; it was over $15,000 and maybe he would prefer to look at others. Karmapa said, "I want to see that one. Is it similar to this one?" Karmapa rolled up his sleeve and showed a watch that was exactly the same. The man was blown away.

Often Karmapa was laughing as he left various shop people in a state of awe. He would often play with the shop owners and bargain. "How much is this? But if I buy ten?" We would say, "But you can't bargain here!" They would start off being very polite and formal; then as it escalated, the manager would come in and bow and then the manager would be blown away.

Karmapa eventually said it would be good for me to do a three-year retreat at Rumtek and he would arrange all permits required for my stay in Sikkim. Just before he got on the plane from New York back to India, he said, "Maybe it might not be right for you to the three-year retreat at Rumtek in Sikkim, maybe you just do the retreat wherever you can." And then he was gone. That was the last time I saw him in that life.

I was in Hawaii when I heard Karmapa had died. I decided that very day to go into a three-year retreat because that was the last thing he said to me.

Karma Pakshi Cave

Before Karmapa passed away, he hinted to me about going to Tibet. After I got out of the retreat in 1986, I went to Karmapa's main seat at Tsurphu in Tibet. At his monastery, Drupon Dechen Rinpoche said I could do a retreat in the Karma Pakshi cave high above the monastery. All 17 Karmapas had either lived, visited, or meditated there. Maybe because of the altitude or maybe because the blessing was so very powerful, I couldn't do anything but meditate throughout the day and night. Karmapa often came to me very strongly in meditation and said, "You will start Tsurphu Foundation." I was reluctant to do it. He won, as always, because I ended up doing it and with his blessing the Foundation was very successful in helping to rebuild Tsurphu.

OM MANI PEME HUNG

KARMAPA CHENNO

WHEN THE IRON BIRD FLIES
by Steve Roth

Steve Roth met the Vidyadhara Chögyam Trungpa Rinpoche in London in 1967, and has been his student since 1970. Steve is a member of the Shambhala International sangha and lives in Boulder, Colorado.

In eighth century Tibet, Padmasambhava made a prophecy: "When the iron bird flies, when horses run on wheels, the king will come to the land of the red man." Twelve centuries later, His Holiness the 16th Karmapa, Rangjung Rigpe Dorje, travelled—by airplane and by automobile—to the Hopi Indian nation.

In October of 1974, His Holiness Karmapa made his first journey to the United States. His itinerary was packed with a great many events, but from the beginning it was clear: one of the top items on His Holiness' agenda was meeting with the Hopi Indians, whom he regarded as practitioners of the Buddhist ideal of non-aggression. A small caravan was organized to escort the Karmapa from Boulder, Colorado to the Hopi Indian reservation in Arizona. He would be meeting with Hopi Chief, Ned Nayatewa.

We rented a gold-colored Cadillac for the occasion. His Holiness rode in the front, an attendant monk rode in the back, and I had the great good fortune of being the driver. We made our way across Colorado, Utah, and Arizona, reaching Hopi Land early on the afternoon of the third day under cloudless blue skies. We followed a dirt road toward a rugged flat-topped hill rising dramatically from the desert floor. The road began to climb, and soon we were spiraling around the steep, rocky flanks of Hopi Mesa One. Ten minutes later, we reached the Hopi village at the top of the mesa, a cluster of mud-plastered stone and brick dwellings huddled together atop a giant flat rock.

His Holiness stepped out of the car and into the 100-degree afternoon. He was greeted by Chief Ned, a short, wiry and weathered man in his late seventies. In spite of all the hardships that had befallen the Hopis, here stood a chief of dignity, gentleness, and presence. When the Karmapa asked how things were, the chief responded, "Not so good." There had been no rain for seventy-five consecutive days. Crops were failing, creating enormous hardship not only for his tribe but for others as well. The Karmapa listened intently, his face filled with compassion. He promised Chief Ned that he would do something about this situation, and that he would pray for all of the Hopis.

Chief Ned then invited His Holiness and entourage to enter the Hopi's sacred Kiva, an underground chamber used for religious rituals. The only way to enter the Kiva was via an old wooden ladder that descended through a narrow opening to the dimly lit cavern below. His Holiness, being noticeably wider than the opening, stayed above; he waved us on as we followed Chief Ned down the ladder. As we were viewing the sacred objects in the center of the Kiva, I had the strangest feeling that His Holiness was present with us. I turned, and there in the shadows I saw him standing quietly behind us, viewing the items with great interest. I became quite disoriented. It was impossible for him to be in the Kiva, yet there he was. I had no idea how he entered the chamber, nor did I have a clue as to how or when he returned to the entrance where we had left him. The only thing I know is that he didn't use the ladder—but the ladder was the only way in.

There followed a warm goodbye between Chief Ned and His Holiness. The Karmapa returned to the front seat of the Cadillac and we began our gradual descent down the mesa under an absolutely clear blue sky. When we were two-thirds of the way down, the Karmapa began chanting in Tibetan. A stillness ensued—and with it, a sense that we were circumambulating the mesa. We reached the desert floor and headed for the Karmapa's eventual destination, the Hopi Motel and Convention Center at Mesa Two. As he continued chanting, I watched in awe as the sky transformed, with impossible speed, from an empty blue sky into a single thick mass of steel grey-black stretching from horizon to horizon.

We arrived at the inner courtyard of the motel after what I thought had been an hour's ride from Hopi Mesa One. I parked the car and turned off the engine. I remained in the driver's seat and watched as one of His Holiness' attendant monks opened the car door and escorted His Holiness the twenty-five feet or so to his motel room. At the exact moment the door to the room was shut, an unearthly clap of thunder exploded overhead, and multiple bolts of lightning lit up the dense black sky. Then the rain came, a rain unlike anything I have ever known. If rain could pour more than buckets, or harder than a waterfall, that's what was taking place at Hopi Land on that October afternoon. (I returned twenty years later and re-traced the exact route we had taken from Mesa One to Mesa Two. I had to drive it four times; I simply couldn't comprehend that what I had thought to be an hour-long drive actually took less than twelve minutes. Only twelve minutes had passed between a clear blue sky and waterfall rain.)

By evening, the Hopis and the Navajos were aware of what had occurred. Many of them gathered inside the motel's convention center and received the Avalokitesvara empowerment from His Holiness. Many Westerners at the event were struck by the similarities between the Hopis and the Tibetans; they looked like they could have been members of the same extended family. The following day two local papers ran front-page stories reporting that the string of seventy-five consecutive days without rain had been broken by the visit of an "East Indian chief" who, among other things, was well known for making rain. (One headline declared "Chief Karmapa Brings Rain to Bless Hopi Land.")

But the newspapers missed the real story: Padmasambhava's eighth century prophesy had finally—and dramatically—been fulfilled.

THE GREAT LIBERATOR: A BIRD'S EYE VIEW

by Steve Roth

*W*hen *the 16th Karmapa first visited the United States in October of 1974, he arrived with a full schedule: visiting with the Hopi Indians, performing Black Crown Ceremonies, conducting empowerments, offering refuge vows, giving audiences in various cities, and meeting with local and national dignitaries. There was another item on his agenda as well: locating—and acquiring—certain kinds of birds.*

Joel Wiley, a close disciple of the Karmapa, was His Holiness' designated "bird man" during that first visit. Within two days of the party's arrival in Boulder, Colorado, Joel's other responsibilities became so demanding that he invited me to take his place as the Karmapa's bird locator. I joyfully accepted. I soon witnessed His Holiness' extraordinary love of birds. It became immediately apparent that his interest was of an entirely different order than that of a bird collector, or even a bird lover. I once asked him, "Why do you like birds?" He replied, "Just try to sense their joy." Birds seemed to be both the recipients of and vehicles for His Holiness' enormous delight and profound compassion.

Steve Roth reporting to HH Karmapa, 1977.
(Courtesy of Steve Roth)

I learned that the Karmapa had a world-class aviary at his monastery in Rumtek, Sikkim, filled with hundreds of birds. When he traveled by airplane during the US visit, he would somehow manage to tuck a few of his newly-acquired tiny birds within the folds of his robes so they could fly with him.

Upon becoming the bird man, I immediately began conducting bird research (and would continue to do so throughout both US tours). When I wasn't driving the Karmapa's car, I was sitting on the floor of his bedroom, at his request, surrounded by phone books, pen, and paper, dialing away on his private rotary phone—sometimes for hours at a time.

(How different it would have been with a computer and cell phone!) My search for bird stores and private aviaries within the Boulder/Denver area soon expanded to include San Francisco and Los Angeles as well. When His Holiness visited those cities, my search continued in much the same way: whenever I wasn't serving as the Karmapa's driver, I was on the phone searching for extraordinary birds.

While primarily interested in canaries—Border Fancy, Gloster, Norwich, Belgium, and Yorkshire—the Karmapa's favorite bird was the Rainbow Finch, also known as the Lady Gouldian Finch. These tiny, exquisitely beautiful rainbow-colored birds usually have crowns of black, red, or yellow and breasts of purple, lilac, or white. His Holiness would explain that Rainbow Finches were the most non-aggressive of all birds. If a fly were inside its cage and came to rest on its perch, rather than pecking at or attempting to devour the fly, the finch would scoot over to make room for it. At one point, I felt that if the Karmapa were to perform the Black Crown Ceremony for the entire animal kingdom, he would appear as a Rainbow Finch.

Instead of placing paper at the bottom of the bird cages, His Holiness would have his attendant use remnants of satin or silk— leftovers from the preparations for his visit—to line the cages. (We had lined the walls of His Holiness' residence with satin; now he was using the same satin to catch bird droppings!) When students would politely express their concern at seeing as many as fifteen birds in a relatively small cage, Karmapa would explain that "they are very social and like company." Jamgön Kongtrul Rinpoche and other travelling lamas told us many times that they had personally seen His Holiness put dying birds into samadhi—a profound meditative state. Rather than dying and falling from their perch to the floor of the cage, the birds would remain sitting upright on their perches.

The Glorious Bird Expeditions

The Karmapa arose at 4:00 each morning to do various meditations in his bedroom, followed by long days filled with meetings, ceremonies, and activities. Whenever he was not engaged in some aspect of his official itinerary, he spent virtually every spare minute visiting private bird fanciers and bird stores.

Private bird breeders typically build their aviaries inside their

HH Karmapa visiting a private aviary, Denver, Colorado, 1974.
(Copyright Michael Scott)

homes, or right next to their homes, and are often a husband-and-wife team. Whenever His Holiness showed up—often with an entourage of monks and Westerners—their reaction was always the same: a combination of awe and wonder.

After looking at their birds for a while, His Holiness would ask me to bargain with the owners in order to obtain the best possible price. At first I felt a bit awkward in this role, but I soon became more relaxed and playful with it. It wasn't really difficult to negotiate a favorable price, since the breeders themselves had become so relaxed and open by his loving presence.

All of this was frequently the prelude to an outrageous and hilarious moment with the bird breeders. His Holiness would quietly say to me, "They are hiding their best birds next door, so just bring that up with them. Let them know I would like to see their best birds." I had to tell the bird owners, "His Holiness would like to see your prized birds as well. He senses they are next door."

They would look at one another in shocked bewilderment and shyness. How could he know? A few moments later the Karmapa would be looking with delight at their inner sanctum of prized birds, often their special show birds. As a grand finale, he would somehow manage to buy one or two of these prized birds, leaving the owners standing there, dumbfounded and amazed.

These bird fanciers—many of whom had been breeding birds for more than twenty-five years—would pull me aside or call me later that day, asking, "Who is he? He knows more about our birds than we do! When is he coming back?" They kept calling me even two years later, adding remarks like: "We will have Rainbow Finches, Dutch Frills, Belgium Fancies, Yellow Yorkshires and Red Factor Canaries for His Holiness to see."

The exchanges between the Karmapa and the bird breeders were always sweet and loving. To a person, they became disarmed, vulnerable, and curious.

Even though they had no idea who the Karmapa was, their good fortune—and good karma—brought them into contact

HH Karmapa visiting a private aviary, Denver, CO, 1974.
(Copyright Michael Scott)

with a dharma king. They had no way of knowing they were dealing with the "Knower of the Three Times," from whom nothing could be hidden—not even their most precious birds!

An Unexpected Blessing

When His Holiness made his second tour of the US in 1977, one of his first stops was San Francisco. A reception in his honor was to be held at a mansion in San Francisco's Pacific Heights district, and I had made arrangements for my mother to meet the Karmapa there. While my father had been very supportive of my involvement in Tibetan Buddhism (he had been very helpful finding the mansion for His Holiness' visit, and had attended a Vajra Crown Ceremony), my mother had little or no idea of its role in my life.

Like so many of us, my relationship with my mother was conflicted. In fact, I'd had a love-hate battle with her ever since childhood, and I held onto a fixed view of how I thought I had been treated by her.

My mother entered the foyer of the mansion just before the start of the reception. His Holiness stood at the far end of the foyer; I was standing off to one side. When His Holiness saw her, his eyes lit up and a big joyful smile appeared on his face. He literally ran over to her and threw his arms around her. I didn't know what to think. He kept holding his hand up to her head saying how tiny she was. (She was barely five feet tall.) He just loved her.

I visited her at her home two days later. She was sitting on her bed, unusually calm and direct. "Who is He?" she asked. There was a long moment of silence, after which she stated—with complete conviction—"He is my King." There was nothing more to say.

During the next fifteen years my issues with my mother went through a process of softening and healing. Somehow His Holiness gave a great healing blessing for us both, unraveling and dissolving some of the painful experiences of my childhood. There is no question in my mind that this healing came as the result of the blessing of Karmapa.

Eleven years later, when my mother was dying of leukemia, I gave her a small amount of salts that contained sacred remains of the 16th Karmapa. I can't explain it, but my sister, Nancy, and I both witnessed our mother's entire face and countenance transform into that of a girl in her teens. She died extremely peacefully, with no painkillers.

A Unique Challenge

While the 16th Karmapa's extraordinary love and compassion for all sentient beings is well known, I once witnessed an event that has continued to haunt and challenge me.

His Holiness loved to visit pet shops in search of particular birds. Because these shops also sold snakes, lizards, turtles, and ferrets, some version of the following conversation would almost always take place:

HHK: "Please find out why there are crickets here."
SR: "The owner says they are sold as food for the lizards."
HHK: "Why are there mice here?"
SR: "The owner say they are sold as food for snakes."

His Holiness would then buy hundreds of crickets and/or mice, and following his instructions, we would release them in the foothills of Boulder.

I later learned that there are many Tibetan Buddhist teachings and liturgies regarding the practice of saving the lives of sentient beings. However, I have never encountered Buddhist teachings— or teachings from any tradition, for that matter—having to do with what happened on one particular day.

His Holiness had purchased a hundred mice from a pet store, and then asked for two empty cardboard boxes. He placed the container of mice between us on the front seat of the car (I was driving him in the gold Cadillac), and we drove to a large park in the foothills of Boulder.

Once the car was parked, His Holiness began separating the mice by gender. He would reach his hand into the sea of little wiggling bodies, lift one up, turn it on its back, look at its genitals and say "male" or "female," and place it into one of the two cardboard boxes. He went through the entire box, separating all hundred mice in this way.

He then gave the box containing the female mice to a Western attendant, instructing her to release them into the heavily wooded area nearby. Then he had me drive to another park a few miles away, where we released the males.

His Holiness wasn't just liberating these mice from a pet store; I believe he was also teaching us about the inevitable suffering of procreation—and about population control. This was back in the 1970s, when the human population was half of what it is now. Separating the male and female mice is the exact opposite of what Noah did on the Ark. After such a devastating flood, it would have been crucial to pair all earthly sentient beings, many of whom were threatened with extinction. Now, however, we are rapidly destroying ourselves and our planet through unbridled procreation. I strongly believe that it was His Holiness' wish that we ponder this.

Every summer since then, I have made it a practice to liberate crickets and mice as His Holiness demonstrated. Engaging in this kind of practice—as well as contemplating how to limit the explosive growth of the human population—always makes me feel closer to the mind and heart of the 16th Karmapa.

The Blessings of the Black Pill

In 1983, my sister called with grave news: our dad had just suffered a massive heart attack. She told me he had been taken to the intensive care unit of a hospital near San Francisco. And then she said, "Steve, he's dying." I immediately phoned the hospital and spoke with the Intensive Care Unit nurses. They confirmed the news. In fact, they said, my dad was so close to death that there was no need for me to rush out from Colorado to see him.

I was living in Boulder at the time. I called Trungpa Rinpoche and shared this news with him. In the middle of our conversation I blurted out, "Rinpoche, maybe I should fly out and give my father one of His Holiness' black pills." (Black pills, or *rilnak* in Tibetan, are tiny pellets made by the Karmapa that contain extraordinary blessings; they are taken when one is extremely ill or dying.) Rinpoche replied, "That would be a good idea."

So I flew to San Francisco with my wife, Catherine, and our year-old son, Spencer. My son had never met my father, and despite the nurses' discouraging message, I wanted them to be near one another for the first, and most likely, last time. We arrived at the hospital and went immediately to the ICU. A nurse accompanied us to my dad's bed. He was unconscious and looked like a bloated corpse. It was hard to imagine that he was still alive; there were tubes coming out of his mouth, and many needles and wires were attached to his body. The nurse left us there; he was all but gone.

After Catherine said her goodbyes, I asked her to wait with Spencer in the ICU waiting room. When I was alone with my father, I held his hand and said, "Dad, if you can hear me, move your index finger." His index finger moved. I then asked his permission to administer the black pill, explaining that it was designed to help people with such transitions—whether he stays or leaves. I said, "If I have your permission, move your finger once." My dad moved his finger once.

At that point, I became aware that the ICU wasn't exactly designed for privacy; it was a round, glass-walled enclosure with nurses and doctors roaming about and often peering in. Someone might see me putting something in my dad's mouth and think that I was up to some kind of mischief, maybe even that I was trying to kill him. I also realized that, given his swollen, dry, tube-filled mouth, the chances of getting even this tiny pill far enough back on his tongue (either for dissolving or for swallowing) were slim.

So I went to the men's room and carefully crushed the black pill, wedging the powder into the tiny space between my thumb and thumbnail. I returned to my dad's bedside and was trying to spread apart the tubes in his mouth when I heard a voice behind me say: "Hi." I swiveled around and there was my dad's doctor, right arm extended to shake my hand—my right hand, the hand which was hiding the crushed black pill. I made my best attempt to shake hands without losing any of the precious powder. After a few agonizing minutes the doctor left the room, and somehow I managed to place the black pill powder into my dad's mouth.

To the astonishment of everyone—including the doctors and nurses—my dad made a full and complete recovery. That was twenty-nine years ago; my dad will be ninety-seven this coming December.

A Pointing Out Instruction
by Dale Brozosky

I started a PhD program in philosophy in the 1970s and left it to dedicate myself to explore spiritual practice in several religious traditions. Most of my training has been in Vajrayana Buddhism. I met the 16th Karmapa in 1974 in Boulder, Colorado, when I was teaching at Naropa Institute; and travelled with him on his tours to North America and England. I returned to graduate school in Berkeley, California in the 1990s and have degrees in theology and interfaith ministry. I am now based in Oakland, California.

The 16th Karmapa was spontaneous and no one knew exactly what would happen or when. As one of the drivers on his 1977 American tour, I would often stay at his residence overnight ready for an early morning assignment.

Before dawn on a day I can never forget, the Karmapa came to wake me up in the dining room where I was sleeping under a table on a makeshift bed. His attendant told me that he wished to make an unscheduled visit to the land donated for a monastery in Putnam County. The week before one thousand people, including the eminent Kalu Rinpoche, had gathered at the site for a three-day ceremony, and it seemed he wanted to go back there and check it out.

Off we went before dawn in a four-wheel drive Jeep—quite a recent model. It was the only way to be sure of getting up the steep dirt track to the land, particularly with a forecast of rain for the day. The entourage with the Karmapa included Jamgön Kongtrul Rinpoche and an attendant monk. The drive would take two hours each way, and my instructions were to be back for his lunch date with Werner Erhard, founder of Erhard Seminars Training, at 2 pm.

The Karmapa sat in the front passenger seat, on which a silk brocade cloth had been draped. Rain threatened, but it remained dry on our way there and the drive went smoothly. I feared that if it rained, the sharply curved dirt track up the steep hills would become treacherous with mud. When we arrived, the Karmapa walked slowly and deliberately for a few hours around the site of the future monastery, assessing its potential before announcing it was time to return to New York.

We had just rejoined the highway, when there was a loud pop, like a small explosion and the Jeep lost momentum. Fortunately, I managed to steer it safely to the side of the road. All of us, including the Karmapa, got out and walked to the back of the Jeep. The rear tire was completely flat. Luckily, the car carried a spare tire; alhough slightly bald, hopefully it would get us back to the city. We spread the silk cloth over a boulder near the side of the road as a temporary seat for the Karmapa. He sat there, relaxed and smiling, while cars zipped by at sixty miles per hour.

After removing the rear wheel, we laid the brocade over it. His Holiness moved to sit there instead of on the boulder, as I put the spare on the jacked-up Jeep. At that very moment, the rain began, and soon it was pouring. His attendant unfurled a yellow umbrella and held it over the Karmapa's head. I shall never forget the image of the Karmapa sitting on a Jeep tire at the side of the road, looking as poised, relaxed, and radiant as a king on his throne. While I was frantically working to change the tire in the pouring rain, the attendant reminded me again of Karmapa's lunch appointment.

At last the spare was on and we continued on our way.

Then the rain grew heavier until it became a deluge making it difficult to see out the windscreen. Oblivious to the difficulties I was facing, my passengers were all sleeping, seemingly confident in my ability to bring them safely home. I felt nervous, as visibility decreased in the driving rain. We were at the Manhattan turnoff; as I took the sharp curve of the highway exit, the Jeep skidded in the rain. Suddenly we were headed toward the retaining wall—as I braked, I lost control. With my left hand trying to steer the Jeep to minimize the crash, I wrapped my right arm around the Karmapa, so that he would not smash into the windscreen. The Jeep hit the wall, at perhaps fifteen mph. and came to a stop. My arm was still holding the Karmapa when everyone woke up.

I was horrified to see that the Karmapa was bleeding slightly from a head wound where he had hit his forehead on the windscreen. However we had avoided a much more serious injury but the Jeep was a wreck! The right side was smashed in, trapping the front wheel, making it imposible to drive. Yet again the attendant quietly reminded me of the lunch appointment. I leapt out of the Jeep, flagged down a taxi, gave the driver instructions to the residence, and escorted my precious passengers into the taxi. From a pay phone, I called the residence to report what had happened.

I took full responsibility for the accident. Driving conditions were very poor, but it was not a hurricane. No other cars had been involved or smashed into the guard rail. I felt distressed and confused because I knew I was an experienced driver in rain and snow. The next hours were very painful, as I felt I had betrayed the trust that the Karmapa had placed in me. After finding a tow truck and a repair shop, I called the residence to get an update. Perhaps they would not wish to see me again that day, or ever. It was an appalling thought.

An English-speaking monk answered the phone. He told me that the Karmapa was fine, and that he had been asking about me many times. He was concerned that I had not taken lunch. He

HH Karmapa blessing Dale Brozosky, KTD, 1980.
(Courtesy of Dale Brozosky)

said that the accident was not my fault, that it was karma, and in fact, my embrace had saved him from serious injury. He gave orders that no one should blame me or say anything to upset me. I should come to the residence as soon as possible to eat lunch and see him.

I arrived at the residence and was taken immediately to see the Karmapa. He had a small Band-Aid on his forehead, but seemed completely fine. He emphasized that the accident was not my fault. I had been travelling with him for many months, he said, and now it was time to receive certain teachings. "Just being with you is enough," I replied. "Your presence is the teaching."

But he insisted that the teachings were now necessary and proceeded to give me the most precious direct teachings a guru can give to a disciple: the "pointing out" instructions on the nature of mind. That moment, as I later realised, was perfect timing because I was in the appropriate mind-state to receive them. The shock of the accident had prepared me to look directly into the nature of mind in a way I could never have done before.

After these instructions, the Karmapa also transmitted Guru Yoga to strengthen the devotional, energetic connection to him and his lineage. He said that there is never any separation between guru and disciple, that whether one is near or far from the guru, the connection becomes vivid through devotion.

Decades later, the 16th Karmapa is still completely alive to me and I now understand the profound meaning of why he is called a Living Buddha.

Meeting the 16th Gyalwang Karmapa
by MJ Bennett (Jangchub Wangmo)

"*A* *cross what stormy seas of grief come those who see your sacred Vajra Crown:*
It is the water cooling the eyes of all who are tired of seeking
The amrit nectar that fills their mind, bringing liberation from suffering."

From *A Garland of Morning Prayers* translated by Gelongma Sister Palmo

His Holiness the 16th Karmapa was one of Tibet's last great Dharma Kings. The Tibet of the 16th Karmapa was still a medieval feudal society, but the emphasis of the Tibetan people was on the connection between man and the divine. Every mountain, every river, every spring was sacred. Carved *mani* stones and prayer flags adorned each mountain pass. From the peasants who worked the monastery lands, to the nomads of the eastern plains, to the aristocrats who ran the capital of Lhasa, the faith and devotion of the Tibetan people opened their psyches to magic and mystery beyond our everyday consciousness.

When His Holiness walked into our world over the Himalayan passes, he came to us from another time and dimension. The

HH Karmapa.
(Courtesy of Lama Surya Das)

16th Karmapa embodied all the magic and mystery of the Lamas of Tibet recorded by the early twentieth-century explorers.

My experience of reality was irrevocably altered from the first time I saw him. It was the defining moment of my life. My lack of self-confidence and fear left me. Gone were the troubled years of my youth, filled with emotional confusion. Once again, my life had meaning and hope. A sense of purpose was born in me. I had been searching for a spiritual teacher, perhaps it was Karmapa. His very being was the compassion and light spoken of by the first psychedelic explorers, hippies and scholars who travelled to India in the 1960s to meet these holy men who had come out of Tibet.

It was the fall of 1974 when I met His Holiness at the Dharma Centre of Canada. I was not living there at the time; I had joined a month-long meditation retreat nearby. One afternoon, our group went there to receive empowerment and His Holiness' blessing. Just being in his presence was an awakening experience. It was as if I was being embraced by total unconditional love.

I then understood the depiction of the aura around all great saints. The luminosity and power that radiated from His Holiness was unmistakeable. I did not return to the nearby retreat. I stayed on at the centre and helped in the kitchen. This was His Holiness' first world tour, his first trip to Canada. This was something not to be missed.

Travelling with His Holiness was an entourage of eight monks, the English nun, Sister Palmo, whom His Holiness lovingly called "Mommy," and a dashing Tibetan translator. This was indeed a magical mystery tour. Sister Palmo was the former Fredi Bedi. She had met her husband, Baba Bedi a direct descendant of Guru Nanak, the founder of the Sikhs, when studying at Oxford University and had lived in India most of her life. After meeting the Karmapa, she became his disciple, took nun's vows and stayed by his side, helping him preserve the Kagyu Lineage.

Each evening after prayers in the temple, Sister Palmo would invite us into the tiny cabin where she was staying at the centre. We would sit around her on the floor while she explained Buddhist meditation and prayer. She gave us a booklet of prayers printed on rice paper that was both beautiful and exotic. She spoke lovingly of the Karmapa's monastery at Rumtek, Sikkim. The monastery

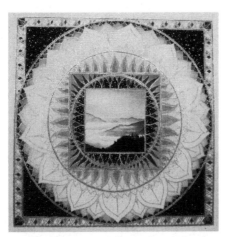

The Old Monastery at Rumtek, painting by Diane Barker.
(Copyright Diane Barker)

wreathed in a thousand rays of rainbow light she would say. We were entranced, enthralled.

During this entire two weeks, we were receiving initiations from the Karmapa, spiritual transmissions into the tantric practices of the Kagyu Lineage. Each afternoon, His Holiness would arrive at the Temple in a gold Cadillac and after each empowerment we would file past his throne to receive his blessing. He would bless each one of us on top of our heads. Then one of the monks assisting in the ritual would offer us blessed saffron water and we would receive a red blessing cord. We were a small group of about thirty people. I could not get enough of this magic. I began to wonder whether His Holiness was the teacher I had been searching for. Was I his disciple? How would I know that this was my true path? Should I ask for a sign?

I knew a Tibetan family in Lindsay, Ontario, Canada. When I heard that His Holiness would visit and have lunch at their home, I asked to be there. The day arrived and I was in the kitchen, helping the Tibetan women of that community prepare *momos*, a traditional Tibetan dish of filling wrapped in dough. My Tibetan friends had purchased a luminous orange chair for His Holiness' visit. Their living room had been cleared for him except for this beautiful chair and a resplendent Tibetan carpet.

After lunch, I watched the people going into the room for an audience and coming out moved and altered. Even the mayor came out with tears of emotion streaming down her face. I realized that this was my time to ask for a sign. Was this my true path and His Holiness my guru? I prayed from the depths of my heart. After a short wait, I was let into the room.

I was aware of His Holiness, radiant and smiling seated in the orange chair, his attendant off to the side. I approached with the traditional white scarf offering and began to prostrate at his feet. He completely dissolved into light. The whole room disappeared into radiance. I fell to the floor surrounded by light and lost consciousness briefly. The next thing I remember was the attendant helping me up, and His Holiness reappearing from this light, still bathed in incredible luminosity. As he smiled at me with total love, I backed out of the room overwhelmed but with a feeling of certainty. This was my sign. His Holiness was my teacher. The Kagyu Lineage was my path.

The Gift of Non-Discrimination

When I was cooking for His Holiness in Phil and Diane Budin's apartment on the upper East side of New York City, many wealthy and influential people would come to visit His Holiness. HH the Dalai Lama had not yet been granted permission to travel to the United States due to political sensitivity, and the 16th Karmapa was one of the first of the great Lamas to come out of Tibet to tour North America.

As a steady stream of influential persons would arrive each morning, I was busy in the tiny kitchen making and serving them tea, as well as doing the meal preparation. It was gruelling work, and after a time, fortunately I had a helper, Elise Frick.

However, having no money and having given up my home and job to come to serve the Karmapa, I was often filled with longing to receive just one of those beautiful gifts that the wealthy were receiving—pure silver boxes with intricate Tibetan stamped silver designs, amulet boxes of solid silver, coral rosaries, beautifully hand-embroidered Bhutanese cloth—all the finest that the Tibetans of that day had to offer. I longed for such a gift.

One day, when my longing was particularly strong, His Holiness appeared at the kitchen door, entered the room, and offered me a scarf. It was an old and rather tatty-looking scarf, perhaps a cravat, and definitely used. It was blue- and white-striped, perhaps silk but perhaps not.

Smiling, he said, "For you." I took it in my hands, bowed in thanks completely nonplussed. He abruptly turned around and left.

I kept that scarf for many years in a wooden shrine box of "special items," but I was never completely sure what it meant, and I never did receive a beautiful silver box or gemstone rosary. But I did receive untold blessings that have remained with me until this day.

Nothing to Hide

After His Holiness invited my husband Bob and I to come to New York, within a week we sold our property, bought a used camper for our pickup truck, packed up what belongings we could, and along with our two Huskies, William and Sam, left the Yukon to meet up with him in Saskatoon, Saskatchewan. Suddenly we were on a very long drive through the Canadian prairies. We arrived in Saskatoon just after their arrival. We parked and slept outside in our camper, but had meals with His Holiness' party in the home. Shortly after we arrived, we were told that His Holiness wanted to see our camper. I rushed out in a panic; it was a mess and I cleaned frantically, stuffing things into drawers, washing and scrubbing and trying to make it look presentable.

Then out of the house came His Holiness, across the lawn to the street, looking with curiosity at our truck and camper. Then he came around to the back. Bob opened the door; His Holiness peered in obviously interested and impressed. We had not only agreed to come and help build his monastery, but there we were, as promised, with truck and camper following him to New York.

Then with an impish grin, looking straight at me, he reached out and opened one of the kitchen drawers near the exit to the camper. It was a complete mess! His Holiness threw back his head and laughed and laughed, ever louder the more I blushed. He loved a good joke. You really couldn't hide anything from him. After all, he was called the knower of the three times—past, present, and future. Busted, I thought! He touched me gently on the arm in a fatherly manner and I had to laugh too.

BEING KARMAPA
by Robert Clendenning

I was a nineteen-year old hippie when I first met His Holiness in 1968 with a group of other Canadians who accompanied Namgyal Rinpoche to Rumtek. After serving His Holiness for several years after he had passed away in 1981, I trained to become a doctor. I practiced emergency medicine for some years, and now do family medicine near Toronto. I've maintained contact with Karma Triyana Dharmachakra and the 17th Karmapa, though unable to devote my "All," as in times before. I'm steering in that direction now, though, and look forward to helping him help everyone again, in a more direct way.

There was no one-to-one contact with His Holiness Karmapa on that initial trip to Rumtek Monastery, but there was a moment which is still vivid in my memory. He had just ascended his throne to do an empowerment and he turned around and looked at the crowd. He looked at me and I felt I was being peeled like an onion. After fifteen seconds gazing at me, he nodded, took off his hat (a tall, yellow hat with a red interior). He put it in his lap, put his right fist into it, and then put the hat back on his head. I don't know what that meant but I can't forget it.

I saw him again when he came on his first trip to North America, although nothing much happened there either. But on his second trip in 1977, one of the dharma students from the Yukon went to New York City to meet with Karmapa again and invited him to come to the Yukon. As we were a small group, half of Karmapa's entourage was left behind in Vancouver and just His Holiness the Karmapa, His Eminence Jamgön Rinpoche, and two of his attendants came to the Yukon.

We were a small group, about thirty of us, hosting him there. The Karmapa and Jamgön Rinpoche stayed in the home of one friend, a delightful two-bedroom bungalow with mountain views, and the other attendants in a home of another friend next door. It was quiet, there was lots of snow, and they were happy as clams. Mary Jane, my ex-wife, was appointed housekeeper and cooked Tibetan food for them.

One morning, Karmapa and Jamgön Rinpoche were playing with bird cages. They called for a carpenter so I volunteered. I came in and bowed. They were both fumbling around trying to make two bird cages into one. I sat down at Karmapa's feet and began to help. I realized what was needed was a miniature tool set, the kind used to make wooden model airplanes. Although I was young and did not have much money, I bought one and arrived with it the following morning. Karmapa was thrilled. He was amazed at my carpentry skills. Mary Jane told me that one morning before I arrived, Karmapa (having heard that she was also a fledgling carpenter) asked her to come into the living room and asked her to use the tools to do some work on the bird cages. She was not very skilled and fumbled around. Karmapa laughed and laughed, telling her that Bob was the better carpenter but she was a better cook! I hung out for many mornings sitting at Karmapa's feet with Jamgön Rinpoche translating.

After several days I began having dreams that Karmapa was my teacher. This was initially confusing to me at the time, as I had always considered Namgyal Rinpoche to be my teacher and had been studying with him for about ten years.

While they were there, Sister Palmo, who had remained behind in India, died. Karmapa was in the car outside, Jamgön Rinpoche was standing beside me. Someone came running out, "Sister Palmo has died." All the monks and Jamgön Rinpoche were very upset, but His Holiness didn't miss a beat, and said, looking at the distraught Jamgön Rinpoche, "*Mintakpa.*" Impermanence. He was expressionless, no emotion evident. In his presence, I felt there was nowhere else to go and nothing to be done. Everything is perfect as it is.

One morning, as I was helping with the bird cages and Mary Jane was in the kitchen, Karmapa said, "You come to New York, help build monastery there." I said, "We can't go; we have a property, with a mortgage. We have to sell it but only to Buddhists who won't kill animals on the land." That really narrowed down potential sales. Karmapa said, "Very good. You keep your promise. Don't break your promise."

The next day, an extraordinary thing happened. The guy who sold us the property came to me and said, "Bob, I want to buy the property back." And he did.

That gave us freedom and money. Karmapa was thrilled. He called both Mary Jane and me into the room. We kneeled at his feet and with Jamgön Rinpoche translating, we officially became his students. To mark the event, Karmapa asked his attendant to bring a small White Tara thanka out of his bedroom. He unrolled it, blessed it, and told us that although it was not of the best quality, that each year on his birthday a certain number were made in just one day for his long life. He gave one of them to us.

We drove off in our four-wheel drive truck with our two Huskies and headed for Saskatoon to meet the Karmapa, continuing to Montreal and Toronto and on to Woodstock. We followed him across the country living in our camper, parked just outside whatever home he was staying in. During that time, Mary Jane was being taught to cook Tibetan food "for a dharma king" by the daughter of the King and Queen of Derge who had immigrated to Canada.

Mary Jane and I spent three years at Woodstock from 1977 to 1980. The lamas bought an old hotel, the old Meads Mountain House, and we got it habitable and made it into a meditation centre.

After three years we told Karmapa we'd like to take a rest and do other things. We had the trailer packed up. That was 1980 and

HH 16th Karmapa in Woodstock.
(Courtesy of Dorothea Fischer)

Karmapa was then in Woodstock, so we went for a last audience with him. We were saying goodbye when suddenly he said, "Bob, don't go, you won't be happy, you come to India." He said, "Meet me in Calcutta, February 22nd."

We were met at Calcutta airport, and taken to the Soltei Oberoi Hotel. In the morning, we were ushered into an opultant white marble room with a water fountain where the Karmapa was seated, radiating as clearly as the white marble. We bowed at his feet. The first words he said to us were, "Where's William?" That was our white husky whom Karmapa loved and who had once prostrated to him. The Karmapa was delighted that we had actually made it to India and the next day all of us flew to Darjeeling and drove up the hill to Rumtek. "Yishin Norbu" (Wish-Fulfilling Jewel), as the

Tibetans called him, had been gone for almost six months. It was a glorious arrival.

We were installed in the translator's old house at the first bend in the road below the monastery. Right away they arranged Tibetan lessons for us. It was really a magical time, as we were the only "Injies" around and were treated like pets. After a while, we blended in so well we were almost unnoticeable. We got to see the Karmapa's household. We had a special six month visa, unheard of at the time. Jamgön Rinpoche was there; Gyaltsab Rinpoche was always around in his room.

We never had a chance to make any plans. We'd be sitting somewhere and someone would come and say, "Bob-la, Yishin Norbu, come, come, come." We'd go running. It could be nothing in particular, or he might have a mechanical problem with some camera or other device.

At that time we could come in any time. Now you have to show your passport and get searched. It's painful. When I've seen the 17th Karmapa, Ogyen Trinley Dorje, in the West, there's almost no contact. You can't get close. I have never had a one-to-one with the 17th Karmapa, though I did have a brief audience some years ago in India. Clearly an amazing being. He's quite other worldly.

I started a clinic shortly after we got there with the co-operation of the General Secretary and Raj Kotwal, a major in the army from Gangtok, who would come over once a week. One day I was called to see the "cow nun," a solitary little old lady who lived by the old monastery and took care of the cows. They said, "Old nun is sick. You must come." Her heart was palpitating. I informed His Holiness and said, "Old nun is sick. We should take her to the hospital." He looked at me sideways and said, "You think? You think it will help anything?" So he smiled knowingly at me and said, "Okay, take her to the hospital." Kotwal phoned me up and said, "She's old, she's dying, you should bring her back home." We told Ashi Choekyi who prepared a little house in the middle of the village, emptied it out, stocked it with food, cleaned up the old nun, and propped her up in bed. The whole town filed past her to say "nice to have known you." She lasted two or three days before she died.

Everybody brought wood for her funeral pyre when they cremated her. But I will always remember Karmapa's knowing smile, "You really think this will help?"

I had a dream as soon as I was back in New York. I dreamed medicine had progressed to the point where we could revive dead people. I dreamed Mary Jane had died and we were waking her up again but we couldn't stop the rotting. It was becoming more and more obvious that she was alive but smelling bad. She finally said she wanted to die. The ultimate futility of medicine was the point of the dream.

Towards the end of our six month stay, it became apparent that Karmapa was dying. He couldn't extend our visas for Rumtek and he was spending more and more time in his room with pain in his abdomen. He asked me to stay in Delhi, and my life would

16th Karmapa, a painting in Rumtek.
(Copyright Norma Levine)

have been very different had I done that. But me of little faith. I didn't want to put my trust completely in the General Secretary. I was a bit afraid of his power and arbitrary decisions. I was out of money entirely so I didn't want to be solely dependent on the good will of Mr Damchoe Yongdu. It was a very difficult decision. I wanted to go to medical school. I said, "I don't have any money, I have responsibilities, I'd like to go to medical school." He said, "Okay, that's okay."

I always wondered what would have happened had I stayed there. Later I contacted Jamgön Rinpoche and asked "Was that a big mistake not going to Delhi?" And he said, "Yes, but you can make up for it."

In retrospect, I feel I was picked up and dragged along. My faith and devotion permitted me to be there. But I have no idea why I was there. Why me? Life is not yet over and maybe it will become clear.

I had a dream of the Karmapa a little while ago. He was sitting on a mountainside with mountains towering above him. Below him was a vast sea of beings. Occasionally, one would reach out a hand; he would grab it and pull him up the mountain. Whenever somebody boiled up to the surface in the sea of beings, he was there to pull them out. When one of them had a moment of awareness and looked up, he was there. What struck me was the absolute dedication of staying there, though there were many other things he would want to do, but this was what he was doing.

Encounters of the Immediate Kind with the 16th Gyalwang Karmapa
by Richard Zelens

*A*t an early age I entered the art world in New York as a ballet dancer.

I went on to study art which led to a career painting in oils, ceramics and hand-painted silk. At that time I became involved in the flourishing of spiritual activity in New York, which led to the connection with the Karma Kagyu.

I now live in Tucson, Arizona where I continue painting, ceramics, and hand-painted fabric.

If my memory holds, it was in 1974. I was living in Sag Harbor, Long Island being creative, without much occasion to read the local paper, the *Village Voice*. Glancing through it quickly one day, I came across an ad announcing that some Tibetan guy was giving a special Tibetan ceremony on Thirty-Fourth Street in New York City called The Black Crown. Coming from a history of teaching yoga with Swami Satchanada and a few years of sitting with an extraordinary Rinzai Zen Master, Isshue Muira Roshi, I took the bait and trundled off to the ceremony.

Bedazzled by the richness of sound and ritual and this "Guy and his Hat," a door was opened, a new world, or perhaps an old world.

A few years later, I was invited to an apartment on Park Avenue—I believe it was the Budens—to help in the kitchen with this wonderful lady, Mary Jane. It was the Karmapa's second visit in 1976 and this was where he was staying.

Mary Jane insisted I go into the living room where "This Guy" was giving an audience. There were about fifteen people present, sitting in a circle—at the head, the Karmapa. A bit of discussion ensued, and it was finally decided that the Karmapa would give the five precepts. Slowly he questioned each person in the circle. When he came to me, I immediately had a vision of myself that I won't go into. Not all five precepts were taken.

Somehow a shift was made; I began studying with Khenpo Karthar Rinpoche at His Holiness' New York Karma Tegsum Choling. That relationship flowered to the point of my living and caring for the center, a chance to be present for the visit of all four of the Karmapa's heart sons as well as the Karmapa. A wonderful, if unconscious, time for a few crazy seeds to be planted.

At this time I was asked to produce a mandala for *One Twelve Workshop,* an avant-garde experimental gallery in Soho. I called it Beginning Sphere, based on Trungpa's teaching of the elements. The mandala consisted of forty-two hand-painted silk banners fourteen inches high and forty-eight feet wide. There were five environments, one for each element surrounded by a ring of fire. (At that time I had a fairly successful career hand-painting fabric for the esteemed decorator, Halston and was associating with local avant-garde artists.) Later, on His Holiness' last official trip, I decided to present him with the mandala.

Arrangements were made to give him the mandala in Woodstock at Karma Triyana Dharmachakra. I took a bus to Woodstock with my bundle of silk banners and managed to get to the top of the mountain for a four o'clock appointment. Nowhere was the

Brocades presented to HH Karmapa by Richard Zelens.
(Copyright Richard Zelens)

Karmapa to be found—some people presumed he was visiting local peacocks. Alas, I was supposed to catch the 5:30 bus back to
New York.

Hopes of the presentation were fading when suddenly, there
he was in the reception room, waiting for devotees who were wait-

ing for him. I was lead into the room, did my prostrations, and prepared to present the banners. Jamgön Kongtrul Rinpoche along with Bardor Tulku and Khenpo Karthar were present. The Karmapa was comfortably placed in a chair. I unfurled the first banner at his feet. A green banner, an air banner. "Ah," he commented, "My essence, Buddha activity." The second unfurled; red, fire. "Ah," he commented, "My burnt karma."

From that moment on, I have no recognition. Totally spaced, consciousness lost. The audience ended at his feet, with my head in his lap being stroked. The mandala was given to the care of Bardor Tulku and used at several of KTD's events.

My last audience with His Holiness was at Karma Thegsum Choling in New York, just before he returned to Sikkim. He questioned the group on the six realms. My answer was that they were visible in our world, if only we looked for it. Each of the audience was given tokens and a brief comment. Mine was "very strong, very strong."

His Holiness the 16th Gyalwang Karmapa Rangjung Rigpe Dorje to this day remains a vital element on my altar. Perhaps some day I will have the priviledge of meeting His Holiness the 17th Gyalwang Karmapa, Ogyen Trinley Dorje.

A poem written on the death of the 16th Gyalwang Karmapa:

Lord of the Dharma
Cloud of Bliss
Dissolved once more into the clear Dharmadhatu
With showers of blessings on disciples
We ask for your return
So sentient beings
Still clouded from Truth
May benefit from your
Enlightened presence

BOOKENDS
by Don Morreale

Don Morreale is the author of The Complete Guide to Buddhist America *(Shambhala 1998),* Buddhist America: Centers, Retreats, Practices *(John Muir Publications, 1988). A freelance journalist, he writes a weekly column for the online newspaper* Examiner.com. *A graduate of the Spirit Rock Community Dharma Leader Training Program, he teaches meditation in Denver, and worldwide on Royal Caribbean Cruise Lines.*

It all started—or jump-started—with a call from my old friend Bonnie Miller, whom I'd known in the late 1960s at the New York Zen Studies Society. "Hey Don," she said, "The Karmapa's coming through Denver in a couple of days. He's going to be changing planes at Stapleton and he's agreed to give a puja. We're all driving down to see him. Wanna meet us there?"

I had no idea who this Karmapa guy was, and only the vaguest notion of what a puja was. Nor, to be honest, did I much care. In the thirteen years since last I'd practiced Zen, I'd fallen into an emotional and spiritual tar pit. Several promising love affairs had gone south, and to say that I'd become something of a grouch would be an understatement. I was pissed off at everything and everybody pretty much all the time. Anger had become my default position.

I remembered something my teacher, Eido Roshi, had said to me on the day I left New York: "Go, and suffer as much as you can." It was good advice, but advice I had no intention of following. Like everyone else in my generation, I'd sought my salvation in the three refuges of the conditioned realm: sex, drugs, and rock 'n' roll. And now here I was, thirteen years on, caught in the gnarly tentacles of samsara.

"Yeah, sure," I told my friend. "Why not? I'll meet you there."

A few days later, I drove out to the airport and found my friends waiting in line outside a small room off the concourse. I was more than a little cynical about the whole business, but I got into the queue anyway, and when my turn came, I stepped into the room.

Sitting on a raised platform was a jolly Tibetan monk, smiling and laughing and trading wisecracks with the American translator who was standing beside him. I have no idea how it happened, but the next thing I knew I was flat on my face, arms outstretched in a full Tibetan prostration, and the monk was patting me on the head and giggling. I got up, and as I walked out, another monk draped a gauzy white scarf around my neck.

Back on the concourse, I stood with my friends and watched people going in and coming out of the room. There was a glow on their faces and a kind of lightness as they emerged. I remember one young woman in particular who stepped out and heaved a huge sigh of relief, as if she'd just dropped a thousand-pound backpack. Everyone laughed as if they understood. I laughed too.

Then the Karmapa came out, trailing his retinue of monks, and we all fell in behind them and walked in silence down the concourse to his gate. There was a festive, happy feeling in the air. Later, it occurred to me that this must have been what it was like when Jesus rode into Jerusalem on a donkey, his followers dancing with joy and strewing his path with palm fronds and flowers. It was a biblical story I had never really understood, but now I got it in a visceral way. Of course they were dancing. Their teacher had come to town. For what is a spiritual teacher, if not a bringer of joy?

I drove home that afternoon and tried to make sense of what had happened to me. There had been, for one thing, something rarified and luminous about the atmosphere in the little room, as though I were breathing light instead of air. But something else had transpired, and it took me some time to figure out what it was. It was as if the Karmapa had held up a mirror, and for the first time in my life I could see myself for what I was. What I saw was not pretty.

High time I did something about myself, I decided. That evening I sat down to practice, and I've been doing so every day since. It was Eido who'd sent me out into the world to grasp the meaning of suffering. It was the Karmapa who invited me back to learn how to overcome it.

HH 16th Karmapa.

HH 16th Karmapa with Katia Holmes, Rumtek.

HH 16th Karmapa wearing the Black Crown, Rumtek.

HH 16th Karmapa in his room in Rumtek.

Karmapa blessing Dale Brozosky, KTD, 1980.

Karmapa "Rainbow Body", Rumtek, February 8th, 1978.

HH 16th Karmapa with Steve Roth, Denver Zoo, 1974.

HH 16th Karmapa at Rumtek.

HH 16th Karmapa.

Jamgon Kongtrul Rinpoche and Bokar Rinpoche at the cremation of HH the 16th Karmapa, Rumtek, 1981.

Cremation of HH 16th Karmapa at Rumtek, 1981.

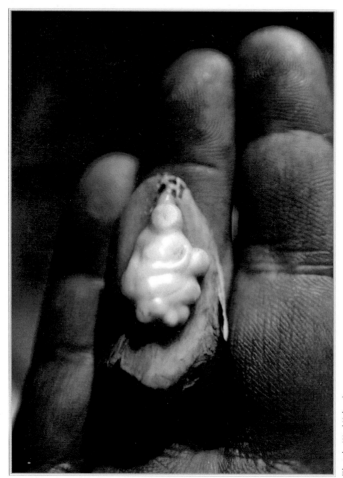

Karmapa Relic: Buddha Bone manifesting in the ashes after his cremation and taken to Tsurphu by Drupon Dechen Rinpoche.

(Photo by Ward Holmes)

Karmapa with birds.

(Painting by Marianna Rydvald)

Chenrezig.

HH 17th Karmapa.

(Photo by Karma Changchub)

Dusum Khyenpa thangka presented by HH Karmapa to Goodie Oberoi.

KARMAPA'S POLITICAL ADVICE
by Lama Surya Das

Once I was sitting with the Karmapa and one or two other "Injies" in his sitting room upstairs at Rumtek in the mountains outside Gangtok. It was autumn, 1976, an election year in the far-off United States. News was scarce in those days outside the major cities of the Indian subcontinent, pre-CNN and Internet café days, although we disciples—busy with our gurus and *ngondro* (foundational) practices—didn't miss news much and actually lacked for nothing. For example, it was months before we heard about the enormous Watergate scandal and President Nixon's subsequent resignation.

Someone asked the Master something about America and the presidential elections, remarking that his parents back home in the West were worried because he wasn't going to partake in that important American democratic process—in which the Washington outsider Jimmie Carter was running against incumbent president Gerald Ford. His Holiness laughed and said, "It's only for a few short years anyway, those American kings. Better be an adamantine (vajra) sovereign of the noble Dharma than a temporary lord of this dew-drop-like world. Look at our good friend the Chögyal (king) of Sikkim!" He was referring to the then recently-deposed king, the Twelfth Chögyal of the small Buddhist principality of

Sikkim, who was a Kagyu tulku married to an American society lady named Hope Cooke. In 1975 his country was annexed by the democratic government of India.

HH 16th Karmapa.
(Courtesy of Norma Levine)

Lord Karmapa continued: "You can help the entire world with your Bodhisattva vow and by becoming enlightened yourself, and not just for a few years or decades. This is the politics of the Golden Rosary of Kagyu Gurus in the accomplished practicing lineage (*Rimay Drub-gyud*)!"

My friends and I elected to stay and vote for Gyalwag Karmapa, our trustworthy Dharma King. We wrote in with our chanted prayers.

No Thought
by Suzie Albright

Suzie Joy Albright did a twelve-year solitary retreat at the Karmapa's main centre at Woodstock, New York. Later she worked as a massage therapist and then retired, living on a boat with her cat. She died in October 2013 after a prolonged illness.

In 1975 I received ten vows and robes from Lama Yeshe with the thought that I would take ordination in the Gelugpa tradition with His Holiness the Dalai Lama. But the following year, the Karmapa came to Chökyi Nyima's gompa which had just been built in Boudhanath, to offer a month-long cycle of Kagyu empowerments, which I attended with Lama Yeshe's blessing.

I felt very close to Karmapa, very comfortable with him. From then on it was always easy to be near him, literally and otherwise. When I went to the Black Crown ceremony, I ended up sitting next to his throne, and my view of him was straight up. There wasn't any thought. You weren't thinking about what you were experiencing; it was just the experience itself. Then he'd bless everyone with the cylindrical umbrella.

Normally, the streamers drop off to one side, but when I went through, the entire banner spread over my head like a hat. I heard His Holiness make a kind of grunt of approval. At another Black

HH Karmapa giving blessings with the water of the bumpa vase.
(Courtesy of Dorothea Fischer)

Crown ceremony, instead of feeling the brocade banner when I went through the line, I just felt the Karmapa's hand on my head. When it's your fate to meet with someone who has the wisdom and compassion to share, with whatever your capacity to receive it, that's blessing.

I did know there was a deep connection. So I decided to be ordained in the Karma Kagyu tradition. At the ceremony I stood next to Karmapa as he offered the ritual objects. I held a bowl with him, and at that point I noticed dirt under his fingernails. I thought, that's Tantra! There is no good or bad, clean or dirty. That was a moment of clarity I'll never forget.

The Karmapa then offered to give me a transmission for *ngondro* if I could come down early in the morning. When I arrived at Chökyi Nyima's gompa wearing my robes, the sun was rising. The Karmapa emerged from the bathroom, having just washed, so he looked like he was materializing from steam and light. It was phenomenal—just he and I and one of his attendants, and the sunrise. He sat down and smiled, and when he realized I didn't speak Tibetan, he just laughed and clapped his hands. In walks Bokar Rinpoche—to translate. It's only in retrospect that you think, "That was amazing!" But at that moment my mind was free of thought.

However, it's not humility but honesty when I say that my realization is lacking. No one knows how ignorant I am more than I do. But having received so many blessings, I find people respond to that. I'm like the dog's tooth. I have been saturated by blessings. If people feel that's from me, it's not my wisdom, but my exposure to those who had wisdom. And though I may be a fool, at least I have enough sense to keep practising. When Sakya Trizin said to me, "Oh, you must be realised now." I answered, "I just keep practising."

She Ate Snow, by Victoria Dolma, Victory Banner Publishing, pp. 24–26, p. 38

His Holiness the 16th Karmapa, the Wish Fulfilling Jewel
by Dawa Lorien

Dawa met His Holiness while a graduate student at UCLA. Inspired by this meeting she undertook extensive travel, study, and pilgrimage in Asia. During her travels she met her teacher the Venerable Kalu Rinpoche and entered a three-year retreat in 1982. Today, Dawa works in social services with foster children and as a Compassion Cultivation Teacher. Her PhD research on three year retreats is being complied for publication

At the time of my first encounter with His Holiness the 16th Karmapa, I was a young graduate student at the University of California, Los Angeles studying dance ethnology and, as students of anthropology, my friends and I attended many ethnic ritual and dance events. For weeks we had seen the announcement of the Black Hat Ceremony and a group of us were planning to attend.

I had spent the previous two weeks in a low-grade depression—mood dark, no motivation. When my friends left to attend the Black Hat Ceremony given by the 16th Karmapa (Los Angeles, California, 1977), I declined to go. Nothing could stir me from my private gloom. I felt a weakened shadow of myself, with my days experienced in various shades of gray. Reports back were glowing and there would be another event, a smaller more private affair in the Hollywood hills, in a few days and, through some circuitous Hollywood connection, I was invited.

We piled into my grandmother's 1953 Packard, and headed up into the Hollywood Hills searching out the Tibetan Rinpoche said to be giving a special initiation. With a penciled address and no directions, we wandered the narrow streets through a neighborhood of elite homes secluded behind their tall hedges and security fences. Our brief glimpses inside revealed mini-palaces on generous green lawns surrounded by manicured gardens. These are the homes of movie stars, I thought—my apprehension growing as we pulled into the driveway towards a huge, starkly white building with strong contemporary lines and large cathedral windows. I parked my Packard alongside luxury cars and limousines and without hesitation, strode into the building as if I was expected, entering into a huge tower-like room with nothing but large Tibetan thangkas (paintings) in frames of brilliant silk brocade— figures both benevolent and furious.

We were soon absorbed into the general confusion and the busy flow of monks in maroon and gold, and their intense Western assistants in business suits, who pulled us out into the garden and set us at the foot of an ornate throne on which sat the Rinpoche, His Holiness the 16th Karmapa. The ceremony began: "I take refuge in the Buddha, I take refuge in the Dharma, I take refuge in the Sangha."

I jumped up in confusion. Finding a monk who spoke English, I hurriedly asked, "What does this mean? Does this mean I am a Buddhist and can't have any other teachers?" Recently I had gone to a talk at the Pasadena Theosophist Center, given by Rolling Thunder, a charismatic and prophetic Native American Elder who was welcoming non-Indians to join his community in the Mojave Desert. I was intrigued and wanted to check it out, or maybe the Sufi Whirling Dervishes I had just met. Certainly I did not want to limit my "freedom" to taste from the spiritual smorgasbord peculiar of California "New Age" culture. The monk's smile seemed enigmatic and promising: "It is a blessing; you need not give up your studies."

I returned to my place kneeling on the grass, as if pulled magically back into the ceremony. I lowered my head for His Holiness to cut a piece of my hair. He placed it carefully in an envelope and I received my new name, "Karma Lekshey Drolma," on delicate rice paper with a red stamped seal. The same English-speaking monk translated the Tibetan as "positive communication," a somewhat imprecise, awkward translation, I learned years later. But now in this Hollywood garden sitting under the throne awash with exotic color and sounds, I was losing touch with my surroundings, and ordinary reality had been replaced with the extraordinary.

My friends and I were escorted out as the ritual was completed. From then on my memories of the event took on a supernormal aura. Oranges in the supermarket so intensely orange, light so clear, bright and radiant—I was swirling with bliss and well-being. This state lasted close to three days and was in sharp contrast to my dark and hopeless moods of the past weeks. I had "come home"—I had seen into my being and found myself whole and connected. Each sensation arose endowed with profound contentment and peace, accented by bursts of bliss and love in the most mundane encounters with reality—cracks in sidewalks, small insects and tiny birds. At night I had such clear dreams I can still remember them now, thirty years later. I dreamed I was receiving dharma teachings on high mountains with Lamas. The teachings were quite specific, and I was later to find their vestiges in actual teachings of Tibetan yogas given to me at a much different place and time, in a three year retreat. This moment of refuge, of naming was extraordinary and from that day forth, I was a Buddhist, a Tibetan Buddhist without any clue to what that meant. I had been caught in an effervescent moment imbued with spirit, mystery and promise. My life was permanently altered and a piece of my identity shifted.

I decided to go on a pilgrimage. I knew I was Buddhist, but without a teacher or teachings. I was a self-taught meditator from the time I was seventeen, learning from books: Paul Brunton's book the *Secret Path* (1935), *Magic and Mystery in Tibet* (1929) and *The Hundred Thousand Songs of Milarepa* (1962). My "pilgrimage" lasted three years and midway, I ended up in Korea teaching English, where I encountered further word of His Holiness.

Songgwang Sa Monastery, South Korea, 1979

I had been in Seoul, teaching English for almost a year when I found my way to the mountain retreat and temple of Zen Master Kusan Sunim (1908–1983). One morning, sitting on my cushion with the sliding doors of my hut open, Master Kusan walked by. I looked and saw a being that seemed to be the essence of a smile, light and sunny, almost floating by. Later that day, during an audience and teaching, he said, "Even if the Buddha walks by, one's meditation remains undisturbed, your resolve should never waver." I was struggling. The Scottish nun who translated for Master Kusan, approached me, "You know that Master Kusan met with the Karmapa; they are friends." She went on to tell me Karmapa had been ill. Immediately I knew, I had to go see him; he was for me the source, the affirmation that I was on the right path. I learned that his main residence was Rumtek, Sikkim.

Sikkim 1980

I knew the name of my destination, but not the way, the territory—neither the place nor the unfolding story. I followed imprecise, vague inner voices, bounded by the small space I had taken and defended as mine. My identity had been packed and narrowed into a bag guarded firmly under my feet.

Arriving in Gangtok in the late afternoon, I was searching for cheap lodgings when a Tibetan monk approached me, and asked where I was going. "To Rumtek to see the Karmapa." "No need to stay here, we are going to Rumtek and you can come with us!" He took me to meet a Canadian woman who was living in Rumtek. Mary Jane was to become my friend and guide and I spent my first night in Rumtek staying with her and her husband Bob. In the morning over a very welcome cup of coffee, a message came from the Karmapa's house on the hill. Karmapa wanted to see Bob and he was to bring the "Injie" (the foreigner)! I was awestruck.

As we rushed up the hill, I was tripping on my long Tibetan dress. When I was called, I entered a room with many rows of Tibetan Rinpoches seated on thrones and Karmapa at the end of the room. I threw myself into my first-ever full prostration at his feet. "So where have you been?" I muddled through giving a rather confused answer about pilgrimages and Master Kusan. "What is it that you are looking for?" Unable to give an intelligible answer, I was ushered out of the temple. After that encounter, a sadness tinged my days in Rumtek. How could I have been so dumbstruck that I couldn't even verbalize my deepest wish, my purpose? I wanted to practice, to meditate, to have a teacher!

I had had my audience with His Holiness, participated in several Black Hat ceremonies, and received the special precious pill to be taken at the time of death. I wandered past the Karmapa's aviary of exotic birds, said to be his disciples or devotees from past lives. The steep slope was headed by the dense Himalayan forest; at its edges stood a large wooden structure with no windows. I walked around the building—no sound, no movement—I could not penetrate the inside nor see any meaning or purpose to the structure. It was forbidding and imprisoning in its silence and refusal to communicate. I asked my family host, "What is that building?" They told me it was a retreat, where monks stayed for three years, enclosed. I thought to myself, "That is one thing I would never do—lock myself away for three years in a place with no windows."

Kalu Rinpoche, painting by Marianna Rydvald.
(Copyright by Marianna Rydvald)

Sonada, West Bengal, India

As I was leaving Rumtek, Mary Jane mentioned that I could go
and study with an old Lama outside Darjeeling in Sonada. I left
feeling uncertain and as the bus wound down mountains, shud-

dering around steep corners, I closed my eyes and prayed, *"Karmapa Khyenno."*

A few months later, when I was living in Sonada studying Tibetan, doing ngondro, and taking teachings from Kalu Rinpoche I had an *experience*: an awareness that clarified my old wordless, unanswered question. I was sitting at the back of the large temple hall with other foreigners and lay Tibetans who showed up for evening puja. Kalu Rinpoche was sitting on his high throne playing his bell and damaru (small drum).

I was gazing at his face when suddenly, I was looking at nothing but clear, brilliant sky—what I'd call his luminous sky-mind. Simultaneously, I was aware that this was the nature of my own mind, regardless of how cloudy and confused it might be most of the time. When I looked away and then back at him, there it was—the empty sky-mind in place of Rinpoche's physical face. His corporeality was transparent—transformed.

I was reminded of this event, when a fellow retreatant told me of his first meeting with His Holiness: "We met Karmapa during his second tour (1976–77). He was giving a Chenrezig empowerment at Harvard. We were all waiting in a big institutional marble hall and each time the large doors would open, the candles on the shrine would flicker and waver. Then Karmapa arrived and, as he walked past the candles, he was transparent; I could see the candles through him! I did a double-take, in case there was something wrong with me. Quickly, I looked around to see if anyone else had seen that! For a few seconds, he'd been transparent. But what really confounded me was that in the very next moment he was just as ordinary as anyone else! Only in retreat did I see the photograph taken of Karmapa during the Black Crown—the camera captured that moment when his body was transparent, dissolving."[1]

---

1 Excerpt from *Assembled Identities: Transformation of Identity in Tibetan Buddhist Three Year Retreats* (Lorien, 2011) unpublished dissertation and used by permission of interviewee.

Bodhgaya, 1981

I had been in Bodhgaya for some days doing prostrations. I ran into Mary Jane in a chai shop. She was distraught. His Holiness was very ill in a hospital far away in the US and it was hard to know what was going on. I was confused. Could a Buddha suffer just like a human? She collected enough money to make a grand offering, lighting up the whole stupa with hundreds of electric lights and butter lamps. After dark we were standing in the street in front of the temple gate. Would it work, or would it blow a fuse? Then suddenly the dark Indian night was bright; the MahaBodhi Temples glowed and radiated. I was struggling to find my thoughts. The Karmapa's Buddha Mind was radiating everywhere, his presence was in each point of light!

Bali, Fall 1981

It was on a beautiful Balinese beach, alone in total collapse that I was overcome with the futility of samara. All my supports, my illusions, my sense of security and self, had been torn apart, leaving me groundless. I had lost my lover, my health, my means of support, my passport, and even some of my newly-acquired Buddhist faith. At that moment all my clinging, my hopes and fears and expectations were released—burned up in the hot sun, washed out of the body in a shivering fever and deluge of tears.

In a flash, I knew, when rock meets bone, all that matters was practice—I thought to myself, when death sits plainly in view, the buddha-dharma was my only refuge. Even today I can relive that moment of clear awareness, the moment of knowing I was going to go into three-year retreat. I knew I had been liberated from all that could hold me back—all my attachments and illusions, and that this was a rare moment, a gift.

In Darjeeling, Kalu Rinpoche often talked about retreats, but I had never considered that I would do one. In Rumtek, the retreat compound had seemed forbidding. But now, not only was I going into retreat, it would be before the year was out, on Salt Spring Island, British Columbia, in June 1982.

When I arrived at the retreat center, Kunsang Dechen Osel Ling, Mary Jane was already there. The night before we were to enter three-year retreat, we celebrated at a local pub dancing, laughing, drinking wine. We raised our glasses: *Karmapa Khyenno!* The Wish Fulfilling Jewel.

DHARMA IN MY BONES
by Sharon Mumbie

I took refuge with Khyentse Rinpoche. Then I met Kalu Rinpoche and we had a small center in Woodstock, New York. The Karmapa's Lamas came to lunch and saw the old hotel for sale on the mountain, which became the western seat of the Karmapas. We joined forces with the Karmapa Lamas and gave up our center. Serving him was a great blessing and a memorable experience. I promised myself that I would do a lot of retreat before I met him again, so after his passing, I did extensive retreats, including a solitary three-year retreat. I now live and practice in one of the Kagyu Centres in California.

I first read about the Karmapa when I was fourteen years old. I had bought a book by Evans-Wentz called *Tibetan Yoga & Secret Doctrines* at Watkins, the only bookshop in London that sold esoteric books. I had started yoga classes and was drawn to anything called "secret." I remember reading the book and not understanding much at all. By the end I thought that if I should ever meet the Karmapa, head of this "Kagyupta," I would ask him if I should have children. I also had a card of a famous thangka with all of the

Karmapas painted in gold that I kept on my wall. I can still see it now in my mind.

Finally I met the 16th Karmapa when he came to Karma Triyana Dharmachakra, Woodstock, New York in 1980. In the intervening years I had a tiny dharma center in Woodstock, and in 1977 he had sent Jamgön Kongtrul Rinpoche, one of his heart sons, to give us a blessing.

One day his lamas came to lunch. One of my companions in this venture (now Lama Surya Das) took them for a drive into the countryside. They saw an old hotel for sale on the top of Meads Mountain Road. Eventually, they bought it with the help of the late great patron, Mr. Shen.

We decided to help them with their center, since Woodstock was such a tiny village in the countryside that two centers on the same mountain didn't make much sense. I became one of the "staff" members, serving the Karmapa frequently in the most ordinary of circumstances.

Every time I went over to the house, it was like stepping into another dimension—like a space ship at supersonic speed. All my molecules were moving in a different way because space and time seemed quite different. The only comparison I could make was to the LSD trips I had taken in the 1960s in London.

The Karmapa was radiating an incredible energy field. When I met him eye to eye, an amazing empathy and love came beaming through that would engulf everyone in warmth, intimacy and understanding. I didn't have to explain anything. His awareness seemed to be totally ahead of everyone, all the time. It was beyond language, but he could always see what was needed. I saw him gesture, clap, or snap his fingers many times when someone was not getting the point.

Every time I was in the Karmapa's presence, my illness and pain from an acute bladder infection went away completely. I felt uplifted, serene, and even had extraordinary dreams. There was a huge sense of blessing permeating my life. We all laughed a lot and felt incredibly happy. I never remembered to ask him if I should have children. The question seemed to resolve itself. I never have had any and have spent as much time in retreat as possible.

The last time I saw him alive was when he was getting into the car. As I bowed to thank him and say goodbye, he put his hand on my head and pushed me down to the point where my knees buckled under me. I had to sit down to recover from the intensity of the experience. It was like he was pushing his energy into my body.

Recently, I had a very profound dream. After my mother's death, I was experiencing great difficulties with the last of her possessions. A relative was trying to take certain things from me, under the guise of being helpful. I had felt a great deal more loss than I could ever have imagined. During this grievous misunderstanding, I was in utter despair, sobbing alone at home. I kept thinking there is no one else who loves you like your mother; if my relative succeeds in taking these things, who else is ever going to leave me such treasures? I was constantly in tears.

The next morning I had a very strong dream about the 16th Karmapa. He was in front of me, wrapped in shimmering rainbow-coloured silk, which kept moving as if he were weightless and floating. Tiny rainbows were emanating from him and he was filled from within with light. He reached out to me and grabbed my arms and shoulders. He held me firmly pressing his arms into mine so strongly that I have to call the dream "bone on bne."

He held me like that until I understood without speech that I should never let family and transient things of this life upset me like this; that he loved me and I had the Dharma deeply beyond everything. He held on for a long time until I got the feeling in my bones. It was so strong that when I woke up I held my arms and thought "dharma in my bones." The dream was so forceful that I sat there holding my arms with the sensation that he was still there.

As ethereal as he looked in the dream it was not like that at all. It was a tremendously physical dream in which the message came across so clearly with the pushing of his bones on my bones, like the last time I saw him in life when he was getting into the car and he blessed me so forcefully.

I think about this and call upon it in my moments of weakness or when I feel depressed. The dharma we have goes beyond lifetimes and is much deeper than all the things of this life.

Karmapa Disappears
by Barbra Jones

At the time of this story I was in my late teens, early twenties. I was working in the film industry as a scenic painter. I am currently a single mother of a 17-year-old son, and a lawyer with a Legal Aid clinic in Ontario, called Advocacy Centre for Tenants Ontario (ACTO), providing extemporaneous advice and representation for the indigent at the Ontario Landlord and Tenant Board. I continue to practice meditation every day and at retreats.

I was helping to cook for the Karmapa's monks while he was in Toronto on one of his earlier visits in the 1970s. As a respite, someone offered him a stay in a farm house just north of Toronto in Whitevale, Ontario. He and his monks all accepted. We had to get up very early, around 5:00 a.m. to get the water ready for their tea and to prepare the food for breakfast. I was in the kitchen one morning and had just put the water on to boil when I heard a voice in Tibetan. Then I heard footsteps and more Tibetan. I thought it was unusual as they were all normally doing puja at this time. I continued with the breakfast preparations.

Very soon I saw His Holiness and his attendant come down the back stairs that led into the hallway, which led to the back door off the kitchen. Immediately I stopped doing what I was attending to and bowed as Karmapa and his attendant swept by me, smiling, nodding and chatting in Tibetan. They went out the back door from the kitchen which led directly to the carport where the car for His Holiness was parked. The next thing I knew they had driven off down the road. I went back to breakfast preparations.

Just before breakfast was to be set on the table a few monks came into the kitchen panic-stricken. As they didn't speak English they just kept saying "Karmapa, Karmapa." I didn't speak Tibetan, so of course our dialogue was limited to gesticulation and a great deal of guess work. I pointed to the back door and stated "car." At this point panic spread to the others. People kept asking where he was and what he was doing ... and of course I couldn't answer except to say that he had driven off with his attendant.

After a few hours of great consternation and very real anxiety His Holiness returned. He was beaming and seemed extremely happy. Apparently the day before someone had informed him that there was an individual in the area that bred very rare birds—I think some form of canary. The Karmapa had decided that he wanted to see them and the only time he had that wasn't scheduled was before breakfast; so he had arranged with the breeder to go to see them at that hour.

It is unclear to me still whether he was secretly disappearing to steal a moment with his beloved birds or whether there was an inadvertent failure in communication. What was clear was not only how happy he was to have spent some time with the birds, but how loved and dear he was to all those who were with him.

HERE COMES THE SUN
by Linda Lewis

Linda V. Lewis met Trungpa Rinpoche in 1972 and moved to Boulder, Colorado to be his student, where she lived for the next 16 years. It was during these years that she had the good fortune to meet his Holiness Karmapa. Following the parinirvana of Trungpa Rinpoche, Linda moved to Karme Choling for four years with her son; then moved on to Nova Scotia where she helped start the Shambhala School, and taught there for 6 years before doing the 3 year retreat at Gampo Abbey's Sopa Choling. Currently she is receptionist at the Halifax Shambhala Centre and studies Tibetan.

On the first visit of His Holiness Karmapa to Boulder, Colorado he gave us all a Vajra Yogini initiation and blessing in the main shrine room of 1111 Pearl Street, going between the spaces of hippies to touch us with his hand and implements, including the little head of my infant son Waylon.

On his second visit, I believe in 1976, my toddler son fell in love with His Holiness, wanting to go again and again to the place where he was staying on Mapleton Hill, which we called the "wedding cake house." My son would say repeatedly, "I want to go to see the big man with the big hat in the big house!"

16th Karmapa wearing Gampopa Hat.
(Photographer unknown)

On His Holiness Karmapa's last visit to Boulder, I believe in 1980, there was to be a children's blessing in the main shrine Room. My son was now 6 years old. His father had fallen asleep and, although he had said he wanted us to wake him up, he was unspeakably angry when we did so. There was a domestic "scene" and Waylon and I were delayed. I was really afraid we had missed the ceremony but felt inclined to go late, rather than to wallow in domestic misery.

Indeed upon arriving upstairs in the main shrine room, it was clear that His Holiness had just finished blessing all the children and giving them candy. His back was somewhat to us when we entered and we hesitated to proceed, but His Holiness felt our presence; that's the only way I can describe it, and for no other reason he turned around 180 degrees. Upon seeing us he gave us a huge welcoming smile and my son ran to him. I can only use an overused analogy to describe what it was like. It was just like the sun coming out from behind a dark cloud and warming us.

Upon returning home I felt I could face anything with a fresh start—not at all how I usually felt after a domestic scene. The power of love of His Holiness was contagious, indeed like sunlight, which shines equally on everything!

Also on that last visit I had a Vajrasattva ngondro group interview with His Holiness at Marpa House. I had just started that practice and after the interview it was His Holiness that animated the Vajrasattva on top of my head. Since my root guru was Trungpa Rinpoche, I felt like I was cheating on him! So I met with Trungpa Rinpoche to sort of confess—and he burst out laughing, saying, "No difference!"

It was the first time I realized that devotion was not just about loyalty but about the personal connection with an authentic Vajra master and how it resonated with one's inner guru—one's awareness. Both His Holiness and Trungpa Rinpoche woke up my mind-heart in the same way.

"YOUR PARENTS WILL NEVER AGAIN BE REBORN IN THE LOWER REALMS"
by Grant Moore

I have been a student of Trungpa Rinpoche since 1975 and have been living in India since 2001, studying Buddhism and working as a massage therapist.

It was June, 1980, and His Holiness was at Rocky Mountain Dharma Centre to perform the Black Hat Ceremony and also to bless a retreat cabin that had just been built.

The cabin nestled among the pines on a hill above the meadow where the vajra guard encampments took place. Because it was one mile distant from the main shrine room building, His Holiness rode to it in a Jeep, while the rest of us, a group of 15 or so, walked.

After the blessing, His Holiness was asked to plant a pine tree adjacent to the cabin. RMDC staff had planted a few pine trees on the land, but they had all died. The Karmapa, however, had planted a pine tree on Marpa Point near the retreat cabin there and it had thrived.

One of the persons in attendance knew something about tree planting and had brought sand, a special kind of soil and perhaps some other items that he deemed necessary. After layering just the right amounts of each into the hole, the tree was lowered into it and the remainder of the "ingredients" added.

This being done, His Holiness then gazed at the tree for quite some time—perhaps a couple of minutes. This completed the ceremony.

We were then very pleasantly surprised to learn that the Karmapa had decided to walk back to the main building instead of being driven. Our group was ecstatic.

There were at least three monks with him, including a Westerner who was his translator. Jamgön Kongtrul Rinpoche was another of the monks, and was in a particularly playful mood. Grinning broadly all the while, he would periodically hit—quite hard, you could hear the thump—the other Tibetan monk on the upper arm.

His Holiness was smiling and totally joyful throughout our wonderful walk which led us gently downhill on the dirt road through the encampment meadow towards the stream that divided the land.

I had brought my camera given to me by my father when I was a boy. An old Kodak model manufactured in 1938, its antique nature stood out in an obvious way. The Karmapa soon noticed it and asked if the camera took good pictures. I replied that it did. Interestingly, whenever His Holiness spoke in Tibetan, the Western monk translated it into English but when I replied in English, it was never translated into Tibetan, as if the Karmapa understood what I was saying. Finally he asked to see the camera, which I handed over. He turned it around in his hands again and again, apparently appreciating it fully, and then handed it back saying, "Very good," in English, which he did say a few times during our walk.

During this precious time together it felt to me as though some extraterrestrial being had spontaneously alit on a remote hillside in Colorado, and we were accompanying him down to be introduced to an unsuspecting world. It was palpably surreal.

The Black Crown Initiation began shortly after we returned to the shrine room. There were more people there now.

After the ceremony had concluded, His Holiness engaged a few of the people in the room. Two of the people he spoke with were the parents of one of the young men in attendance. After briefly chatting with them he turned to the young man and said, "Your parents will never again be reborn in the lower realms."

At the very end of his visit to RMDC, as he was standing outside in front of the shrine room building, His Holiness was handed an enormous bowl of rice. He then ceremonially tossed into the air some of this rice, a handful at a time, further blessing the land and, in fact, the entire environment. This was a very dramatic moment for all of us and, indeed, many of those present gently wept.

A moment later he departed, and it suddenly felt as though it had all been a dream.

I LIVED ALONE
IN THE MOUNTAINS
by Paula Breymeier

Paula Breymeier became a student of Chögyam Trungpa Rinpoche in 1972 while studying at the University of Colorado. She met His Holiness Karmapa in 1974 when he came to Boulder, Colorado during his first trip to the United States. Trungpa Rinpoche suggested she become an oil painter. She now paints and lives in Boulder where she continues to practice and study Buddhism.

I lived alone near Boulder, Colorado in a mountain cabin 20 minutes from the nearest road. The Karmarpa came to Boulder to teach at Karma Dzong, Trungpa Rinpoche's center and I came down from my retreat home to see him.

The stars were especially brilliant at night from my cabin because I was so far from town. So I would often go outside to study the sparkling sky and to marvel at the stars. The question of how such a vast space could exist often came to mind. How could such brilliance that seemed so small but was so large, that was so far away both in space and in time be a part of our world? The Karmarpa was the only person I had ever met who seemed possibly to have the wisdom to explain the mystery of the universe.

When he met with a small group of students to answer our questions, it was the perfect opportunity to ask him to explain this conundrum but I felt very stupid and embarrassed to speak of such things in front of all the intelligent people there who were asking sophisticated questions about the Dharma. So instead I just asked him the question in my mind. I never spoke it out loud.

At one point he gazed at me and without a word answered my question. He revealed the vast space of mind and the uncompromising truth of non-duality. He showed me how the unoriginated space and brilliance of the universe is the same as my own mind. He showed me that the preoccupations and discontent with which I filled my mind simply covered up who I really am. He showed me that I was in fact missing the reality of my life by focusing on those thoughts and then trying to fill what I thought to be the holes in my life. I felt as if the life I had lived previous to seeing the truth of my true nature was a lie. It was devastating.

He finished teaching and left the room. After he left, I ran out of the building, my eyes filled with tears and stumbled down the sidewalk, numb with despair at recognizing my own ignorance and my wasted life. After a while I calmed down and returned to the building, my mind empty and shorn. I did not know how I could continue to even exist with such a vacancy inside. As I entered the building, he was just leaving, tall, regal with his entourage following behind. He looked at me as I hovered against the wall, cringing before his commanding and brilliant presence. Without breaking his stride, he instilled my heart with perfect confidence to go forward in life without any reference point of thought. That it was possible to be as he was, totally full but without anything to depend upon.

This has remained with me, vivid and unadulterated for more than three decades. I have continued to practice meditation. In spite of his blessing and my practice, my habitual thoughts of discontent, past, present and future continuously arise and obscure my mind and life. But at the same time in the midst of all my sufferings, I have an understanding that it is simply waves on the ocean of my humanity. I still have access to the wisdom he revealed to me and how my lack of contentment is self imposed.

I am so grateful to the Karmarpa for his kindness and generosity. He expanded my life and showed me the confidence that has allowed me to live without regret or looking back.

But make no mistake. This wisdom that he revealed to me is not the exclusive provenance of the Karmarpas. The golden cup into which this wisdom was poured was beaten and fashioned by Trungpa Rinpoche and the elixer of wisdom I tasted has been continuously replenished by every authentic linage master with whom I have met or studied since then. This is the birthright of every being even though we don't recognize it. But it was the Karmarpa's powerful and vast activity that brought it directly before my eyes.

BLESSING POWER
by John Tischer

I have been a student of Chögyam Trungpa since 1972 and helped to build Karme Chöling, Rocky Mountain Shambhala Center and Gampo Abby. I was a plumber for 30 years. Now I have retired to Tepoztlan, Mexico.

In 1974 the 16th Karmapa visited the Vajradhatu Seminary taking place in Snowmass, Colorado, which I attended. At the time my mother was diagnosed with terminal cancer.

I was a server for the Karmapa's monks one morning when Freda Bedi, the Karmapa's secretary, was there. I told her about my mother, and couldn't keep myself from crying.

She grabbed me and literally threw me at the Karmapa's feet and spoke to him in Tibetan. He was smiling the whole time, and gave me a blessing. The next day I was given a protection cord for my mother, but it was different. It looked like a tiny macrame, about three inches long, with many knots. I was instructed to have my mother wear it. I attended my mother the last couple of months of her life. She wore the cord for some time. My mother was schizophrenic, but when she died, her mind was clear as a bell.

A BEAR BLESSING
by Stefan Carmien

I spent my years 15–19 (1966–1970) trying to wake up chemically. After that I lived in silence and meditation in a Catholic priory connected with Thomas Merton. I felt a need for more personal direction and travelled across the country looking for a teacher. I went to Boulder and staffed the first year of Naropa in 1974. Then I followed His Holiness Karmapa to Vancouver. At the time I was sitting Zazen, doing Sufi dances, sitting the Nyintun at the local Dharmadhatu, and going to Mass at the Jesuit rectory in Berkley. So you can see why Chögyam Trungpa's book, Cutting Through Spiritual Materialism struck me to the heart. In short, I was a very accomplished spiritual consumer.

PS. I had decided to follow Karmapa to Vancouver and took refuge from him there. Interestingly he had refuge names for men and for women, and when he came to me he pulled the top one off the stack read it, looked at me again, returned it to the top of the stack and pulled the one off the bottom and handed it to me, with a smile.

Now I am 60 years old, still completing my ngondro (after a 20 year gap) and living in San Sebastian, Spain. I have doctorate in computer science and cognitive sciences, and work on systems supporting the daily life of adults with cognitive disabilities.

From HH 16th Karmapa's visit to Karme Choling in Vermont

In 1980 (or 79 or 81, it's a bit fuzzy) at the end of the North America tour of the 16th Karmapa, we were told that the Karmapa was asking wherever he went, "Are there bears here?" So the staff took it upon ourselves to rent a bear costume and I got into it. The Karmapa would often spend the early afternoon looking out over the land from the landing in the converted dormitory; and so on this day we arranged for me to amble towards the barn from a retreat cabin and then had the Vajra Guards chase me out of the woods and capture me. I lumbered up the outside stairs to the top and pulled out a white offering scarf and offered it to him. He blessed my nose and I will always remember seeing, through the restricted eyehole of the bear head, his hand reaching out to gently bless his bear.

DISCOVERING BUDDHA NATURE IN DISNEYLAND
by John Welwood

John Welwood, Ph.D., is a psychotherapist and teacher specializing in integrating Eastern spiritual wisdom and Western psychology. His books include Journey of the Heart, Perfect Love, Imperfect Relationships, *and* Toward a Psychology of Awakening. *This chapter was originally published in New Age Journal, June, 1977.*

Disneyland is not the kind of place where one would normally expect to learn about the relation of samsara and nirvana, the world of illusion and the world of awakened perception. But then my first visit there was hardly a normal one.

In the mid-1970s I had the opportunity to experience Disneyland in the company of His Holiness the 16th Gyalwang Karmapa and his party of Tibetan lamas and monks. His Holiness was the head of the Kagyu lineage of Tibetan Buddhism and one of the great spiritual figures of our time. During the days of the "holy man jams" of the sixties where smiling bearded men in white robes proclaimed the message of all-is-one, I had become somewhat suspicious about holy men in general. The term "His Holiness" grated on my ears until I came into contact with the man himself and realized that there was no other title that did him justice.

His Holiness' presence had nothing to do with any stereo-
typed images of ethereal piety or blissed-out otherworldliness. He
was something far more refreshing, an embodiment of grounded
awake vitality that had no discernible limitations or boundaries.
To put it simply, he was the most powerful and enlightened human being I have ever encountered. His very presence commu-
nicated enlightenment without his ever having to mention that
word. This quality of enlightenment, which is very hard to grasp
or pin down, had something to do with his not being able to be
encompassed by any thought categories. Somehow he surpassed
and overflowed anything you could think about him. This was
his power over you. His compelling presence beckoned to you to
surrender your beliefs about who and what you were. His smile
pierced through everything you were clinging to.

As part of the community hosting him on one of his visits
to Los Angeles, I was surprised and somewhat dismayed to hear
that His Holiness not only wanted to visit Disneyland but that he
wanted to spend an entire day there. The source of my discomfort
was an old determination never to set foot in Disneyland, a place
that had become a metaphor for me and many of my generation of
what was worst about America, for which we coined a new usage
of the word "plastic." However my former vow fell to the way-
side amidst the bustle and excitement of preparing for a day-long
journey to a place that was beginning to seem, in this context, an
exotically foreign American territory.

As the motorcade carrying His Holiness and party sped across
the Los Angeles freeways to Anaheim, I was uneasy about the day
ahead of me, with a certain familiar malaise I tend to feel with
full-on encounters with unabashed Americana. I wondered about
how these Tibetans who never saw a single road in their native
land, were experiencing the freeway culture, the endless miles of
concrete stretching out in all directions. And I wondered how they
imagined the place they were going to. We tried to prep the monks
the night before with stacks of Disney comic books, which didn't

HH Karmapa and Jamgön Kongtrul
Rinpoche with Pluto at Disneyland, 1976
(Photographer unknown)

seem to make much of an impression.

Disneyland was prepared for His Holiness. When we arrived, a large gate was thrown open, and the whole party was greeted and ushered in. Special hostesses and hospitality people, their white-teeth smiles flashing in the bright sunlight, escorted us to the Disneyland Town Hall, where Mickey Mouse and his cohorts gave His Holiness a warm welcome. A small crowd soon formed and he was escorted inside Town Hall to sign the register, amid much hubbub and picture taking. This was but the beginning of the royal treatment Disneyland gave us all day. I understood that they did this because of the Karmapa's high diplomatic and political position, but since this political position in Tibet implied and was secondary to his spiritual attainment, it also seemed that the Disney world was recognizing and paying homage to the realm of the spirit, just as the mayor and police department of Los Angeles, along with other dignitaries and celebrities had been doing all week. Something strange and exciting appeared to be happening here in this intersection of different realities.

A double-decker bus with a fringe on top pulled up to the Town Hall, the whole party climbed aboard and we were soon on our way into the heart of Disneyland. We covered an enormous amount of territory in just a few hours. This fifty-four year old man, who had the energy to bless thousands of people individually in the space of two hours without a sign of fatigue, took Disneyland by storm. The shiny all-American hostess had planned out a selection of the high spots, leading us through every major event from the Jungle Cruise to the 360-degree film of America the Beautiful.

As he did everywhere he went, His Holiness created his own space around him. The Tibetans in their wine-red robes cut a colorful swath through the crowds of tourists, which parted and dispersed before them. His Holiness formed the head of a snake-like procession, whose sinuous body was shaped by clumps of monks and students following at various intervals behind. In the rear of the procession the monks would scurry off in all directions to check out the flora and fauna along the way, and several times the party would have to stop to rescue a stray monk from the seductions of a popcorn-seller or a cowboy-hat stand.

By noon, while His Holiness and the monks were off to the Disneyland Hotel for a catered lunch, I had to retire to the cool recesses of a local bar, along with some of the other American students, to let the kaleidoscopic impressions swirling through my mind settle out a bit.

From all appearances His Holiness and the monks were having a great time. They were able to give themselves to the rides with a child-like abandon and amusement that I envied. I kept wondering how they were experiencing things, what the whole place meant to them. There was no telling. It seemed to me a far cry from the images of a fierce Mahakala, or wrathful Tibetan deity, dancing on the corpse of ego in a circle of purifying flames, or a bloated hungry ghost, swollen with its own insatiable craving for what it does not have, to the cartoon world of spooks and skeletons of Disney's Haunted House, but such considerations did not seem to faze His Holiness and his monks.

One important stop after lunch was the enchanted Tiki Room, a Polynesian hut sponsored by Dole Pineapples filled with mechanical singing and talking birds. His Holiness was known for his attunement with animals and was a great lover and connoisseur of birds in particular. The Tiki Room put me through some rough moments. I half expected His Holiness to storm out in disgust and outrage at the sheer plasticity of it all, especially when the birds all sang to the syrupy sing-along, "Let's all sing like the birdies sing, tweet, tweet, tweet, tweet, tweet." But he seemed to love it, while I and the other Americans were cringing in our seats or looking around for the exits.

On our way out of the park His Holiness paused to rest on one of the front porches on Main Street, and a monk served him Tibetan tea from a thermos. Soon a small crowd gathered around the framed veranda, and someone asked me "What's that?" You mean, "Who's that?" I asked back. "Yeah, what's that?" the questioner persisted, obviously trying to figure out what Disneyland character His Holiness was. "He's a very high Tibetan Lama," I replied, to keep it as succinct as I could. "Oh," came the disappointed response as the questioner turned and shuffled off, somewhat irritated by this intrusion of reality into his Disney Day.

Sitting on a bench in Town Square, near the front gate of Disneyland, waiting for His Holiness to depart, I felt exhilarated, exhausted, yet deliciously unsettled in some way. And I reflected: We in America are prisoners of a world that has been so over-symbolized, over-packaged and over-consumed that we can barely see things as they are anymore. What we tend to see instead are symbolic complexes about things—media images, what someone has told us to look for, our ideas of how we should respond—rather than the things themselves. We have lost our direct and immediate sense of what is, of what things are in their very being, unmediated by the culture's symbolic machinery. Disneyland is a highly developed form of this symbolic world. Not only is Disneyland not the "real" world, it does not even attempt to represent the "real" world. All of the mechanical animals and talking birds are re-creations only of the Disney world, a world of shared fantasies, hopes, fears, and images of what things are like. This puts Disneyland at least three removes from any kind of reality. For some, it must be a relief from other tourist attractions, such as Death Valley, where they anxiously try to "appreciate" the view, to align its sheer presence with their expectations and images about how it should look. Since the Disney world is unreal to begin with, no one feels any pressure to have any "real" experiences there. Disneyland is designed to accommodate the desire to dwell in fantasies.

I was attracted to Buddhism largely as a reaction against all that Disneyland stands for. Yet here I was with the supreme embodiment of the Buddhist teachings in Disneyland, the last place I would ever plan to spend a day with a living buddha. Moreover, he was thoroughly enjoying himself. Maybe he saw Disneyland at some level that turned its abstractions back into reality. Perhaps he saw it as "camp" in some spiritual sense that was beyond me. Or, possibly he was seeing it as a child would, without any conceptual filters at all, simply as an extravaganza of the phenomenal world. Or could it be that his experience of it had nothing to do with anything that I was thinking? In any case, his piercing smile intimated some discovery of buddha-nature, even here, in Disneyland.

Evening was settling in and lights began popping on in all the shops and streets. I was exhausted by the day's events and ready to leave. But His Holiness lingered; exchanging gifts with his Disneyland hosts, who seemed to be enjoying his world, as thoroughly as he was enjoying theirs. They presented the monks with Disneyland souvenir books and His Holiness with the Story of Walt Disney. His Holiness in turn, presented Disneyland with a booklet on Tibetan Buddhism in America.

Some of the monks had scattered to go shopping in the stores around the square, while others were carrying on with Goofy. His Holiness bought some balloons and was writing something on them. As he released them into the evening sky, it seemed that something inside me was also letting go.

BIRDSONG
by MJ Bennett (Jangchub Wangmo)

Those with the good fortune to be close to the 16th Karma-pa knew how much he loved birds. The aviary behind his summer palace just above the monastery in Rumtek opened onto a "lingka," a beautiful garden of flowers and pathways with ponds of gold fish. It was covered with netting and the birds flew freely in the air, filling it with birdsong. It was a magical place. Funded in part by the government of India, it was advertised as a tourist attraction in the Sikkim state brochures. Busloads of Indian tourists would visit in the afternoons to delight in the beauty of the gardens and the various species of birds. But in the early hours of each morning before the monks in the monastery and the villagers in the town below had awakened, the summer palace and its aviary was even more special with the presence of the Karmapa.

Those early morning hours in the first six months of 1981 when I was alone with His Holiness and the two monks who tended the birds, are some of my most treasured memories. I still have a recording of him chanting the Vajrasattva mantra in the aviary. The sound of birdsong is almost louder than the Karmapa's deep melodious voice.

His Holiness loved all birds, but his favourites were gouldian finches for their stunning colours and canaries for their song.

Inside the summer palace was a special room filled with cages of finches and several varieties of the most delicate canaries. His Holiness lovingly visited each bird daily. He would talk to the birds, sometimes take one out; once he had me hold one while he gently cut its toenails. He would reach into the cage and just cup the bird in his hand to take it out. There was never a fuss or flapping of wings. Usually he gave it a kiss on its beak before putting it back. If a bird were sick, he would blow on it to make it well.

I first began helping His Holiness with the birds on his final North American tour in 1980 in Woodstock New York. Shortly after his arrival at his North American Seat, Karma Triyana Dharmachakra, he began making trips almost daily to search out birds. He visited all the pet shops in Kingston, New York, a half hour drive from the monastery; as well as specific breeders within a hundred mile radius. At his favourite pet shop in Kingston, he became known affectionately as "The Chief" because of his majestic presence and entourage. His Holiness would decide which bird he wanted, step into the flight cage, put out his hand quickly and with a deft movement catch his chosen bird. It was during these trips to the pet shops in Kingston, New York that His Holiness discovered that the mice in the cages were kept for people to buy to feed to snakes. He immediately began buying up all the mice in that town!

One morning, His Holiness had me bring a small cage with canaries and another small cage with the mice into his interview room and place one cage on each side of him. Then he handed me his Polaroid camera, and asked me to take a photo of him. He gave it to me, and said: "This is how I always want you to remember me."

Since the Karmapa was already in poor health at that time, many of the staff of the monastery were concerned about these trips. They wanted him to rest. But at any break in his schedule, he would sneak off to look at birds. He would simply disappear, much to the organisers' dismay, and return an hour or two later.

At any break in his busy schedule on that last trip to the West,

Copy of photo from a newsletter of HH Karmapa with a canary on one of his last world tours to the West.
(Photographer unknown)

the Karmapa would fit in a journey to look for birds. Early one morning, as I was cleaning bird cages around the swimming pool of the home where he was staying, while his birds bathed and sang in the morning sun, he said to me: "I don't have to buy birds you know. I just have to look at them and be with them. Being with them is my best medicine." I could see that was true. After any journey to visit animals of any kind, His Holiness would return with a rosy glow on his face.

When His Holiness lay dying in a hospital near Chicago, one of his close disciples, a driver and bird procurer, Steve Roth, brought a rare purple breasted gouldian finch and left it in his room. The joyful sound of birdsong would accompany his passage to parinirvana.

THE DREAM FLAG TRAVELS
WITH THE 16TH KARMAPA
Deborah Luscomb

*In 1974, when I first met His Holiness, I was a young, single seam-
stress... and a new student of the Vidyadhara's. Today, I am an
old, single, mother of three, grandmother of one (and one on the
way) seamstress... and still a student of the Vidyadhara's.*

At the request of my teacher, Chögyam Trungpa, Rinpoche, I was
in charge of the national textile production for the 1980 visit of
His Holiness, the 16th Gyalwang Karmapa, and in that capacity
had the opportunity to do some personal sewing for him.

For his stay in Boulder most of Marpa House had been turned
into visit accommodations. Early on in the visit, I was called to
His Holiness' suite and asked to make a new brocade cover for the
box housing the Black Crown. Unfortunately, due to long-stand-
ing tradition, my gender prevented me from measuring the box.
Measurements were given to me by a male attendant (the only
kind in existence at that time) and brocade was chosen. I mentioned to His Holiness that I could not promise a reasonable fit
since I was unable to obtain the measurements myself. He did not
seem worried. The project was taken on by my colleague—a most
accomplished seamstress—Susan Drommond.

On the day of the scheduled Black Crown ceremony, I was again called to His Holiness' suite only to learn that the new, perfectly constructed brocade cover for the box was too tight. This time I was invited into the bedroom with my tape measure. I had only 4 or 5 hours before the ceremony to create another cover.... which included some shopping for lining and notions. When His Holiness asked me if I could complete the task that day, I replied "I will try." My answer was obviously unsatisfactory. He asked again... and I said, "Yes."

Anxiety filled my afternoon as I worked to construct another new cover for the Black Crown box. Imagine a slip-cover creation... a three dimensional piece, with (hidden) zippered cover, for a deep, round, hat box. The project was completed at about 7 pm and I quickly changed for the ceremony, where I arrived at about 7:30, to a huge, packed hall at the University of Colorado. I sent the cover backstage.... and about 10 minutes later a monk appeared on stage carrying the hat box—with the new cover—on his shoulder to the appropriate place for the ceremony. His Holiness appeared shortly thereafter and performed the ancient Black Crown ceremony for the benefit of all. I had absolutely no idea that the ceremony was waiting on the new cover... I really had assumed it was a travelling cover.

Sometime in mid-June I was summoned to the suite where His Holiness presented me with several small sketches of a flag which he had seen in a dream. He had used blue and yellow pencils and was quite specific about the colors. He asked if I could make the flag, adding "Everywhere the flag flies, the dharma flourishes."

The design appeared very symmetrical, vertically, horizontally, as well as diagonally, in the sketches and I found it challenging to render a pattern. I called upon my mathematician friend, Michael Lewis who suggested using graph paper to make it accurate.

When I showed it to His Holiness he said, "Perfect!"

The next challenge was to enlarge it to 4 by 6 feet so that it would be a full size flag without losing the perfect proportions.

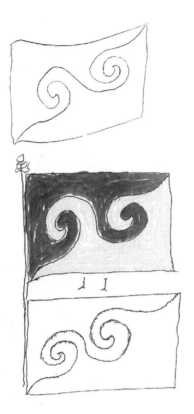

Dream Flag original drawing by Deborah Luscomb.
(Copyright Deborah Luscomb)

I went to the Boulder Public Library to use an overhead projector and, with a sheet tacked up onto the wall, was able to enlarge the design without distorting it.

In the meantime, plans were being made to raise the first "Dream Flag," along with the (currently in production) Tibetan tent at our annual Midsummer's Day celebration, which would be attended by His Holiness and party. In addition to the usual flying of the US flag, the Colorado flag, the Mukpo Standard, and the Shambhala Standard, a fifth flagpole was needed.

The Dorje Kasung assured me that there would be five flagpoles ready and waiting, and as the day approached, I stayed up two nights in a row finishing the first Dream Flag, as well as ceremonial saddle blankets for Chögyam Trungpa Rinpoche and his wife, who would both be riding in a procession to open the event.

The construction of the flag presented yet more challenge. In appearance the yellow and blue just meet. In practical terms, one needs to overlap the other—or be "appliqued"—to be able to join them together. For this first flag, having cut both colors, I used iron-on glue, yellow on blue, before stitching. (By the second one, I had developed a simpler, and more efficient method.)

After the second night without sleep I arrived at the ranch south of Boulder for Midsummer's Day with flag in hand. The celebration was beginning. There were hundreds of people and the weather was perfect. The completed Tibetan tent had been raised and was in use. I was dressed in khakis, holding the flag folded properly, feeling slightly delirious (read exhausted). While hunting for the Color Party I saw that there were only four flagpoles!

I turned around, walked back to the parking lot, and drove back to Boulder in tears. At Marpa House I noticed that no flags had been raised. So I stopped and raised the Dream Flag by myself and then went home and slept.

Soon after, however, His Holiness requested several more flags in different sizes. By the time he left Boulder, they were even flying from his car.

The following month, to my utter astonishment and delight, I was included in the entourage accompanying His Holiness as he travelled through California—visiting sanghas, holding audiences, performing the Black Crown ceremony, and sight-seeing. He thoroughly enjoyed tourist adventures, like fireworks over the ocean near Los Angeles, and touring San Francisco Bay where he piloted the boat for some of the trip. And shopping—yellow jacquard silk with tiny horses to make into monastic shirts, gifts to take back to Rumtek, and of course, buying special birds to add to his extensive collection.

Dream Flag made by Deborah Luscomb.
(Copyright Deborah Luscomb)

During a visit to an art gallery in San Francisco, as His Holiness was receiving visitors and I was kneeling at his right side, suddenly he took hold of my hair and began knocking on the top of my head ... telling me something important. "Learn to make all the monastic garments," said the translator, "and when I come back I'll teach you how to make the Gampopa Hat."

A little more than a year later, the coffin holding Karmapa's body was flown from Chicago to Rumtek. His body was wrapped in the original flag.

I continue to produce Dream Flags, commonly known as Namchen Banners... and today they fly all over the world. And, true to his prophecy, the dharma is indeed flourishing.... as I wait for the 17th Karmapa to teach me to make a Gampopa Hat.

Europe

The 16th Karmapa in Europe
by Ken Holmes

THERE HAVE BEEN SEVERAL milestone events during the two and a half thousand years of Buddhism. Following its own rich development in India, it spread across Asia, from Alexandria to Japan, reaching Tibet in the 7th and 8th centuries. It was annihilated in India in the 12th century and, in the 20th century, finally arrived in all the other continents of the world.

From an historical perspective of forty years, it is clear that the three tours of His Holiness the 16th Karmapa to the West in 1974, 1977 and 1980 were powerful and defining factors in the West's awakening to Tibetan Buddhism in general and to the Kagyu tradition in particular. In a broader context, his activity, like that of His Holiness the Dalai Lama, created favourable circumstances ensuring the survival of the ancient Tibetan traditions.

Buddhism first found its way into Britain in the 19th century through translations of scriptures from the various schools in different parts of the east. In 1879 Sir Edwin Arnold compiled an epic poem, *The Light of Asia*, describing the Buddha's life. Allan Bennett returned from Sri Lanka in 1898 as Ananda Metteyya, the first

Englishman to be ordained as a Buddhist.

In 1907 a group of people got together and formed The Buddhist Society of Great Britain and Ireland. This was succeeded in 1924 by The London Buddhist Society, a lay organisation founded by Christmas Humphreys. It was the first really successful organisation in Britain to provide a platform for all schools and traditions of Buddhism.

The year 1967 saw the founding of Samye Ling, the first Tibetan Buddhist centre in the West, in southern Scotland, by two Tibetan lamas: Trungpa Rinpoche and Akong Rinpoche. Their arrival in the UK was facilitated by Freda Bedi (later to become ordained as the famous Sister Palmo)—an English woman married to a Sikh.. She founded the Young Lamas Home School in Dalhousie, India, to care for the young, newly-arrived reincarnate lamas and to save them from the difficult conditions of the refugee camps where many Tibetans were dying. She became a personal secretary to His Holiness Karmapa and with his guidance, she appointed Trungpa Rinpoche as its director and Akong Rinpoche as its manager. By 1963, she arranged for these two to go the UK and obtained a grant for Trungpa Rinpoche to study at Oxford.

By the fascinating power of coincidence (interdependence), an early and interesting seed for this had been sown in 1958, on the 16th Gyalwang Karmapa's return from Beijing to Tsurphu when he stopped over at Palpung Sherab Ling, in Kham. Almost a hundred reincarnate lamas (*tulku*) were gathered there to see him and receive his advice in those dire days. It became known that during his stay he would impart, as he does only once in a lifetime, very secret transmissions of protector practices, giving the empowerment in the night to only thirteen people. Among the chosen few were the Trungpa and Akong tulkus. The Karmapa counselled both tulkus to leave Tibet before the arrival of the Maoist troops.

It only took a few years for the two Rinpoches to move on from being invited to teach in other organisations to seeking to found their own centre in Scotland. By a series of good fortunes, they were able to do this in southern Scotland, in 1967, in what had been for some years a Buddhist community, called the Johnstone House Trust under the guidance of the Ven. Anandabodhi—a Canadian born Western teacher. Anandabodhi trained first as a Theravadin monk and, following a pilgrimage to the 16th Karmapa, became known as Namgyal Rinpoche. He arranged for Johnstone House to be offered to Chögyam Trungpa and Akong Rinpoches, who re-named it Samye Ling, "the place of the inconceivable," after the first monastery in 8th century Tibet.

In the late 1960s, while Samye Ling was still in embryonic form, the two Rinpoches, Trungpa and Akong, visited the Karmapa in India on several occasions, both together and separately, seeking advice on how best to further Samye Ling, and invited him there.

In its first decade, Samye Ling grew slowly and, to a limited extent became an "in" place. The famous psychiatrist R. D. Laing and the singer Leonard Cohen were among its visitors, as was David Bowie. Flower-power was bringing a wider interest in spirituality and things Eastern and the prevailing mood of many of its adherents was one of integrating any sort of religion into a broader, more cosmic, view of things, rather than of making a deep commitment to one faith. Nevertheless, some of its residents and visitors were practising Kagyu Buddhists while others, already dedicated to other spiritual movements, came to learn more. And there were the many people who had read and believed the fantastic novels of Cyril Hoskins, an Englishman posing as a Tibetan, Lobsang Rampa.

Trungpa Rinpoche, who returned in visionary mode from a trip to the Tiger's Nest, a Guru Rinpoche cave in Bhutan, had no wish to be the iconic master simply performing to the tune of the various expectations of 1960s seekers. He preferred an uncompromising, often challenging and direct, interaction with people. He wanted new dharma prayers in English and did not feel inclined to establish Tibetan Buddhism in the UK in a progressive, step-by-step way, along very traditional lines, as clearly preferred by Akong

Rinpoche. They disagreed irreconcilably about this and turned to the Karmapa for guidance. Under a lifetime seal of secrecy, the instruction and counsel given to each of them by His Holiness was to shape the following decade of Kagyu dharma in the USA and Europe, bringing different but suitable responses to the immediate situation in each continent. The "traditional approach" was chosen for Europe: something to be confirmed repeatedly in the 1970s by Kalu Rinpoche and the Karmapa, in the 1980s by the Tai Situpa and Gyaltsabpa and in the 21st century by the 17th Gyalwang Karmapa, Ogyen Trinley Dorje.

Trungpa Rinpoche left Samye Ling in 1969 after a severe car accident which left him partially crippled. He preferred thereafter to use his teaching skills as a married layperson. He went to the States in 1970. Akong Rinpoche took on the direction of Samye.

The early development of Kagyu dharma in Europe took place principally in two ways: through what spread from Samye Ling and through the activities of returning Europeans who had spent significant time in India or Nepal with refugee Tibetan lamas.

Wishing to lay the best foundations for the future, Akong Rinpoche requested—either directly or via the Karmapa—some of the finest Kagyu scholars and meditation masters to come to Scotland. The first major response to this were the 1973 and 1974 visits of Khyabje Kalu Rinpoche ("Khenpo Kalu" as he was known then), who had been instructed directly by the 16th Karmapa to visit Samye Ling in particular and Europe more generally in order to help strengthen dharma but especially in order to prepare the way for his own visits in a near future.

Kalu Rinpoche's arrival marked a huge change in European dharma and, as planned, paved the way for the 1974 and 1977 visits of the Karmapa. There was effectively a "before Kalu" and an "after Kalu." The reason for this was the scale and nature of his visits. In 1974, he arrived accompanied by a large monastic party of over a dozen, including five Bhutanese lamas, fresh out of three-year retreat. They were fully-equipped with ritual and musi-

HH Karmapa with Kalu Rinpoche, 1973.
(Photographer unknown)

cal instruments, huge smiles and much enthusiasm: a very power-ful dharma team indeed. They arrived on the day of a full moon. That night, sitting on the front steps of Samye Ling, they played the long *radong* horns and oboe-like *jaling* well into the clear, still night, letting the very typical, unique Tibetan sounds resound along a European valley for the first time ever.

Kalu Rinpoche gave Refuge, lay precepts, the Bodhisattva Vow, many comprehensive dharma instructions and empowerments, setting a whole wave of people on the special Kagyu *ngondro* foun-dation practices. His maturity, sparkle, authority and charisma quickly drew many people to dharma. He had meditated for some fifteen years in caves in Tibet, and seemed to embody the yogic path. There were stories of him speaking directly to animals telling them not to kill.

Through his teachings on Marpa, Milarepa, Gampopa and the early lineage masters, Kalu Rinpoche brought a vivid awareness of the special qualities of the Kagyu traditions and in particular of the unique Karmapa line.

The Buddhist scriptures explain that when the mind, or the situation, is ready, the Buddha will come. They compare this to the cleansing and preparation of a palace before it is fit for the visit of a Universal Monarch. The foundation work of the lamas, helped by the generous support and enthusiasm of the few hundred Europeans whose karma had awakened early and drawn them into Tibetan Buddhism, had, by 1974, sufficiently prepared Europe for the 16th Gyalwang Karmapa's historic visits.

Although these were still very early days, His Holiness did, in those powerful visits, what the Karmapas have always done. He inspired the creation of, or consecrated, the vital supports of Buddhism—its temples, monasteries, images and scriptures—by such acts as his own sponsorship of printing a new edition of the complete canon (*tripitaka*) and donating it to new centres. He developed the sangha, giving Refuge widely, as well as the bodhisattva vow and lay and monastic precepts. He implanted the Kagyu lineage, giving empowerments for its main *yidam* and *protector* practices, as well as inspiring, supporting and counselling the activities of its *gurus*. These deeds are referred to traditionally as "establishing the supports of the *Three Jewels* (Buddha, Dharma and Sangha) and the *Three Roots* (gurus, yidams and protectors).

Although this is indeed the work of all Tibetan gurus, the Karmapas incarnate the very radiance of the final result—enlightenment—and perform these tasks with unique magnificence: teaching by being. They do not talk *about* it; they *are* it. The Karmapa's main teaching was not through discourse but by directly manifesting enlightened qualities and spiritual activity of a buddha. Part of this were his unique activities known as "bringing liberation through seeing, hearing, touching or recollecting." These included sharing awakened presence through the ceremony of the Vajra Crown and helping people through the sacred medicine known as Karmapa Black Pills.

The first visit, in 1974, followed directly on from His Holiness' first trip to America. The Karmapa and his small party flew into Prestwick airport and quickly remarked how small everything—the houses, the cars, the roads—seemed after the US. Sister Palmo, shocked by the changes in a Britain she had not seen for a while, was a main facilitator in the UK. The Karmapa stayed in Samye Ling for over three weeks and continued to London, then on to France, where he was given a major gift of land in the Dordogne by the millionaire inventor Bernard Benson. He visited the newly-formed centres of Kalu Rinpoche. He also visited Pope Paul VI, in a private meeting in the Vatican, facilitated by Namkhai Norbu Rinpoche.

In the light of this first trip, His Holiness asked Akong Rinpoche, who had accompanied him throughout, to organise a more thorough trip, lasting some six months, during which he would visit more countries and dharma groups and meet more civil and religious dignitaries. This happened in 1977 and many of the stories that follow occurred then. He was able to accept some of the many invitations he had received and to preside over the consecration of his new land in the Dordogne, a major event attended by almost a thousand followers. There was a third, final, brief visit through London in 1980 when HH Karmapa was ill with cancer, barely a year before he left his body in 1981.

The clear success of the Karmapa's two main European tours was first and foremost due to his own radiance and that of the impressive Lamas and monks accompanying him. However, it is certain that there would have been far less impact without the help of some well-placed people, such as politician Jean-Louis Massoubre in France, or without the liasons established by those familiar with the groups already active in various countries and able to interpret for them, such as Ole and Hannah Nydahl with their contacts throughout Scandinavia. It was truly a team effort, where a network of those with the good fortune to be with and help the Karmapa had the chance to be part of the extraordinary karma of bringing his blessing to a new continent.

For both Tibetans and Westerners looking back at the Karmapa visits, the impression is the same: they marked the real implantation of the Karma Kagyu tradition in Europe, sealing the work done by many before. The seeds blown by the wind of fate had now taken firm root, ready to provide nutritious fruits for generations to come.

Memories
of the Buddha Karmapa
by Ken Holmes

Ken Holmes is a dharma teacher, writer and translator. He left engineering to spend a year in India, with Tibetans, in 1970. Since 1971 he has been based full-time at the Samye Ling monastery in Scotland, where for many years he has been Director of Studies and through which he helped organise the Karmapa's 1974 and 1977 European visits.

It was my very good fortune to have spent altogether some seven months in the daily company of the 16th Karmapa, first for some weeks during his 1975 visit to the UK, then for the entire six months of the 1977 European tour and finally during his brief visit to London in 1980.

Following the first momentous visit, the Karmapa had instructed Chöje Akong Rinpoche to organise the forthcoming 1977 Europe tour. Akong Rinpoche appointed me as trip co-ordinator, visa-fixer and advisor to the groups and centres we visited, helping them understand who the Karmapa was and how to receive him properly. That second tour was without doubt the highlight of my whole life and I have only one regret, namely that I was too young and naive to appreciate it to the full.

HH Karmapa on tour with the Hat Box, Berlin, 1977.
(Photo by Gunter Denk)

In their curiosity, it is the anecdotes and extraordinary events of those six months that people want me to recount. There were many and I am usually happy to oblige.

However, infinitely more important than these, in my mind, was the continuous radiance of the Karmapa's presence and the very nature of his constant activity. Like all the Karmapas of the past, he was a power-house establishing, promoting and healing with the buddha-dharma, in all its forms.

His presence was totally striking and unmitigated. His "job description" was to be buddha for us and for the world—a task he accomplished in unbridled splendour. Most lamas and rinpoches we had met before him (and since) were fairly self-effacing and might declare they did not remember past lives, had no special powers and were just picked by someone else and given the reincarnation name they bore. The Karmapa, by contrast, shone without any of these reservations and let his enlightened radiance illuminate the world around him. Like the Buddha, he taught by being more than by words. That language of being speaks directly to everyone and we saw it overwhelm people of all beliefs, politicians of little belief and simple everyday people who had no idea of the credentials of the person before them but an immediate feeling of his majesty. It also spoke to animals and, I'm fairly sure, to many other beings beyond the range of our senses.

The presence was most powerfully felt during the Vajra Crown ceremonies. I must have attended at least thirty of those, if not more. Buddhas have many manifestations and in particular those of the three kayas or forms.

The Vajra Crown ceremony was a precious moment in which the Karmapa left the smiles and warm presence of his usual form-kaya activity and entered profound meditation in which "voidness has compassion as its heart essence," quietly turning his crystal mala with the left hand and holding the deep blue crown so characteristically with his right hand. These were the most powerful and meaningful episodes, leaving an indelible imprint that will surely go far beyond this life. It was unique inasmuch as it gave the audience a chance to experience what normally happens only when a Vajrayana guru gives a "pointing out" or deeper empowerment.

During his tour of Europe, the Karmapa rarely gave formal dharma teachings and had a dharma master (Khenpo Tsultrim Gyamtso) flown over specially to give any dharma talks that were required. The rare teachings that the Karmapa did give were jewels and even now, over thirty years later, I can hear the unique intonation of his voice shaping the words in the particular way he did, using the lips more than most Tibetans do to speak. If you have ever seen a photo of him speaking to his birds you will know what I mean.

On the subject of that voice, one of the most moving moments of the tour happened in the back of a stretch Mercedes, lent to His

Holiness, in which I was in the company of Jamgön Rinpoche. With a cheeky look, so often seen on his face with its high cheek bones and frequent smile, he produced a cassette from his shirt pocket and slipped it into the cassette player next to the bar. It was a recording of His Holiness singing: minutes of exquisite celestial sound. I've often wondered if a copy of that exists anywhere, having only ever heard since then the minute sample clip Sina Vodjani made into a CD track.

His authority was majestic. I had the privilege of driving him in the UK and in Paris. At one point I took him to a cathedral[1] as the special guest of the Archbishop. The cathedral itself was closed at the time and the Archbishop showed us around very kindly. He seemed rather daunted by the Karmapa's presence. When we reached the high altar, the Karmapa asked what took place there and, to make things simple, the Archbishop replied "We pray." "Pray," said the Karmapa, in a commanding voice and with a not-to-be refused gesture of invitation with his hand. The Archbishop got down on his knees and prayed, very sincerely, looking up from time to time like a small child, awaiting permission to complete. After what seemed an unendingly long time to me, overtaken by embarrassment, Karmapa said, with a huge smile, in English, "Very good" and beckoned the priest to rise. It was such a touching moment, bringing this high figure of the church to a humility and sincerity that the latter, to his great credit, obviously appreciated. It also appeared that the Karmapa was having fun bringing whatever sublime light was appropriate to those in his company.

The 16th Karmapa had a unique laughter and he laughed often and did have fun. The most hilarious moment of the tour, for me, occurred in Regent Street, London. We were out shopping. We had just left the Rolex shop where HH had asked to see the most sparkling diamond-studded watches and spooked the shop assis-

---

1 Possibly St Mary's Episcopal, in Edinburgh, but my memory is not good enough to be sure.

tant by taking it out into the street to see it in the sunlight. After looking at a couple of models, he giggled, said, "Thank you" and exited. He just wanted to see the twinkles.

He then asked to go a bag shop to look at largish suitcases. We ended up in the basement of a luggage store where HH asked for a specific type of case: Samsonite, if my memory serves me well. The young assistant, who was quite taken by the Karmapa, took the appropriate model down from a rack. Then HH said he had seen an advertisement where someone jumped up and down on top of the case to prove its strength and he asked the boy to do it. Without question, the assistant put the case on the floor and started to jump up and down on it, at which point the manager, a rather sour-looking shrivelled businessman, came down the stairs and gave the lad a sharp telling-off. Even so, the young man was still impressed by the Karmapa and I gave him a leaflet for the Crown Ceremony taking place that evening. I was so pleased when he came along. Such connections, the Karmapa said, bear fruit, sometimes in this life sometimes in a future one. The connection is what counts, even the negative ones of those who try to harm or insult the Karmapa, as one of the stories below recounts.

The Karmapa's sense of humour was not always easy to deal with. I had a miserable little goatee beard at the time. He would often grab it and make a gesture of striking a match and saying "num," the Tibetan word for *petrol*. He would do this when I was driving him and, once or twice, did not let go but pulled my head lower and lower until I had difficulty seeing over the dashboard to drive. I was completely torn between my duty of driving him safely and my disciple's duty of accepting the guru's treatment, whatever it was, without question. Just as the situation was reaching crisis point, he would let go with a huge laugh.

The worst such dilemma happened at a red traffic light in Princes Street, Edinburgh. Our car was stopped, first in line. In English, Karmapa said, with some force, "Go!" and I was torn between the guru's command and all my driver instincts, not to mention fear of being arrested in that very public place with HH on board. Remembering Gampopa hesitating before Milarepa's command to drink alcohol, I took off the handbrake and drove forward. There is no handbook or higher authority to turn to in such situations: just you and the guru and a choice to be taken on the spot, for better or for worse.

Sitting next to him in the car was like being mentally naked. He knew everything, not only the thoughts going through one's head but everything. Once he said, through interpreter Achi Tsepel, that I had previously killed birds and that was very bad. Then he actually said, "very bad" in English: not at all joking. I now realise what skilful means it was for him to have me as driver on many expeditions to buy birds, helping me purify that karma. It made me remember what I had long forgotten: shooting birds with an air gun when I was a kid and killing chickens, for the table, during a time when we had chickens in the back yard at home. He must have seen it as clearly as he saw my ridiculous beard.

He was there to help us purify our karma. He would often give people money, as a token of helping them through their poor "finance karma" to reach prosperity in the end. I know one or two cases where this really seemed to have worked. They probably did not realise this at the time and just took the gift as a kind gesture and as a sort of "relic" from him.

The Karmapa's teaching simply by presence has certainly helped me understand the way the Buddha must have taught in ancient India and I can never envisage it as simply "talking." It was 1977, in the Château de Chaban, Dordogne, France. Karmapa was holding group interviews. As one of his secretaries, I was hovering outside the room in which they took place, having ushered the group in. When the party (of mixed nationalities) emerged, an ecstatic lady came straight to me saying, in a very strong accent, "I had no idea he spoke Italian ... and so beautifully and so perfectly. And, it's incredible, he spoke just about what was on my mind!"

I too did not know he spoke Italian. During my six months with the Karmapa, these instances of mind-to-mind communication, which people automatically "heard" in their own language, were so numerous as to seem normal after a while. It helps us understand such things as why, in the list of the Buddha's sixty qualities of speech, it is said that the teaching can be heard in all tongues and by those at the back of a huge crowd just as clearly as by those at the front: impossible if it is only a question of sound-waves.

Paris, 1977

Mainly because of having just inherited a superb Citroen DS (the same model as the French President's), I got to drive the 16th Gyalwang Karmapa in Paris, a city with which he was totally unfamiliar. One day, he wanted, as he often did, to go and buy birds. We were told that these were sometimes reincarnations of his previous disciples, with the mixed karma of being reborn an animal but an animal nevertheless close to the Karmapa Buddha. I took him to the famous Quai de la Mégisserie, with its row of bird shops but he quickly perused all of them without interest. We left and he started directing me, "Left here, now right…" into completely unknown territory. After some ten minutes, I assumed he was having a huge joke at my expense with a random sight-seeing tour in the bargain, as there was no way he could have any idea of the layout of Paris. My tangible anxiety at being totally lost changed briefly to relief and a sense of triumph when he said, "Left" and I could see the street sign saying it was a cul-de-sac: game over, joke over. I stopped the car. Delighted, he immediately got out and walked straight to the pet shop at the end of the street and, once in the door, directly to the birds he wanted.

Back in the car, with the birds on board and seeing me completely lost, he directed me skilfully home to where he was staying. I simply marvelled. Better than SatNav? Of course—who

HH Karmapa and Pope Paul VI in the Vatican, Rome, 1975.
(Photographer unknown)

wouldn't want a SatNav with the Karmapa's beautiful voice and protective presence?

The tour included meeting with eminent politicians, such as Chancellor Bruno Kreisky of Austria, and Christian leaders, such as the Roman Catholic Archbishop of Westminster and the Dean of Westminster Abbey (who, to our surprise, had a bell and dorje on his mantelpiece). The Karmapa had already been taken by Akong Rinpoche to meet Pope Paul VI in 1975.

Tibetan Buddhism was very new to Europe, having only arrived with the two young reincarnate masters Chögyam Trungpa Rinpoche and Chöjé Akong Rinpoche, who co-founded Samye Ling monastery in 1967. His Holiness met with various leaders of the Theravadin and Zen communities, already well-established on the continent. These included probably the most well-known Zen Buddhist in Europe at the time, the Japanese master Taizen Deshimaru: an impressive figure in the true "here and now" strict style, it was said. I acted as go-between for meetings between him and the Karmapa.

As chance had it, my first trip to him and his *dojo* was on the day in France when they celebrate Epiphany, the visit of the Kings.

I found, to my astonishment, Deshimaru wearing a golden crown and heading a large table of disciples. I discovered later that he had the slice of traditional almond pie with the hidden magic bean that makes its finder "king for the day." He subsequently met with the Karmapa on several occasions and was invited to attend an empowerment that was to take place in an immense public hall.

I had been present on several occasions when Tibetan Rinpoches—seriously-respected masters in their own sphere—became like children with their daddy when in the Karmapa's presence. He would pull them around by the hair, tease them and teach them with alternating sunny humour and great seriousness. His authority was always total and natural: it went without saying. His task was to be buddha for them and pointer-out of whatever remained, in their remarkable minds, to be dealt with.

At the empowerment, Taizen Deshimaru was given a place of honour, along with some of his monks, on the stage, almost directly in front of the Karmapa. Deshimaru was trying to look relaxed as if taking it all in his stride as a Zen master should. I was right next to the stage and I saw him, as the ceremony evolved, growing increasingly uncomfortable with being in the amazing aura of the Karmapa and the empowerment. He seemed to be oscillating between being a magnificent master and being an open-hearted learner. At one point, Karmapa picked up the *damaru* (hand drum) and chanted as he beat it slowly from side to side, now looking directly at the Zen master, whose cheeks were starting to flush. At the end of passage, Karmapa gave the powerful final flourish of the drum, like a thunderclap, and the master literally jumped. Karmapa smiled. The master relaxed and seemed to recognise something. Able to exhibit every mood necessary to help and guide anyone, the Karmapa is a teacher of teachers even to guide the most advanced to a state of simple beginner.

The *connection* with the Karmapa is all-important, for future lives and for the death of this life. I think we were in Birmingham at the time, towards the end of the trip. Throughout the journey, the Karmapa had been buying birds and I sometimes accompanied him on bird-seeking excursions. Jamgön Rinpoche explained to us that this was not just a foible of His Holiness but that the birds were his former disciples, now blessed to be born close to him. I have particularly fond memories of evening returns from long avian sorties, with the Karmapa next to me and Jamgön Rinpoche behind, fulfilling their daily commitment to Mahakala practice, reciting it by heart, making mudras and occasionally clapping their hands as I drove them through the dark.

One evening, Tsultim Namgyal, Karmapa's personal attendant at the time, sought us out to usher us into a dimly-lit room in the house lodging the party. He made a gesture to keep quiet. There was a bird cage on the far side, with two largish birds on a perch, next to each other, physically dead but mentally in deep samadhi. The feeling around them and all over the room was one of immense stillness and the sort of profound interiorisation that cuts through everything and carries you into somewhere timeless.

When birds die in normal circumstances, they keel over and you find them dead—stiff on the cage floor. The fact that these two died *together* and standing so perfectly in samadhi was a living proof of the Karmapa's power of "liberation through contact" and of his ability to draw beings into his inconceivable blessing. The birds stayed in samadhi for a couple of days. Then, their minds liberated, their bodies eventually fell down.

HH found true delight in finding and buying his birds. I must have accompanied him on at least a dozen such trips, if not more. By the quirks of karma, the birds he chose were not only his former disciples but also fine specimens in their own right. I recall driving him to one breeder, way out in the English countryside. The birds were in old converted mobile homes and trailers, on the back of his property. As he ushered us into one of them, HH lit up and simply plonked himself down cross-legged on the not-too-clean floor, to the horror of his attendants. Within seconds he was pointing to the birds he wanted, among about a hundred

In Honolulu, Hawaii 1977, these peacocks came to Karmapa who fed them. (Photographer unknown)

in that aviary. HH was even pointing behind himself to cages in the corner out of his line of sight. The breeder was totally amazed. The Karmapa had not even gone all around the cages and there he was, asking to see his finest birds. Even experienced breeders have a rather clumsy way of catching the bird in the cage. It involves cornering it and then making a skilful grab, around the wings. When a breeder went to do this, HH would often indicate them to stop and then simply put his finger inside the door of the cage. He spoke to the bird and it would hop over to him. The professionals were stunned to see this.

One bird trip was a local one to the home of the garage attendant in Lochmaben, near Samye Ling. The house was a modest semi-detached and they had obviously just had new fitted carpet installed in the hall. As we were leaving, they asked HH for his autograph. Tibetans, at the time, used the old fountain pens, prone to clogging up. I shuddered as the Karmapa shook it to free the ink flow: little black spatters appeared on the carpet. But the couple were so enthralled by his presence that they were truly happy he did it, just as Tibetans would have been to have such a "relic." Every time I filled up the car, for years after that, the attendant would ask affectionately after "the Bird Man."

However, the reaction was not always entirely positive. His Holiness was travelling with a party of some fifteen lamas and monks and a bus had been specially converted for the tour, with one side of the seats stripped out and replaced by two huge armchairs, for HH and Jamgön Rinpoche, and cupboards for the birds and their stuff. As the Karmapa bus reached the Danish frontier, the senior border guard was called over on account of the unusual assortment of travel documents I presented to him. These were not all passports and included two Bhutanese "travel passes" consisting of a single foolscap-size sheet of hand-made rice paper, looking as though they had been made with a child's printing outfit. The guard turned out to be a very reactionary Christian, who kept asking why we needed to bring our religion to his country, which did not need it. I am of a rather soft nature but was duty-bound to be strong with him. We were held up for several hours, with phone calls going back and forth to their Interior Ministry.

Even more worrying was the arrival of the bus at Dover, having crossed the Channel. The Karmapa had gone ahead by car and it was late in the evening. The customs wanted to open the box containing the Vajra Crown. Zimpon-la, the Karmapa's personal attendant, simply stood in front of it and said, "You'll need to kill me first. No one except the Karmapa has ever touched this, in all its history." The situation heated up and eventually a senior Home Office official had to be called at his home to make a decision. His Holiness was travelling on a diplomatic passport and a decision had to be made as to whether the Crown could be viewed as diplomatic baggage. In the end, it was.

But the worst time was in Belgium, trying to get German visas. There were few dharma centres in Europe at that time and many of our destinations were hosted by small, local religious groups. One German host was not well-viewed by the local German secret police. This was the time of the Bader-Meinhoff terrorists and the consulate was very jumpy with over-the-top security. It took me six visits, including two personal meetings with the Consul, in order to get the papers. Each visit involved being frisked at the end of a machine gun. The Consul himself was a true aristocrat and very apologetic, saying that the local secret police had to have the final say. In the end, I had to get thousands of US dollars together in a suitcase to take to him to prove we could support ourselves during the visit. I also had to be a little inventive with the rice-paper travel documents, which had no more spaces for new stamps. The only Bhutanese representation at the time was at the UN, in New York. All turned out for the best, because once we had the German visas, other countries found no trouble in following their example.

I witnessed a very touching and predictive moment in that famous bus. There was the Karmapa, Khenpo Tsultrim Gyamtso and just myself with one other Tibetan. Karmapa asked Khenpo-la to sing him a Milarepa song. Once sung, he then asked him to explain it to him. Khenpo looked a little embarrassed but, of course, obliged. As he went through it, from time to time His Holiness interrupted him, very sweetly and gently but nevertheless with authority, making slight corrections. Although Khenpo Tsultrim has since become well-known for his spiritual songs, this was not the case at the time. Before his arrival, the word was that he was very severe and tough. And during the six months of the tour that was the only occasion I heard him sing a doha.

The Karmapa was famous for his foresight and it was sometimes unusually expressed. The sky would be clear and he would say something like "Such heavy rain." Next day, it poured. The miracles also sometimes took time. In Samye Ling, Akong Rinpoche asked him to make a footprint in a rock, at the site of the future retreat. His Holiness placed his foot on the rock but the footprint took years to slowly appear. It is now quite distinct. He also teased Akong Rinpoche, calling him "Africa Lama." We assumed it was because of his Afro hair style at the time but, in retrospect, it is doubtful HH would have known of such things. Akong Rinpoche was to become his representative in Africa a few years later but that was completely "off the cards" at the time. He has since guided the

Kagyu centres in Southern Africa for thirty years.

It is said that karma—actions—carried out in the presence of a buddha are very powerful and are some of the few that produce the famous "instant karma." One incidence of this seemed to happen in Denmark. Karmapa was due to stay in the house of a certain Axel Jensen, a man who, among other things, produced magnetized water for healing. He had "approved by Kalu Rinpoche" marked on the bottles. Our advance party went to Mr Jensen's house to check that all was appropriate and Akong Rinpoche found the bed intended for the Karmapa to be not at all adequate—far too small and "used." It would need to be changed. Axel Jensen could not accept this and said, "If it's good enough for me, it's good enough for the Karmapa." He would not budge. Plans were rapidly changed and HH and the whole party stayed elsewhere. There was little space and Katia, my wife, and I ended up sleeping in the vegetable garden, in sleeping bags. The entire entourage were totally shocked, saying how it was such an honour (and unheard of in Tibet) for the Karmapa to stay in any individual's home and that Axel Jensen had made terrible karma for himself. By "coincidence," the very next week a national newspaper ran an exposure article on him, with a cartoon of him bottling tap water and making a fortune. He was ruined.

Today, memories of the Dordogne are the most painful ones. The donation to the Karmapa, by Bernard Benson, of Dhagpo Kagyu Ling, a magnificent piece of land around his Chateau de Chaban, had been a feature of the 1975 and 1977 visits (particularly the latter). It was full of hope: the new seat of the Karmapa in Europe. I remember the Karmapa, accompanied by the whole party, choosing the site for the future monastery, on a high hillside. He had found a large stone that naturally resembled a snow lion and placed it at the centre-point of where he thought the structure should be. He also pointed out a forest in the shape of a heart on a distant hillside, directly opposite. The Karmapa gave a series of empowerments while we were in Dhagpo, in a huge marquee. We cooked for five hundred at the inauguration and there was a general sense of celebration. That the whole site has now fallen under the control of the Shamarpa faction is an unbearable thought to those of us who were there in those magical days of hope. One evening, in the inner courtyard of the Chateau, towards eleven-o-clock at night, Karmapa was walking with a few of us to take the night air. He stopped and said something to his attendant. He knew that there was someone prostrating outside the gate, beyond our sight and sound, and sent the attendant to give the person a small gift.

The 16th Karmapa passed briefly through London in 1980 and once again I was part of the organising team. Through government contacts, his departure happened through the VIP lounge at Heathrow. I recall Prime Minister Edward Heath was in the lounge at the time. The Karmapa had always been warm and smiling towards me throughout the five years of our acquaintance. However, in a little moment before his departure directly onto his plane, somehow we were alone together for a few moments and he looked at me very differently: quite severely and sadly. That look is burned deeply into my memory. In the few seconds that it lasted, I suddenly knew I would never see him again: a thought that had never crossed my mind. It also had a strong feeling of disapproval yet protection. In the few years that followed, I made some silly but important mistakes in my dharma responsibilities and I now know that in his omniscience he foresaw it all; and was both warning me yet caring for me throughout. As he disappeared onto the waiting car on the tarmac, there were many tears in my eyes and shock throughout my system.

THE KNOWER
OF THE THREE TIMES
by Rager Ossel

Rager Ossel is owner of Gentle Bridges and founder of In Touch, a Dutch company based in Amsterdam providing advanced customized networking solutions to businesses throughout Europe.

In 1976 I got off a truck at Rumtek Monastery. No one knew I was coming but apparently His Holiness asked a monk to go down into the fields to pick me up. The monk took my luggage as we ran uphill towards the Karmapa's summer palace. They pulled me, "Come, come, come." As I passed the guesthouse the jalings started. His Holiness was outside in front of the summer palace, sitting on a small throne with a wall behind him, holding the Black Crown in his hands. He waited for me to sit down in front, looked at me and then he put the Crown on his head. I had no idea about anything. That was the first meeting and there and then I went into his being, his world. His Holiness entered into a deep meditation and it seemed as though we had melted into one. From then on, everything danced very spontaneously. It was synchronized; the timing was exact.

The next incident happened in Europe in 1976. We were going shopping for birds in the countryside of Holland driving towards a well-known breeder. En route we drove through a small village. His Holiness said, "Stop here." We went to the door of a very simple house and rang the doorbell. The wife opened the door. I asked if they had birds. And she said, "Yes" and invited us through the house to the back yard. Her husband was there. Birds were sitting on his hands and shoulders. His Holiness especially loved gouldian finches. This man was at one with his birds and soon both he and His Holiness were both talking continuously to the birds. Their sound was so beautiful; it was an experience to hear it. The man brought out a huge bird cage and placed a very ill bird into His Holiness' hands; when His Holiness touched it, immediately it flew away. The man put a few birds into a cage and gave it to His Holiness. So we got his birds but we never made it to the shop and we actually didn't meet the big bird breeder at all.

On another occasion I was driving to Antwerp to meet His Holiness. I saw a rainbow; every time I went to see His Holiness there were rainbows. He used to give me presents all the time, all kinds of things. While I was driving I thought of a very nice Chinese lacquer pen and how I would like to have such a pen. When I arrived I prostrated to His Holiness. I saw his hand go into his shirt. He was picking up a pen and then his hand was going in my direction to reach out. Suddenly he looked at me with his huge laughing face and put his other hand around his hand and pulled it back again. His smile and personality melted everything. My thought was gone for all time. It was an essential teaching for me. His Holiness was invited by Trungpa Rinpoche for Losar. Karmapa wanted to sit there all day and talk together with Akong Rinpoche and Chögyam Trungpa. There was no way for me to get past the guards so His Holiness put me under his chuba and wrapped his arms around me very tightly; and we walked like that up the stairs. I was there from morning till evening with him.

HH Karmapa with Trungpa Rinpoche and Jamgön Kongtrul Rinpoche. (Photographer unknown)

In '79 near Lille (France) I found myself on the road looking for a hotel in the middle of the night. I had just been released after three months confinement following a very big mission for His Holiness. I was responsible for some important articles belonging to him and had been out of circulation for some time. No one knew where I was. After half an hour I found a hotel. Of course I didn't have a reservation. As soon as I entered the room, the phone rang. It was His Holiness! He was calling directly from wherever he was through the reception to my room.

I was still quite confused by the situation that I had found myself in during those three months. He gave me encouragement about my practice and confidence that everything was fine. This episode was timeless and extremely profound.

A HOLY MOMENT
by Maia Saabye Christensen

*I was 6 years old when I met the 16th Karmapa on his first visit
to Europe in 1974. It was the first Black Crown Ceremony in
Denmark. Times were different then and my parents and I spent
hours in the informal company of His Holiness each day. Similar
blessed circumstances prevailed during the Karmapa's second visit
to Denmark in 1977. The day I started high school, at 14, I began
the ngondro with the instructions of the 16th Karmapa and Ven.
Tenga Rinpoche.*

*I studied documentary filmmaking at the Danish Film Studios.
My lifelong study of Buddhist methods and views and its association with the behavioral sciences and related research on meditation
and mindfulness is the foundation of my work as writer, program
editor and filmmaker.*

*I've worked with the Danish Ministry of Foreign Affairs, Save
the Children, UNICEF and other groups.*

*Currently I have two documentaries in progress; "Parliament
Karate Club" & "900 Years of Wisdom" and am working as film
consultant on issues related to the Buddhist science of mind.*

I met the 16th Karmapa when I was 6 years old in Denmark on his
first trip to the West. At my first meeting he gave the Black Crown

ceremony. I remember every second of that ceremony crystal clear as if it were yesterday. There is a quality to that ceremony that makes it so fresh—it doesn't fade. It's as if there have been no time layers since then. In retrospect, I would say this quality of now-ness is the state of being as awake as you can possibly be.

There was a huge courtyard in front of the palace where the ceremony was to be held. The monks had been given bicycles and they were riding the bicycles in the yard. I showed them how to cycle. Then we went into a palatial hall with pillars. I remember the excitement in the voices of the people and a feeling of expectancy. There was a lot of incense in the air. The sun came in through the huge windows and made rays like angel hair. I remember how it came into the room and lit up the incense smoke. Then we went in and sat down in the midst of it all.

The ceremony started. All the monks went to do different things in the enormous room. I wasn't so focused on what they did—I was only a child and didn't have any expectations. Then Karmapa entered the room, smiling and radiating light in all directions. He was outshining the sun's rays. When he took the Black Crown to his head, there was total silence in the room. Time stood still. I was mesmerized by this man and the Black Crown.

From that moment I remember every detail in the room, the sound, the smell, the way everything happened and in which order. Afterward we all passed by him and I thought I was seeing the biggest person that could ever exist. He filled the whole room. I thought to myself, "this is as holy as anything can be."

The Karmapa liked children. When I came up to him, he gave me a huge bright smile and nothing else existed except me and him at that moment. That meeting had such a deep impact that very often, and even now, I dream that the Black Crown is floating inches over my head and blessing are flowing through me. As a child I remembered these dreams clearly and how the next day I felt I was walking on air.

The next day we were going to meet him again. All the peo-

HH Karmapa with children.
(Photographer unknown)

ple were sitting in this little room. But I waited outside because
I thought he was so huge he wouldn't be able to fit into that room.
Then he came and he went into the room just like everybody else
and I was a bit disappointed. Away from the ceremony he looked
just normal.

In the days following, my parents, sister and I went to see His
Holiness several times. Again my memories are that he was an al-
mighty being, huge and shining like the sun. The Karmapa had
some sweets and was very focused on us children. He immediately signalled us to come up to him and was very playful: smiling
and laughing a lot, squeezing our cheeks, holding our heads and

hands. Time always seemed to transform into something timeless. There was oceans of time. So I just sat there in his lap for most of the meeting with him, feeling totally awed and happy.

TEARS OF COMPASSION
by Vicki MacKenzie

Journalist and author. Since taking a month-long meditation course in 1976, her primary interest has been to make Buddhism accessible to the general public. Her books include:

Reincarnation: The Boy Lama,
Reborn in the West: The Reincarnation Masters
A Young Man of The Lama: A Tale Of Drugs, Hot Sex, and Violence in The Fall Of Tibet
Cave in the Snow: A Western Woman's Quest for Enlightenment, 1999, *(a biography of Jetsunma Tenzin Palmo)*
Why Buddhism?: Westerners in Search of Wisdom
Child of Tibet *(Co-authored with Sonam Yangchen)*

I met the 16th Karmapa at Kham House in the late 1970s very soon after I had first been introduced to Tibetan Buddhism. I wasn't at all aware who the Karmapa was but I found myself in the front row as he performed the Black Hat Ceremony. As he held the Black Hat above his own head, I noticed tears were pouring down his face. There were no sobs or histrionics, just this stream of quiet weeping. Nobody would have seen it from further back. I realised then that he was weeping out of sheer compassion and love for all the suffering sentient beings in the world. This is what I remember of the 16th Karmapa, and the image has never left me.

KARMAPA ROCKS
by Tony Visconti

Tony Visconti was a foremost record producer in the 1970s, residing in London, England. His clients then were David Bowie, T. Rex, Thin Lizzy and many more. In 2011 he is still producing records and resides in New York City.

Chime Rinpoche gave me my first meditation instructions in 1970 and I took my Buddhist vows from him in the same year. My given Buddhist name is Karma Lodrö Thaye. Those who know Chime know that he is a wonderful storyteller and I believe the lessons of the Dharma were always conveyed in his voice no matter what subject he is talking about. Every story had a lesson built in. He once told us, his students, how he was in an advanced inner circle of young Tulku lamas (in their late teens, early twenties), two of whom were Trungpa Rinpoche and Akong Rinpoche, who were receiving instruction from the 16th Karmapa. One day, Karmapa was solemnly foretelling each monk in turn, the specific circumstances of their deaths. One will die of old age, the next will die young, in an auto accident, etc. His delivery was extremely somber. But Chime said, "We were all Tulku lamas, we had died many times, and the result of Karmapa's predictions was having the entire group break out into a fit of laughter." This was my introduction to the mythical, legendary 16th Karmapa.

In the summer of 1975 the 16th Karmapa and his entourage of about 12 monks and lamas visited the UK. Chime encouraged a group of his students, including me, to drive out to Luton airport for his arrival. We were extremely excited and didn't have to wait long for him to appear. Like a rock star, parts of his entourage appeared first from the exit, unmistakable in their maroon robes, and one was carrying a very ornate box, to which Chime exclaimed, "That's The Black Hat!" And then Karmapa appeared in the middle of the entourage. Although there was considerable distance between him and us, he immediately turned our way and recognized Chime and his group. He was wearing, like a rock star, shades, or more commonly known as sunglasses. We simultaneously felt a surge of energy in our minds and bodies that almost seemed to make us levitate; this was confirmed when we later spoke about that initial contact. In the moment I turned to Chime and said, "That was incredible, that feeling," and Chime said with the timing of a veteran comedian, "That's nothing, wait until he takes off the sunglasses!"

A day or two later I was with the same group of students walking into Chelsea Town Hall in London finding a seat amongst about 500 participants eager to be part of the famous Black Hat Ceremony. The stage was beautifully set with a special throne covered with ornate fabrics woven with Tibetan motifs. Monks were seated on both sides of the throne, and Karmapa was led on stage by two attendant monks who helped him climb onto the throne; there he settled into a lotus position. Everyone was silent with anticipation as he began to recite a sutra, as this was the beginning of the Black Hat Ceremony. Karmapa intoned in a strong voice, sometimes picking up a dorje and other times ringing a bell.

Then the moment came. The monk in charge of the Hat carried the same ornate box we saw at the airport and presented it to Karmapa. Karmapa opened the lid slightly and put one hand inside, careful not to open it anymore than need be. He took out the Black Hat and placed it on his head, securing it with one hand while with the other he held a crystal rosary. Instantly his demeanour changed to an open, relaxed expression. It is said that the Karmapa goes into a complete state of samadhi after he places the Hat on his head. And that is the way he remained for what seemed like an hour, never changing position, perfectly still. The audience meditated as best as we could with him. Afterwards we were invited to form a queue and get a blessing from him. I received a red string to wear around my neck and was given a second Buddhist name. But I took away much more from that ceremony, a feeling of fulfillment for having been through a rite of passage.

It is said that the Black Hat is woven from the hair of dakinis (enlightened women, sometimes described as fairies). It must stay in the box because the Hat would fly away. This is why Karmapa must hold it on his head throughout the ceremony. Chime told a story that once one of the monks in charge of caring for the Hat accidentally left the lid open and the Hat floated to the ceiling. With the help of some other monks and a tall ladder they retrieved the Hat from a high corner of the room.

A few days later I received a phone call from Akong Rinpoche who ran the Samye Ling meditation centre in Eskdalemuir, Scotland. I had met him whilst attending two retreats there. He asked me if I would like to host an evening in my home for Karmapa and his entourage. I said yes immediately

HH Karmapa with a miniature dog.
(Photographer unknown)

and told my wife, Mary Hopkin, that we were having 12 Tibetan monks to dinner. What do you serve Tibetan monks for dinner? Akong told me that they liked Chinese food; the spicier the better.

The entourage arrived punctually at our house in Shepherd's Bush, and I led them up to the living room. Karmapa immediately asked if we had any dogs (in Tibetan, as he spoke almost no English). He was known to love animals of all kinds, but particularly dogs.

I felt embarrassed that we had none, nor a cat or a canary, but we had a two and a half year old son. I answered, no, we just have him, pointing to our son, Morgan. He made a disappointed face but he then smiled at Morgan. We took our places at the dinner table after our local Szechuan restaurant delivered food for our large party. Akong had taken on the duty of boiling water to make "tsampa" from strong black Tibetan tea with salt and butter added. I knew they loved to drink this stuff, but even in the middle of summer? It was an amusing dinner, a little intimidating to be sure. I think half the monks were Tulkus—and here we all were in a semi-detached house in Shepherd's Bush, London.

When dinner was over we relaxed in the living room again. I didn't have enough chairs so some of the younger monks graciously sat on the floor. For entertainment I put on a BBC documentary about Tibetan Buddhism in the VCR and they seemed to like it. Some of it contained very old footage of, I think, the previous Dalai Lama and other high lamas that the monks seemed amazed to see on a British television set.

Afterwards, Karmapa beckoned to my young son to come to him and sit on his lap. Morgan did so, almost obediently, as if he had no choice. Karmapa and Morgan looked deeply into each other's eyes as some unspoken message seemed to pass between them. Karmapa reached for a grape from the fruit bowl and put it into his own mouth. He then took the grape from his mouth and offered it to Morgan. Morgan took it from him and put it in his mouth and ate it. I know this appears really odd, and concerns of hygiene come to mind, but this was a very deep blessing from Karmapa, his gift to our family. (I am proud to say that Morgan, now 38, grew up to be a fine upstanding man, successful in his career.) A few minutes later Karmapa announced it was time to go. In a further few minutes there were no Tibetan lamas in our house. I will never forget an evening that can only be described as surreal.

A SHRINE ROOM IN THE BLACK MOUNTAINS OF WALES
by Diane Barker

In the 1970s I was a young hippie learning my craft as an artist. Now I am a Sufi aspirant, an artist and photographer, and also CEO of British charity Heart of Asia.

High above the river Wye, at a place known as Middle Wenallt (but named "Karma Naro" by its owners), in the wild Welsh borderlands is a very special Tibetan Buddhist shrine room.

It is in an old Welsh farmhouse. In the '70s a wealthy Tibetan Buddhist couple—Kurt and Maggie Schaffhauser, owned the house. Kurt was from America and Maggie from Scotland, and they were devoted followers of Chögyam Trungpa Rinpoche. They created a beautiful small shrine room in their home and filled it with magnificent paintings and calligraphies that they had been given by Trungpa and Tai Situ Rinpoche; splendid thangkas and exquisite ritual objects. They invited local Tibetan Buddhist friends to come and meditate and take part in prayers there.

In 1977 His Holiness the 16th Karmapa visited Europe and was invited to visit Karma Naro. To our astonishment he came. I was living in Hay-on-Wye, a nearby village, and along with many

Prayer Flags at Karma Naro, painting
by Diane Barker
(Copyright Diane Barker)

other friends, was invited to attend the ceremonies performed by His Holiness.

To be honest, I didn't know much about the Karmapa or Tibetan Buddhism, and I found a lot of the talk of magic and mystery by my Buddhist friends, and the thangkas of wrathful deities that I'd seen on visits to Kurt and Maggie, rather unnerving. However, I was in love with a Tibetan Buddhist man at the time so I went along because it was his world and I wanted to be part of it. I was also curious to find out what all the fuss was about. In those days I was a rather timid, retiring person, so to go along at all was in fact an act of enormous courage.

On New Year's Eve 1977, seventy-five people crammed into the tiny 12 feet by 12 feet room to take part in the Karmapa's Black Crown Ceremony. I will never understand how the room accommodated His Holiness and his throne, Jamgön Kongtrul Rinpoche, monks, a nun, the Schaffhausers and an assortment of English Buddhists and local hippies (two with their dogs). Everyone who was there swears, as I do, that the room expanded so that we could all sit comfortably.

I had not a clue what was going on. I was a dazed hippie who had been raised in a Christian but not church-going household and my dabbling with eastern philosophy was confined to reading Chinese and Japanese poetry and the I Ching. The colour, ritual and chanting, the palpable atmosphere of spiritual authority and the effect it all had on my heart, was deeply unnerving—even disturbing. I felt both fear and awe, as if the ground I knew had fallen from under my feet in the presence of this Lord of Power.

I was deeply impressed by the Karmapa in a way that was beyond my own normal, very limited comprehension. Something transformative and deep was going on, but I had no idea what.

During the Black Crown Ceremony everyone was solemnly chanting and among the Buddhists there was a sense of great solemnity. I looked up, feeling extremely bewildered and noticed a Lama with a very long moustache holding rice in his hand. He caught my eye and, grinned as he started to bounce grains of rice

Black Mountain view, painting by Diane Barker.
(Copyright Diane Barker)

Monk meditating in mountains, painting by Diane Barker.
(Copyright Diane Barker)

off the top of the bald man's head in front of me. This compound-ed my confusion. Later sweets were handed around and I remember thinking: "What is that all about?"

Later many of us were encouraged to "take refuge" with the Karmapa. Again I had no idea what was going on, but was told it was a great blessing so I was more or less shoved back into the tiny shrine room. I remember tearing off a much-cherished silver bracelet and giving it to the Karmapa as an offering, precisely be-cause I was so attached to it. He cut off a long lock of hair from the crown of my head so that I had a funny short little aerial of hair that stuck up for ages afterwards, and plucked at random from a hat a new refuge name for me. Karma Chökyi Lhamo. Apparently I'd become a Buddhist.

A few days later the Karmapa and his entourage left, and then I heard tales of his visit. I was very moved to hear that he had liked our wild Welsh borderland and had said that the nature spirits were still alive there. I had always felt the power and mystery of this land and was encouraged to find a reflection confirming my intuition about my beloved local landscape.

I also heard that Kurt had presented the Karmapa with a tract of land on top of the mountain behind his house and that the Karmapa had buried a vajra in the land predicting that one day a big stupa would be built there. (That prediction has yet to be fulfilled.)

Life changed radically for everyone I knew in the intervening months. Relationships dissolved and re-constellated in different configurations, as if the Karmapa had picked us all up like a deck of cards, given us a good shuffle and thrown us down in a different order. Life was never the same again as patterns were blown apart. Something had happened.

Shortly after, I left the Welsh borders for a life in London. Kurt and Maggie divorced. Maggie moved to a Trungpa Rinpoche community in Nova Scotia, and their three children grew up and left home, leaving Kurt alone at Karma Naro. In the intervening years I heard that the number of local Buddhists who met in the shrine room had dwindled. Only Lama Lodrö's annual visit from Birmingham Karma Ling, to perform a Naga puja, temporarily boosted attendance for three days every June.

Some years later I returned to the area for a visit and went to see Kurt. He ushered me into the tiny shrine room and showed me an extraordinary phenomenon. The beautiful offering vases on a shelf near the shrine contained a crystalline substance that over-flowed the sides of the vessels. Kurt explained how this had happened spontaneously, to his immense surprise, and that it was apparently a most auspicious occurrence. When it had started he glassed the shelves over, so the offering vases could not be touched and still more of the crystalline substance had appeared along with ringsel, little pearl-like beads.

The room itself remains remarkably powerful. I've visited it several times in the intervening years and have always been struck by its potency and a low hum that sounds in the air.

For many years after that, I had an inchoate desire to paint, which was linked to meeting the Karmapa. Just after I met him I prayed to be able to paint mandalas for him. I didn't want to turn out traditional Tibetan paintings but something that reflected his brief but palpably powerful input into my life.

In the early 1980s I met the Sufis, and with their loving encouragement, I began to paint in my own original style. What emerged were mandalas with poems written around the perimeter and visions, landscapes, even buddhas in the centre. After some time I realized that my prayer had been answered, in its own way. Like the crystalline substances that had formed in the shrine room, some powerful energy was working to guide me along my own maverick path, Sufi with strong Tibetan connections.

In 2000 I met the 17th Karmapa, Ogyen Trinley Dorje, for the first time in a private audience (invited along by a friend), and to my astonishment he leaped to his feet and greeted me as if I was someone he knew. I was deeply moved. Though I had only met his predecessor all too briefly, it seems that the connection was eternal.

Horatio: *O day and night, but this is wondrous strange!*
Hamlet: *And therefore as a stranger give it welcome.*
There are more things in heaven and earth, Horatio,
Than are dreamt of in your philosophy.

Hamlet Act 1, scene 5, 159 – 167

BLACK CROWN, BLACK MOUNTAINS
by Norma Levine

At the time of meeting the 16th Karmapa I had dropped out of academic life and was managing a shop which I had set up selling whole foods in Hay-on-Wye, Wales, now famous for its international literary festival. After living for 5 years in India I returned and set up another business, Windhorse Imports. I've written three books and continue to write, live, practise and travel on pilgrimage to remote places by the grace of the Buddha Karmapa. More information about my projects can be found on www. earth-mudra.com.

In 1977 I met the 16th Karmapa when he was invited to a farmhouse in the Black Mountains of Wales. If there is one event which you can say changed your life, this was it—the Black Crown ceremony.

A monk wearing a yellow-fringed hat shaped like a half moon prostrated three times while the assembly started to chant a liturgy. The ritual master was piling rice onto a gold plate and offering it up to Karmapa. Two monks blew long Tibetan horns in a haunting wail so loud and long it startled thought patterns, blowing them away like clouds. The sound went beyond words into primordial memory.

The Karmapa slowly opened the Black Hat-box, took the black heavy silk crown in his hand inspecting it with his gaze, and put it on his head holding it down with one hand, elbow up forming a salute. With the other hand he fingered a crystal rosary moving it deftly, twirling the beads around three times. The horns continued while he gazed with eyes that seemed to dissolve the fiction of time and the boundaries of space.

Time was standing still. There was a feeling of expansion, everything stretching like elastic; a sense of openness as if nothing were fixed or substantial. It was the experience of "the world in a grain of sand ...infinity in the palm of your hand and eternity in an hour." Compassion was a presence you could almost touch.

The horns stopped, the rosary stilled. Karmapa removed the Black Hat and put it carefully back into the box. People got to their feet unsteadily and formed a queue holding white offering scarves and envelopes with offerings while the monks chanted the mantra *Karmapa Khyenno*: Karmapa know me. With lowered heads we went to the throne to receive a red cord with a knot in it that we tied around our necks. Karmapa looked at every person and truly seemed to know each one.

The experience of being fully complete, of oneness, in the eternal present was mystical: Karmapa showed it to us so powerfully that it was hard to miss. "Words are liars," said Karmapa in the final line of a commentary on ultimate wisdom.

In the afternoon, there was to be an empowerment of Karma Pakshi, the second Karmapa, and I was invited to attend. It involved a commitment to the Buddhist path. In my heart I knew I was a Buddhist, but what did all these ceremonies mean?

"What is an empowerment? And who is Karma Pakshi? And why should I go?" I asked Jamgön Kongtrul, the young incarnate Lama accompanying the Karmapa. "You don't need to understand it," he replied beaming with great compassion. "Just go." He smiled so sweetly I felt I was with my original family at last; people I could trust to the core. So I went.

Jamgön Kongtrul Rinpoche, painting by Diane Barker.
(Copyright Diane Barker)

Karmapa was on the throne this time wearing a ceremonial brocade hat. He recited a Tibetan text and suddenly he seemed to transform into another Karmapa, a yogi from another life. As he got down from his throne I looked down at his bare feet and then up to a skullcup in his hand. He took a long handled silver spoon and poured a small amount of liquid into our cupped hands; and as he moved from one to the other of us—there were only about seven people in the room—he was dancing joyfully like a wild yogi drunk on the nectar of liberation.

From *Chronicles of Love and Death, My Years with the Lost Spiritual King of Bhutan*, Vajra Books, 2011

Amazing Grace

After meeting HH Karmapa in Wales on his first visit to the UK, three friends and I set out from the village of Hay-on-Wye on the Welsh borders some time in 1977 (I'm not sure of the precise date) in a converted ambulance. Our destination was the Dordogne in France where the 16th Karmapa was going to consecrate his land and establish his European seat.

I had met the Karmapa several times and had experienced the Black Crown ceremony; but I never felt it was possible to have personal communication with such a supreme being. He was the embodiment of absolute reality.

It was to be a long trip, crossing the channel from Kent, driving through Paris and onwards hundreds of kilometres to the Dordogne. To my dismay, I was the only driver and as we drove through Paris on the maze of intersecting motorways I felt exhausted with the sheer weight of the vehicle. The diesel engine was so noisy we could hardly talk; the steering wheel was making my arms ache with each movement. I felt like the captain of a cargo vessel steering a consignment of human freight through turbulent waters. I was desperate to be released.

Several hours after Paris, we were off the motorway on a country road when suddenly the engine made a clanging noise and stopped. It sounded serious. We got out of the ambulance and saw a thick black sticky line on the road behind the vehicle. It was oil. We looked at each other in horror. The engine had seized and it was the end of our journey.

We walked a few paces ahead to see where we were. There was no village in sight. A petrol station, a farmhouse, nothing else.

Suddenly we saw a sign that made us all stop in amazement. The sign said, "La Grace de Dieu," the Grace of God, exactly at the spot where our ambulance had come to a halt. "What did it mean?" we wondered. Should we go back? Should we continue? We found a farmer who towed the dead ambulance to his farm-

16th Karmapa from his first tour.
(Courtesy of Norma Levine)

house, and after deliberating for some time, decided to continue. All our money had been spent on food and transport since we planned to eat and sleep in the camper. We loaded up our rucksacks with the bare necessities, left our temporary home behind and set out on the road, penniless hitch-hikers. We became pilgrims taking whatever food and shelter came our way, and after two days and many adventures, arrived at a large marquee in the centre of a field. The Karmapa was sitting regally on his throne where he performed the Vajra Crown ceremony and gave initiations.

I pondered the significance of La Grace de Dieu for many years as I continued to meet the 17th Karmapa under the most timely circumstances. In the mandala of the Karmapa there is perfect synchronicity; timeless spontaneity. Even when things look wrong, everything is right. Amazing Grace.

THE OWL
by Marianna Rydvald

I was a young dancing dakini at the time of this story, and I am an old dancing dakini now. The only difference is squeaking bones. It all works, thanks to the grace of the Guru and Mother's Bliss, Om Ah Hung Om Ah Hung Om Ah Hung

www.dakiniart.com

In the early 1970s I was painting in an art studio in the south of Sweden. A North American medicine man came for a visit and presented me with an owl feather and said: "The owl will speak with you." I received the owl feather and contemplated its meaning. Soon afterwards friends from Oxford invited me to travel with them to Findhorn, Scotland. Findhorn was a spiritual community famous for its organic gardens. A timely art commission enabled me to journey there with my daughter Anana.

Whilst in Findhorn, I saw many owls, and was reminded of the medicine man. As we left Findhorn, a friend in the car said, "There is a Tibetan temple around here." I pleaded with them to take me there. When we arrived, we saw that many people had gathered at the Tibetan center, called Samye Ling, and we were told that His Holiness the 16th Karmapa was arriving the next day. I had already been to India with my daughter and met precious teachers, but had not yet met with the Karmapa. I was so happy and grateful

Flight of the Pueo, painting by Marianna Rydvald.
(Copyright Marianna Rydvald)

for this auspicious coincidence. We found a place for the night at Samye Ling. In the evening I went for a walk in the forest, and an owl came swooping down to where I was standing.

In the morning, the Karmapa arrived and Samantabhadra's blessing clouds descended upon us. Later I had an audience with His Holiness and offered him, a "kosa," a wooden water bowl that my father had carved in Sami tradition. At the audience, we exchanged mantras. Karmapa gave me the mantra of fearlessness and to my surprise, I replied with the Guru Rinpoche mantra. Karmapa found it so amusing that he laughed with delight. The following day, after the teachings, the Karmapa told me through a translator, that he wished me to go to an abandoned house on the left side of the road, up into an attic, open the windows and release an owl that was trapped inside. The Karmapa and his Lama pointed out the road to me.

I was very excited because of the experience with the owl

Karmapa with birds, painting by Marianna Rydvald.
(Copyright Marianna Rydvald)

feather gift from the North American medicine man. It felt auspicious that the great Karmapa was magnetizing students in this miraculous way, and releasing birds at the same time. As I walked out, two young men asked me what I was doing and

I told them of my mission. They became curious, since they also had a connection with owls and wanted to walk with me on this quest. I gladly invited them to do so and soon we saw the abandoned house on the left side of the road. The house was locked and the only way to get into it was by climbing through a window, which the young men did very quickly. I stayed outside, since I knew that they were going to open the windows in the attic to release the owl. The owl flew out and I felt great joy that we all were part of a wonderful journey through the blessings of the Karmapa. The Karmapa is known for his amazing communication with birds and had a large collection of singing birds. The birds sometimes travelled with the Karmapa and he could even put them into meditative absorption!

The meeting with Karmapa inspired me to paint many Tara paintings. I had already painted Tara from a young age, but since I grew up in Samiland (also called Lapland), my first Taras were derived from the indigenous wisdom of my own region. The first Tara I showed Karmapa had birch shoes on her feet, and when he saw the painting, he again was amused. "You probably thought she was cold up there in the north." He gave important advice about my paintings: "Be true to your own style," he said, "study the old traditions, and work on the transition from the old to the new."

Karmapa also inspired me to paint birds. After the owl quest, he told me to paint singing birds, a parrot and a raven. I painted many singing birds and parrots, but only recently have I finally painted a raven. It came into a Vajra Yogini scene in the Chod Gompa of Venerable Ani Tenzin Palmo, at Dongyu Gatsal Ling, in Himachal Pradesh.

Once in the early morning after a black Vajra Yogini initiation, I woke up to the sound of a raven, repeating a mantra with a strong, raven like voice just outside the window. I was startled and happy, and thanked His Holiness for sending birds to wake me up.

May the Karmapa's enlightened activity be with us always!

A HIGH NOTE
by Grandfather Kurt

Kurt Schaffhauser, formerly married to Maggie Russell, was born in the US, but lives in Wales on a farm re-named Karma Naro. He was initially a student of Chögyam Trungpa Rinpoche. In 1977 HH the 16th Karmapa stayed at Karma Naro, for several days giving the Black Crown ceremony and an empowerment of Karma Pakshi. The land at the top of the site was offered to the lineage of the Karmapas.

Grandfather Kurt is a very secretive man with some interesting stories to tell about his meetings with His Holiness the 16th Karmapa. If we hadn't met in a dark corridor one evening at Sherabling when the electricity was down, he would never have revealed a single word. But on that auspicious occasion our minds joined and I jotted down his personal memoir.

When the 16th Karmapa was visiting one day he told me he wanted to buy some mules. "What on earth do you want mules for?" I asked him. He explained that these are not the mules we all know as mules; they are in fact a cross between a canary and a wild song bird which are noted for their enchanting song. By chance we found some breeders of "mules" nearby in the heads of the valleys. After a short journey, we knocked at the door of the Jones' house and Mrs Jones invited us in. The Karmapa was in robes of course and Mrs Jones looked at him with friendly curiosity. Soon we were sitting down and having tea with the Jones family; everyone was in high spirits. Mr Jones showed us his rare crossbreed collection of "mules." The Karmapa selected a few birds and they were put into cages to travel home.

As he opened his wallet to pay for the birds, a sudden gust of wind swirled through his wallet lifting the notes. I ran after them trying to catch as many as I could. The Karmapa was watching and roaring with laughing as I ran to and fro over the garden driven by the wind. I returned all the notes I collected to him. Thereupon he gave me one back. I looked at the £50 note which was a lot of money in those days and said no, I could not keep it. But the Karmapa insisted. After three attempts to return the money I decided it was useless to argue with His Holiness. "I have kept it all these years treasuring the moment which ended on such a high note!" Grandfather Kurt smiled with delight and winked mischievously.

A Butterfly in Winter
by Nina Finnigan

Nina is a long term student of Akong Rinpoche, having lived in an isolated cottage near Samye Ling Monastery in Scotland from 1972 to 1978. It was here that she and her five children met and took refuge with His Holiness the 16th Karmapa. She recently spent four years at Tergar Monastery in Bodhgaya as a student of Yongey Mingyur Rinpoche, where she helped Rinpoche organise his winter teachings and set up a school for his 250 young monks. Now back in Wales, Nina continues her association with Tergar, supporting the school and doing the English announcements for the Kagyu Monlam.

On a chilly late afternoon in the Scottish border hamlet of Eskdalemuir, an amazing event was taking place. Hundreds of people crowded into the tiny village hall, where His Holiness the 16th Karmapa would perform the Vajra Crown (Black Hat) ceremony. We were all waiting expectantly, the children as hushed as the adults, while the typical sounds of a Tibetan puja rose to the wooden rafters and out into the clear northern sky. I looked up and above His Holiness' head, a solitary butterfly fluttering around, perhaps one of a flock seen on Karmapa's arrival at Samye Ling, but an unknown sight at that time of year. I noticed His Holiness watching it, his gaze fixed on it until it slowly settled above him and stayed there, unmoving throughout the ceremony. I wonder if anyone else had noticed this small act of great compassion.

We left the village hall, my toddler son disappointed that the Black Hat, made from the hair of dakinis, had not flown around the room as he had expected! Then we saw the rainbow around the full moon....

A MYTH BECOMES REALITY
by Josef Kerklau

The first time I met HH Gyalwang Karmapa Rangjung Rigpe Dorje was in 1976 when I was a student. After finishing my studies I travelled with my wife in India and Nepal in 1978/1979 and spent six weeks at Rumtek around Losar 1979.

I have studied Educational Sciences and am currently employed at the youth welfare office.

In 1977, friends took me to Langwedel near Kiel, North Germany. His Holiness the 16th Karmapa was on his second European trip and gave a Milarepa initiation in a Buddhist center at Langwedel. We all sat in the newly opened temple. His Holiness passed between us and blessed everyone. In Kiel he performed the Black Crown ceremony.

It is almost impossible to talk or write about the experiences with His Holiness. The experiences are beyond time and space. All the old stories and legends about the historical Buddha, of Padmasambhava, the Indian and Tibetan yogis and Mahasiddhas become real. Infinite wisdom of thousands of years embodied in a human form, transparent, clear and indestructible as a diamond; at the same time tender and soft as a lotus flower.

A few weeks later on a meditation retreat in Switzerland I had a spontaneous experience as if my mind had dived into a lake of Karmapa's mind. The result was an unshakable faith and devotion to His Holiness.

In December 1977 I went to Samye Ling, Scotland, to see Karmapa. There were again Black Crown ceremonies, teachings and initiations. I was lucky to get an interview with His Holiness. He answered my question about which lineage to practise with his famous bright smile directly in English: "no problem, just mixing water with water."

In 1978 and 1979 I traveled nine months through India and Nepal. In South India I met my teacher and spiritual friend, the Ven. Drupgyud Rinpoche who had met three Karmapas in this life. As an infant he was blessed by the 15th Karmapa Khakyab Dorje, he was a disciple of the 16th Karmapa Rangjung Rigpe Dorje and is now a disciple of the 17th Karmapa Urgyen Trinley Dorje. Drupygud Rinpoche once told me that one of the Karmapa's qualities is "liberation through seeing": by the mere sight of His Holiness the mind can open and beings can spontaneously attain liberation.

During Losar 1979 I spent six weeks with the Karmapa in his monastery at Rumtek in Sikkim. There were daily teachings, initiations and Black Crown ceremonies. During the Vajra Crown ceremony His Holiness Karmapa connects with his transcendental aspect and with his audience. There is a genuine dialogue, the encounter of his mind with the audience. After the ceremony there is always a blessing for all the devotees. I was able to sponsor the Black Crown ceremony three times and I was sitting with some sponsors in the front row. This ceremony is a very powerful experience. For a moment, His Holiness shares his buddha-nature and gives us the possibility to recognize the true nature of our mind, one's own buddha-nature. His Holiness then blessed me by putting his whole hand on my head and sent an unimaginable rain of blessing through my body.

His death in 1981 shook all of his students, while there was the hope and joy of an early rebirth.

In 1993 Lama Tashi showed the video of Ward Holmes "Return to Tsurphu" at Kamalashila Institute. I got goose bumps, my hairs stood on end. Since I had been waiting so long for the rebirth, I immediately booked a flight to Kathmandu and from there traveled to Lhasa and Tsurphu monastery. I saw His Holiness the 17th Gyalwang Karmapa, Ogyen Trinley Dorje, in the daily public audiences. Crowds of pilgrims from all over Tibet came daily to Tsurphu to receive his blessing. I was fortunate to be taken to an audience into his private rooms where he blessed us with the sacred objects of all sixteen Karmapas, for example the meditation hat of the first Karmapa, Düsum Khyenpa. He was only eight years old but his blessing had the same force and meaning as that of the 16th Karmapa.

For me there is no difference between 16th and 17th Karmapas—the same eyes, the same emanation of wisdom and compassion. A look into his eyes (he is called Yishin Norbu, the Wish-Fulfilling Jewel) is like looking into eternity, beyond time and space. He is a fully enlightened being in a human body.

THE DREAM
THAT CHANGED MY LIFE
by Eva Krebs

*Before receiving HH Karmapa's blessings in 1983 I had come to
India and studied with several teachers, especially the previous Kalu Rinpoche. However, I was still oscillating between a samsaric life and my longing for a spiritual life. I believed in some petty
pleasures of this world, not understanding the dimension of bliss
and happiness that can be gained through true spiritual practice.*

*In 1983 HH Karmapa appeared in my dream in Bodhgaya,
and since then, I have never had a feeling of loneliness. I have been
guided from within knowing what to do, where to go and how to
work with my mind.*

*In 1986 I met the third Jamgön Rinpoche who again became my
beloved guru and most perfect friend.*

*Later when I met HH the 17th Karmapa, Ogyen Trinley Dorje, both in Gyuto monastery and in Bodhgaya in the year 2000,
I had a strong feeling of continuity. I knew that his activity had
never stopped since that day of the dream in 1983.*

I am deeply grateful to HH Karmapa's inspiration and activity.

It started in 1983 in Darjeeling during the Rinchen Terdzo series of empowerments given by Kalu Rinpoche in Sonada.

During a break in the empowerments I had been planning to go with a friend to Nepal. But on the morning as we were about to leave, a monk came to my door saying: "Don't go to Nepal, go to Bodhgaya. It is a good opportunity to go." My friend agreed so we went off to Bodhgaya instead, the three of us: the monk, my friend and I.

It was July and we stayed at the Lotus guesthouse, which was almost the only guesthouse in Bodhgaya at that time.

That night I had a very vivid, clear dream of HH the 16th Karmapa whom I had never actually met. In the dream I was bowing down and he put his hand on my back and blessed me. Then he said: "Now you are finished with boyfriends, now it is the Buddha's time."

When I woke up my whole body was pervaded by an inner fire and my mind remained in a very special state for hours. I felt blessed as never before. I thought: "Truly the Karmapa came to visit me in the dream." But being very new to Tibetan Buddhism and being a child of the sixties, I also thought, his blessing was truly awesome but he couldn't possibly mean that I was not going to have a boyfriend anymore; that wouldn't make sense.

However, after that there were many years in which quite naturally no relationship with a boyfriend came into my life. I met my root lama, Jamgön Kontrul Rinpoche, and was able to learn the dharma very one-pointedly, thanks to the blessing of HH Karmapa.

Karmapa Becomes
the Medicine Buddha
by Christine Maero

*I met His Holiness the 16th Karmapa in Nice while I was at
university studying for my Master's degree in French literature.
I then lived in London for 20 years working for Morgan Stanley
as a trader and later in the equity department of Credit Lyonnais.*

*I am now back in Nice, looking after the same dharma centre
and working in my own interior decoration boutique.*

I was eighteen when I met the 16th Karmapa. He came to visit the
centre which we had just opened in Nice in 1976. At the time we
were very few followers but we were extremely fortunate. When
Karmapa scheduled the Black Hat ceremony, we put an article in
the newspaper, because it was 1976 and Buddhism was not as famous as it is today.

Karmapa performed the Black Hat ceremony at our centre and
also at a hotel in Nice. One woman wanted to take photos during the Black Hat Ceremony but we told her no pictures were allowed. However, after His Holiness put the Hat on and while he
was reciting the Chenrezig mantra, her camera suddenly flashed.
The next day she told us the photo came out black. There was
nothing on it.

I remember Karmapa stayed in a hotel room with all his birds. It was beautiful to see the birds living with him in his own bedroom.

During his brief stay the Karmapa was requested to give the Medicine Buddha empowerment by a surgeon.

The empowerment was held in a small temple in the back garden of a large house in Cannes. There were about 12 or 15 people in the temple and the Gyalwang Karmapa seated on his throne. I was sitting, eyes closed, concentrating on the empowerment. During the ceremony I opened my eyes to look at Karmapa and saw that he was a very deep blue, the colour of lapis lazuli.

I thought I was dreaming or there was something wrong with me. So I opened and closed my eyes all the way through the empowerment; but still he remained the colour of lapis lazuli. It was the form of Karmapa and something else as well; his form without being his form. When the empowerment was finished, he went back to his room to rest.

I turned to my close friend and said, "I saw something strange. Karmapa was blue." And she said, "Yes, I saw it also!" It turned out that all the people in the room saw the same thing. That was the power of the Karmapa.

After the Medicine Buddha empowerment we all had a private audience with Karmapa. We had to go into the room one at a time. He put his hand on our head for 10 minutes and gave us our personal yidam. That was another very special experience. It was an experience of the nature of mind, the true dharmakaya.

After Nice I went to London with my sister. I had just arrived at Victoria station when I saw a tiny picture of His Holiness wearing the Black Hat posted on a tree. The ceremony was an hour later. I didn't know London at all. My sister and I took a taxi and arrived just in time to see the Black Hat ceremony again. Afterwards Karmapa blessed us with his mala. He took my mala in his hands, opened his eyes and recognised me from Nice. It was wonderful to be in his presence again.

Medicine Buddha painting by Marianna Rydvald.
(Copyright Marianne Rydvald)

I have had many dreams and visions of him at times in my life when I was experiencing a lot of obstacles. He came into my dreams in such a way that it was a tremendous blessing. One of the most powerful dreams I had, occurred when I was having some financial problems. Early one morning—always the period when I dreamt of His Holiness—I dreamt I was in the middle of an empty room. A man came up to me who was all black with hair standing straight out. He grabbed me and it felt like he was pumping out my life force. Immediately I prayed to Karmapa and he came into the room in his robes and Gampopa hat. He looked at the man and then at the ceiling. A huge crystal vajra emerged from the ceiling and exploded onto the man's head shattering it into a thousand pieces. Karmapa took me by the hand and said, "Come I will give you a teaching." We left the room together. The black man was, I believe, a malicious spirit. When the vajra crashed onto him it destroyed the obstacles.

Every time in my life when I needed help Karmapa was always there. I do the practice of Guru Yoga every night. I see him last thing at night and first thing in the morning. I have a little shrine and I look at it. But now he's always there. I don't need to look at it.

Now Ogyen Trinley Dorje has come to continue the limitless activity of the 16th Karmapa for the benefit of all sentient beings. My sister gave me the photo of the 17th Karmapa when he was a child and I saw the face of the 16th Karmapa. I actually saw the head of the 16th. I told my sister what I saw and she said, "But this is the 17th."

In 2006 I went to meet the 17th Karmapa Ogyen Trinley Dorje. I was sitting with some Spanish people who had also known the

16th and 17th Karmapas.
(Photographer unknown)

16th, and His Holiness singled out each one of us and came to each of us separately. He looked at me in such a way that I knew he recognised me, and in his look I saw the 16th Karmapa. Afterwards I spoke to the Spanish disciples who confirmed it. We all had the same experience.

BAD IS GOOD
by Billy Gomez

*In 1972 I became a Buddhist. I was out on the streets of New York
hustling to survive. In 1974 I moved to Europe and met HH
Karmapa. From the time he told me to do the ngondro (prelimi-
nary practice), I became a practitioner of Tibetan Buddhism. Now
I am a care worker for old people in Denmark.*

In 1974 His Holiness was in Denmark for the first time and I went,
together with a group of Danish people, from Denmark to Norway to the airport to receive him. His Holiness stood there smiling,
looking very beautiful. The whole group of us said in one voice,
"Wow!" It was like another planet. We were in a state of bliss.

We travelled with Karmapa's entourage to different places,
and then to a castle in Norway. While the monks were performing a Mahakala puja, I felt a lot of anger. I had all kinds of dark
thoughts which I couldn't stop. I wanted to throw everything
down, smash everything. I looked at Karmapa and he was smiling.

After the Mahakala puja was completed, I said to Lama Lodrö,
(Kalu Rinpoche's monk in Denmark), "I am no good." He said,
"No no, come and see the Karmapa." He took me to Karmapa
who was sitting in a huge room in the castle with twenty other peo-

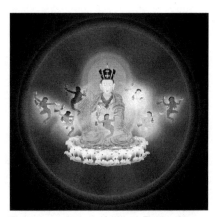

Thangka painting of Mikyo Dorje, the 8th Karmapa.
(Artist unknown)

ple. I made one prostration, then crawled over to him and held onto his feet, crying and crying like a baby, for what felt like half an hour. People were trying to pull me away, but I said, "No, leave me alone!" I cried until I couldn't cry anymore. I felt guilty that in the midst of all these holy rituals I was having hateful thoughts.

The whole room was very silent I looked up at Karmapa and said, "I'm no good." He said, "Gooood" and smiled. He took my face in his hands and raised me up very close to his face, so close I thought he was going to kiss me, but he blew very forcefully in my face. My negative thoughts scattered completely. He gave me one string with 5 knots.

From there we went to Goteville in Sweden. I was with Erik Pema Kunsang, the translator. He said, "Let's go to His Holiness and ask him who our yidam is."[1] I didn't know what a yidam was and I was too shy to tell Erik I didn't know. We went into a room and I saw His Holiness sitting in front of us. We began prostrating to him. After the third prostration I got up and looked at the front of the room where I expected His Holiness to be sitting. He was not in front anymore but sitting on a chair in the back, smiling. We were completely amazed that he was at the back of the room. We turned around to face him and asked, "Who is our yidam?"

And he replied "Mikyo Dorje."[2]

---

1 Personal guide or deity, believed to bestow siddhi or attainments.

2 Mikyo Dorje was the 8th Karmapa, 1507–1554

Afterwards I had many dreams. Whenever I wanted someone to meet His Holiness, I would dream about it and they would be with him in the dream. When I was travelling with His Holiness from Sweden to Copenhagen sometimes I would be feeling sad. His Holiness would catch the moment, knock on the window of the bus and make a hand movement to catch my attention. It would make me laugh and blew the thoughts from my mind.

In another dream he was coming down the stairs holding a rose with a bent stem in his right hand. Then I understood it was a sign not to talk so much about my experiences.

UNDER KARMAPA'S BLACK CROWN
by Joost Willems

After having lived in the USA, Belgium, and the UK, I am now a communication manager residing in Germany with plans to move soon to Middle-America. I am a member of Shambhala International.

The Karmapa was due to arrive at Charles de Gaulle airport in Paris on June 11, 1977. I was part of a group organising a coach for his party in Belgium and we all went down to Paris to receive him. I had heard many stories and was very curious to see him.

He came off the plane and got into a limousine driving towards the VIP reception hall. He got out of the car about 50 or 60 meters from the outside stairs leading into the hall. I could see him getting out of the car and noticed that he was aware of the circular waves of movement created by the 120 or so people standing around his car. As he walked through the crowd up the stairs in my direction, I felt embarrassed because I was somewhat taller than him. So I bent my knees and as he came by he brushed my bended knees. He turned his head to the left in recognition and broke into thunderous laughter while slapping my shoulder. It was shocking but funny and I felt relieved at this joyful meeting.

HH Karmapa giving blessings with the water of the bumpa vase, Vienna, 1977. (Courtesy of Oskar Kornmuller)

In the press conference hall he introduced a Tibetan lama whose Rayban sunglasses made him look somewhat mafioso. He had just arrived in Paris from India. His Holiness said: "This man is going to be very important in the West," and introduced him: "Khenpo Tsultrim Gyamtso Rrrrrrrrrrrinpoche," emphasizing the rrrs of the last word. He then continued: "You will hear from him in the future."

A few days later the Karmapa was at the Dordogne in France. Unexpectedly I witnessed my first Black Crown ceremony. When the Karmapa gave the abhisheka[1] afterward he used only one small bumpa[2] for close to 400 people, while pouring the abhisheka water lavishly. While I was travelling with him, I noticed that this phenomenon happened frequently.

One event in particular stands out from his tour through Europe. His Holiness was invited to Leewarden, a small town in the north of Holland. The Black Crown ceremony was scheduled to

---

1 A Sanskrit word meaning a ritual libation in which consecrated water (or milk, ghee, etc) is used to confer a blessing to devotees. The ritual conducts a transmission of the lineage and acts as an empowerment to begin a certain meditation practice.

2 Vase or container.

be held in a small sports hall. On this occasion just 80 or 90 people were present. Looking at it for the 20th time or so, I watched His Holiness and the monks chant introductory prayers until the Black Hat was about to be raised to his head. At this essential part of the ceremony the Karmapa had a mischievous smile on his face. Holding it on his head in a challenging way, he smiled and surprisingly lifted his head slightly upwards a few times showing underneath a smaller hat, with all the colours and gold lines of the hat above it.[3] I couldn't believe my eyes and asked other people for their perception of this ceremony. They confirmed what I saw: "Yes, yes, yes, did you see that as well?!"

That time was unforgettable. I haven't met the 17th Karmapa yet but I'm eager to see him... again.

---

3 This refers to the naturally arising, "invisible" Black Crown which is said to be always on the head of the Karmapas. There are rare occasions when various people have reported seeing it, for example, the Chinese Emperor Yongle (see p. 10) and the 13th Dalai Lama (see p. 32).

How the 16th Karmapa Transformed and Saved My Life
by Katia Holmes

Katia Holmes is one of Akong Rinpoche's earliest students. These days, whenever possible, she works as a dharma teacher, translator and interpreter for Kagyu Samye Ling in Scotland and its associate centres in Europe and in Africa.

Samye-Ling was two years old and I was twenty-two when the mysterious workings of karma took me there on a random holiday visit in 1969, in the aftermath of the sweeping student movement of 1968 in Paris, which changed the lives of quite a few of us and certainly mine. After a golden childhood and teenage years with no awareness of suffering, I had discovered the wish to change society to make a better life for all, but gradually came to realize that even well-intended changes are forever limited by self-interest: this became obvious in Paris and can be observed in the history of revolutions. It became clear that change had to start from within: a total shift of perspective. This led me to leave Paris and university lecturing in the fall of 1971 to come and live in Samye-Ling, the first Tibetan Buddhist centre in the West.

The 16th Karmapa's First Visit to the West

I had been working in Samye Ling for over two years when one day, in early 1974, Akong Rinpoche announced with an infectious sense of wonderment that his guru, the great 16th Karmapa, now based in India, would visit us and that this was a most extraordinary event. In the past, Tibetans would travel on foot for months just to catch a brief glimpse of him, so we should realize how incredible it was that he was coming to the West and to our small community!

We were told he was a mahasiddha—a great master with miraculous powers—a buddha and, not least, a keen bird lover and collector. Great preparations were undertaken under Rinpoche's hands-on direction, as none of us Westerners had much experience of hosting such a being: we were all fairly new to Tibetan Buddhism.

Sadly, I have no precise recollections of how it felt to meet the 16th Karmapa for the first time, to receive his empowerments or even to witness the Vajra Crown ceremonies during that first visit. Even though these were major events for me at the time, all traces are gone, for two reasons: a coma later in the early 1980s erased a lot of my memory, removing whole episodes of my life at random, and the worsening of a serious, congenital eye condition in 1974 meant that I was living in a blur at the time I met the Karmapa: anything beyond half a metre or so just faded into a haze, undefined and remote. Yet, despite all this, the imprint of His Holiness' presence is there, thanks to what happened to my mother, Andrée, and my father, Max.

Holding the Head of a Buddha

At the time, Andrée was a bright, warm, independent-minded woman of 63, with a strong leaning towards spirituality and an enlightened approach to the Christian tradition. She had been disappointed—to say the least—in my own choice of paths. Why would a fairly sensible girl throw away a promising future in academia, diplomacy or international journalism to embrace a foreign religion, bizarre and perhaps dangerous. A cult, maybe? However, being an intelligent person as well as a loving mother, and seeing me happy in my new life, she decided to come and see Samye-Ling for herself, during the 16th Karmapa's visit, in late November 1974.

The handful of us living at Samye Ling at the time were told there would be no private interviews during this trip: we could gather in the shrine-room and file up in front of the Karmapa, one by one, and ask a question or two, with Akong Rinpoche as translator. However, for some reason, Rinpoche arranged a private interview for my mother in the Karmapa's own room. She had recently lived through a difficult situation with my father and had just retired from her dental practice. Akong Rinpoche was there but I was asked to translate into French, whenever necessary.

It seemed strange that the Samye-Ling residents had only ten public minutes at most to speak with the Karmapa and here was Andrée, freshly arrived, not even a Buddhist, having a private interview with him. The Karmapa talked kindly with her for a while then offered some suggestions. Aware of her former profession, he also mentioned that a part of his upper denture was causing him some discomfort. Could she check it? Had I not been sitting on the floor, I would have fallen over! Andrée got up and stood behind the seated Karmapa in order to examine him. To my utter wonderment, she took his head in her hands, rested it against her and asked him to open his mouth. She took out the offending denture and examined it.

I was so overwhelmed that I cannot remember the detail of what happened next but what I do recall is that she ended up filing the denture, smoothing it down, trying it on and off as she worked on it expertly, until the fit had improved enough for it not to cause any more discomfort to the Karmapa.

When we left the room, possibly a good hour later, I felt like I was walking on clouds. Andrée seemed to be her usual self, finding it all quite natural. I went back to work, we had lunch and then I heard Andrée calling me. "Quick, come and see! There are hundreds of exotic birds of all colours in the trees in front of the house!" I knew Andrée was a very sensible person, quite down to earth, not usually given to visions or supernormal experiences. This was a Scottish December, cold enough for the bare trees not to attract many flying guests, let alone the ones she was describing. I told her the birds she had seen must be due to the Karmapa's blessing, but she insisted they were "real." By the time my partner, Ken and I got to the tree, there were no birds to be seen, of course. She insisted she had definitely seen them there. We had absolutely no doubt she had—after such a morning. How often does one get the chance to touch a buddha's head the first time—or any time one comes into his presence? When asked later, the Karmapa simply commented that the birds she had seen were a manifestation of dharma.

Extraordinary events, such as visions or sometimes miracles, are ways in which the power and beauty of dharma, so perfectly embodied in the Karmapa, are unforgettably impressed upon those who connect with him. His presence has triggered such affirming experiences throughout his seventeen reincarnations, the most well-known perhaps being when the Chinese Emperor Yongle first saw the famous Vajra Crown above the Fifth Karmapa's head.

As for my father, he had been sympathetic to my Buddhist choice from the start, though he himself was on a vaguer, syncretic wavelength. The student revolution had touched him too, eventually turning him into a bright-eyed, freedom-loving hippie at 65.

He drove five hours to attend the evening ceremony of the Vajra Crown at Aix-en-Provence in 1975. As it happened, he died eight months later and I felt so grateful that he had seen Karmapa and the Vajra Crown before his death. He left an oral message for me before he passed away: "Tell her I feel ready for the great transhumance (migration)..."

A Celestial Dove

There was an interesting follow-up to my mother's experience. In 1980, Andrée came to join me for the last part of an Indian pilgrimage led by Akong Rinpoche and, on the day she arrived, we went to Sikkim House in Dehli, where the Karmapa was staying. I was going there to pick up some books from him for Akong Rinpoche. We were standing in the entrance hall of Sikkim House, waiting for someone to turn up so I could make my request, when His Holiness came out of his room. By this time he was quite emaciated—already sick with cancer and recovering from an operation. Seeing us from a distance, he waved and signalled to us to come over. He invited us into his room and called for tea. He had recognized Andrée six years after she had first been in his presence. He sat her down and spoke with her as with an old friend, very directly and intimately.

He asked her if she was still a Christian: "Yes," she said, to which he replied "Very gooood" in English, in this wonderful way he had of saying it, where "good" sounded like the sweet cooing of a celestial dove. These were the very few English words he used but, spoken by him, they were one of the nicest sounds I have ever heard: they made you feel instantly happy and fulfilled, and could convey a great wealth of meaning—whatever anyone needed to hear or understand at the time. He added that, once you have a faith, it is good to deepen your understanding of it and you don't need to look for anything.

So, on her very first day in India, Andrée received her second gift of a private moment with the Karmapa! This was also the nicest possible present for my birthday, which happened to be that very day.

Karmapa's Second Visit to Europe: July–December 1977

By the time HH Karmapa came back to Europe, fortunately I had some vision in one eye and the prospect of "seeing" him, as though for the first time, was wonderful.

After a week or so in the Dordogne, where Ken and I had joined Akong Rinpoche to organize the visit, His Holiness started his six months' tour of the Kagyu centres in Paris. Ken and I had driven up from the Dordogne. To our immense surprise, Ken and I were told to accompany him on the entire tour, travelling in the bus specially converted and painted cherry-red for the trip, discretely emblazoned with the Karmapa's crest and the Tibetan words for "spreading and developing the Kagyu dharma." My specific task was to promote the Karmapa's new seat, in the Dordogne, in each destination and advertise for the consecration ceremonies due to take place in November. In the light of this, Ken and I next requested the possibility of exchanging some English for Tibetan with some of the lamas travelling with the Karmapa. The response, again from the Karmapa himself, was to wait until Khenpo Tsultrim arrived and to learn not colloquial but dharma Tibetan with him.

How Karmapa Launched Serious Dharma Text Studies in Europe under Khenpo Tsultrim Gyamtso

On tour, as is the tradition, His Holiness bestowed empowerments and the Vajra Crown Ceremony but rarely gave teachings. These were mostly given by Khenpo Tsultrim Gyamtso, specially invited for that purpose. His Holiness gave the Gampopa empowerment in Stockholm in August 1977. This was felt to be particularly significant because Gampopa, whose teachings have remained fundamental for all followers of the Kagyu Lineage, was the guru of the first Karmapa, Düsum Khyenpa. After the empowerment, His Holiness decided that Khenpo Tsultrim Gyatso should teach Gampopa's Ornament of the Precious Liberation daily to the handful of Westerners travelling with his party. In so doing, Khenpo-la showed the extraordinary teaching skills that were later to attract so many students and make him famous.

At the end of six months of hard work, Khenpo Tsultrim Gyamtso was very pleased with the results. Feeling now that Westerners were worthy of studying original Tibetan texts in the traditional way, His Holiness decided to set up a six-month course in the Dordogne to teach two of the fundamental classical texts used in the Kagyu lineage. His Holiness sent over Dharmacarya Tenpa Negi, who was fully fluent in Tibetan, English, Hindi and Sanskrit. I was told I would have to interpret for the students and, together with Ken, research the texts in close collaboration with Tenpa Negi and Khenpo in order to prepare a translation for publication. The first text taught was Gampopa's *Ornament of Liberation* and, from then on, Gampopa and Khenpo Tsultrim Gyamtso went from strength to strength in the West. That core study group was also to seed some key translators and Tibetologists. The second text was Maitreya-Asanga's work on buddha nature, the *Uttaratantrashastra* (known as *Gyud Lama*). In accordance with His Holiness' wish, both translations were eventually published after much further work with KTG and later, Thrangu Rinpoche.

The Guru's Command:
A Prerequisite for Transmission

In November 1977, His Holiness was in Belgium. A young Tibetan living there at the time had been asked to translate for KTG in a public hall in Antwerp, before the Vajra Crown Ceremony. The poor man was completely lost—and so was the teaching. Everyone felt awkward. Suddenly one of HH Karmapa's attendants came and whispered in my ear: "Holiness says you must do it." Shock: impossible! How could I, I knew so little, I had only been studying with KTG for three months. Not to mention barging into this poor man's brave attempt. There are times when it is hard to obey the guru's order. But if you do, you can leave it to him to take care of the situation: this was the lesson I was taught—the hard way. The next one came a few days later.

Transmission Power

At the Antwerp centre, His Holiness was about to give the Vajrasattva empowerment when he decided to say a few words before starting. He gestured to me to come up and translate. I nearly fainted on the spot. I looked at Khenpo Tsultrim Gyamtso for support, like a desperate child turns to his mother for help. And somehow, supported by his kind care and by Karmapa's telepathic communication, I managed to do it. I have no memory of the moment but a lingering taste of the total amazement caused by that powerful summons, of the strong feeling of loving support from the Khenpo, and of Karmapa's mind transmitting the meaning to me. I was to experience this sort of transmission again later, with other great lamas, provided my mind remained totally calm, trusting and open.

One of the Gifts of the Karmapa is to Set People on their Special Path

Up to that point, Ken and I had been studying Tibetan identically. As part of my memory loss, I have no recollection of what follows but Ken, who witnessed it, reminded me of it. It seems that, after these two incidents, His Holiness told me that I had a special karma from the past for translating and, somehow, this opened a door for my learning; very powerfully so. Ken tells me that my Tibetan shot ahead disproportionately from that point onwards. Whether one considers it as a word empowerment or simply a blessing, it led to an immensely productive period, before the coma, in which I assimilated much material and went on to translate texts and interpret for the eminent masters who came to Samye Ling in the late seventies and early eighties, such as Tai Situpa, Shamarpa, Khenchen Thrangu Rinpoche and others.

HH Karmapa with Katia Holmes, Rumtek.
(Courtesy of Katia Holmes)

Cosmic Laughter

Being with the Karmapa every day for six months made his presence familiar but it was a presence that was never spoiled by familiarity. It had a sunshine quality that made everything look brighter and more vivid and that made you feel joyful and more alive. Looking back, I feel it was as though, while one was with or near him, he could make you aware of the perfect purity of all things, the "pure appearances" one tries to achieve through developing pure perception in meditation and action. It was like being given a preview of what is truly there in the moment but cannot be perceived yet. Being given the confidence that this is possible—the certainty that opens one to the blessing of the mighty sun which ripens the buddha-seed inside.

Although so many of my memories have gone, His Holiness Karmapa's laughter still resonates so freshly in my mind. I can still tune into it any time. He laughed like no one else: his great, vibrant, warm laughter rippled through you, filling you with joy and lightness. A cosmic laughter. Liberating. I always felt that the whole universe was rocking with its happy reverberation.

Karmapa Becomes Transparent

There was one interesting manifestation of this wonderful purity in apparent human form. Peter Mannox, a student of Akong Rinpoche's, was often around as a photographer, particularly in the Dordogne, in Britain and at Rumtek, and had taken quite a number of photos of His Holiness during ceremonies, as well as some formal portraits. One day, Peter was working on a formal portrait of His Holiness Karmapa on his throne and it seems Karmapa, who knew him well, was in a playful, teasing mood. This was long before digital photography, of course. When the photos were processed, one of them showed a extraordinary phenomenon: Karmapa's body was entirely see-through; one could see the brocade throne behind it even though the body itself was clearly visible! Indivisible unity of voidness and manifestation.

There could have been no manipulation: these photos were taken with a professional camera requiring individual plates for negatives and any possibility of double exposure or sudden movement was ruled out by experts. When shown the photo, His Holiness only allowed one hundred copies to be made while he was alive, to be given to reincarnate Lamas and a select few. Since his passing, it has become widely available through the internet. Curiously though, the original was "lost" when it was given to a commercial photo-lab in Birmingham.

The Power of Connection

The 16th Karmapa's visits to Europe established a powerful connection with him and, through him, with the entire Kagyu lineage. Behind the various activities—crown ceremonies, empowerments, informal meetings, refuge, bodhisattva vow—there was always this underlying importance of making a connection.

Wherever Karmapa went during the six months of his 1977 European, he was welcomed with joy and deep reverence. Arrangements were always the finest anyone could (or sometimes could not!) afford, such as for instance the lavish display of offerings presented by the Tibetan community of exiles at Rikon, in Switzerland, where a few ingots of pure gold were shining preciously on top of an enormous pile of other offerings, such as brocades, carpets and so forth.

Yet, the wonder of Karmapa's compassion is that even a negative action, such as the unfortunate incident of the Danish man evoked by Ken, establishes a link with him, which will help the person in the long run. His Holiness would say that whether someone was generous to him or angry at him, the main thing was that a connection had been made: this would bring benefit in future lives. His compassion embraced all, without bias, whether they offered him gold or denied him hospitality. The difference is on our side: we were told that our devotion is like a ring and his compassion like a hook to pull us out of samsara. He is constantly ready to help, but how much help and blessing we get is up to each one of us. Karmapa is present wherever and whenever one calls to him.

A Dharma King in His Own Seat: Rumtek, Sikkim, 1980

The Karmapa had the dual nobility of his spiritual stature and his aristocratic birth, evident in his noble bearing. Nowhere is a king more at home than in his own palace and I had the joyful privilege of spending a further two months near him at his Dharmachakra monastery in Rumtek, in 1980. A couple of assignments he gave me while I was there may have been part of his wish to leave a spe-

Procession at Rumtek, 1980.
(Courtesy of Katia Holmes)

cial legacy before his passing, in the form of information about the Karmapas' presence in other worlds, and details about the unique Karmapa activity of making rilnak, the Black Pills.

Karmapa in Former Lives and in Other Worlds

I had arrived as part of a pilgrimage party from Samye Ling, led by Akong Rinpoche. We stayed at Rumtek through *Losar*, the Tibetan New Year of February 1980. One feature of the celebrations are the famous masked dances, performed by the lamas in the main monastery courtyard. Besides these, His Holiness had instituted several days of theatrical performance which took place in the garden in front of his summer residence and was enacted by lay devotees. These sacred plays were based on stories of former lives of the Karmapa before he became known as such. His Holiness attended the event from his balcony while carrying on with his daily duties (lamas, dignitaries, monastery staff, visitors would appear at his side from time to time, for brief or long exchanges). As I was watching the performance with interest, His Holiness Karmapa sent an attendant to tell me to come up to see him. He then told me that the play was based on a story of a previous life and he wanted me to work on an English translation of it with Khenpo Chödrak Tenpel, his nephew. This was the *Dzalendara* story, spontaneously told by the 16th Karmapa one day when he was travelling through Jullundur, in North-East India, concerning his former incarnation as the mahasiddha-king of Jullundur. Unlike most mahasiddha stories, which are just a few lines long, this was a full life story in three parts.

The Khenpo and I managed to complete a draft of the Dzalendara story before it was time to go to Delhi to fly back to the UK with the group and to put my mother, Andrée, on her flight home. His Holiness, pleased with our progress, suggested I stay on to translate *Sakarchupa*, a set of ten stories about the Karmapas in other time-space realities as told by the 15th Karmapa.

A rapid trip to Delhi sufficed to accomplish the necessary formalities. In those days, one needed a special permit to stay in Sikkim, which only five years formerly had ceased being a kingdom to become an Indian state in a militarily-sensitive area bordering China. By the time of my visit, the Karmapa's presence had permeated and dominated Sikkim. He was simply adored by both the people and their officials. At the time, it was complicated and often long-winded for a Westerner to get the standard week-long authorization to visit Rumtek. I had a demonstration of the Karmapa's amazing authority and power: a simple phone call from him immediately produced a letter to show someone in Delhi and I was granted a longer permit on the spot. This happened again in Rumtek later on, so that in the end I stayed for some two months, just on his word.

In Rumtek, the Karmapa was like the Buddha at the heart of his own mandala, accompanied by his great Rinpoches as main deities, including some of the young reincarnations that he nurtured so carefully and personally and that have become the lights of Kagyu dharma today. Jamgön Rinpoche was particularly close to His Holiness, like a son, and I was blessed to be with them both on various occasions. Being allowed to be even remotely part of this enchanted mandala was most inspiring and joyful.

At the time, two books of biographies of the sixteen Karmapas had been published. In getting me to put *Dzalendara* and *Sakarchupa* into English (*Stories from the Former Lives of the Karmapas*), the Karmapa, already unwell and probably very aware of his end, left the world a vaster vision of who the Karmapas are. Those stories go far beyond this planet earth and its known history and, like many Mahayana sutras, take us into multiple, parallel worlds in time and space, showing vast enlightened activity of the Karmapas through specific, poignant stories.

The Black Pill Legacy
—after HH Karmapa's Passing—1981 onwards

The extraordinary blessing of Karmapa's presence in our lives did not stop with his physical death. He continued to inspire and support our lives in the way needed by each one of us. In my case, his blessing, in the form of the "black pills," simply saved my life which nearly ended at the age of 35, and was to be its only support for years to come.

Personal Evidence: When Sincere Practice Meets with Great Blessing

The meeting of great blessing and sincere practice can have the power to ripen karma quickly, giving one a chance to purify while having the best possible conditions of a "precious human existence," with the dharma and perfect teachers. The difficulties or sufferings that may occur in the process should not be seen as a failure of practice, but as a fantastic opportunity to settle a lot of old debts speedily, so that the essential purity of one's being can gradually manifest in all its beauty and fullness. Rather than having to experience the painful results of past negative actions in the lower states of existence.

A Mother Pill Saved me from an Early Death

By the end of Summer 1981 in Samye-Ling, my health collapsed after several years of intense work in sometimes difficult conditions. Karma was ripening in the sunshine of powerful blessing. Karmapa's physical death in November 1981 coincided with my entering a long phase of illness and struggle.

In early 1982, I was in France with Andrée, my mother, who was kindly doing her best to get me medical treatment, but I was getting worse and worse as the tentative diagnosis did not seem to match the problem. Around April, Akong Rinpoché told Ken I should come back to Samye-Ling as soon as possible: my life was in danger. I was so ill and weak that the mere thought of going anywhere was impossible but, prompted and supported by Rinpoché's urgings, I managed to fly to London, where Ken had driven from Scotland to pick me up and drive back up in the same day. The next day, Akong Rinpoche advised that I see a consultant in Carlisle Hospital. They kept me in and, the same evening, I fell into a coma.

This coma erased a good part of my memory—quite at random—which is why I have lost trace of many events of my life, including most of the details of that particular episode.

However one moment has remained clear. Whatever was ailing me was causing a violent need to vomit, although I never did vomit—it was just air and agonizing retching for hours on end, making me dizzy and weak. That night, I spent ages doing just this in the toilet of my hospital room, feeling desperately sick and feeble, until I realized I was close to slipping into unconsciousness. I came out of the toilet and went back to bed.

I lay there and felt that I was resting my head on Karmapa's lap. I had a strong feeling of his presence: he was there, supporting me. I felt peaceful and happy, completely safe and cared for. No fear, no worry, I was in his hands. Total certainty, he was taking care of me. Whatever happened was fine. Just peace. Whether these feelings came before I lost consciousness or after, I cannot tell now. What matters most is that Karmapa was there, at the moment of death, when I needed him; as he is, no doubt, when anyone calls upon him at that time.

The hospital phoned Ken in the middle of the night, telling him I was in a coma and he had better come over because I might not live until the morning. Ken must have awakened Akong Rinpoche with the news, and Rinpoche gave him a "mother black pill" to put in my mouth. Ken drove through the night and did just that. It seems I came out of the coma after 24 hours or so. Ken and a friend who saw me unconscious told me later I looked like a real picture of health, a bit like Snow White asleep.

Black Pills as Only Life-Support for Years

Not only did the mother-pill save me from an early death but the little black pills were to be my life-support for over ten years of struggle.

The black pill rescue had left me incredibly joyful and positive, but it was no easy task to get used to living again... differently. Ongoing physical problems, a large memory gap and the flame of intellect dimmed to a fragile flicker, as when getting words mixed up in a rather amusing way. Life became a "one day at a time" job.

With extraordinary kindness and wisdom, Akong Rinpoche took charge of me, both as a Tibetan doctor and as a wise guru, advising whatever was most appropriate at each step. After saving my life by giving me a mother pill, he kept on giving me a little pill each time I got worse, which could be once a month at first, then every two or three months, during the many years when nothing seemed to help my condition. This was the most precious of gifts since no "new" ones could be obtained now that Karmapa was no longer physically present. They were my only medicine, my lifeline. (Ken used to joke saying that my body should be boiled down after death to collect black-pill material from it.)

When His Holiness 17th Karmapa was found, Tibet and later India were still out of bounds for me. By the time I managed to go and see him, in 2007, his black pills had already given me an extra 25 years of life.

A Black Pill Miracle

Interestingly, just as I am writing this, I hear of a recent black pill miracle. When teaching in South Africa last October (2010), Ken and I heard of a friend, a Centre member, who had terminal cancer, having been through several remissions and was now very close to the end. He had been told he should put his affairs in order: a question of weeks probably. I had a black pill with me—I always carry one in case of emergency and as a protection. We decided to offer it to this friend: it would support him and help him to connect with Karmapa at death. A year later, he is alive and looks much better than last year. Ken just saw him today: his inexplicable remission has totally puzzled his doctors and not having radio-therapy and chemotherapy has enabled him to pick up some strength and have an extra lease of life he will no doubt use positively. He said he realized he wasn't as ready to die as he had thought last year and that he really appreciated having that extra vital time to prepare in every respect. He knows his own case well and has no doubt whatsoever that the black pill performed a miracle for him.

During my stay in Rumtek in 1980, HH Karmapa had suggested I work on a document explaining the making of the sacred "Black Pills" (ril nag) of the Karmapa. I did this again in collaboration with Khenpo Chödrak Tenpel. For those who are not familiar with the black pills, here is a summary of what is so special about them and how they are made.

An aspect of Buddha activity

An important aspect of the Karmapa's enlightened activity is his power to set beings on the way to liberation by the mere fact that they think of him, see him, hear him, are touched by him, wear or ingest a sacred substance made by him. His *rilnak* (Tib. *ril nag*) or "black pills" are part of what liberates through wearing (*btags grol*) or through ingestion *(myong grol)*, i.e. the liberating blessing is received by eating the sacred substance.

How do they work?

The *rilnak* bring extraordinary blessing from the Karmapa, through the power of interdependence, to those who wear them or ingest them. Worn on the body in a locket or a relic-box, they offer a constant blessing and protection. They can also be ingested when one is stricken by a life-threatening illness or about to die.

As protection

There have been vivid examples of the power of protection. For instance, direct witnesses recount that, when fleeing Tibet in 1959, people who carried a black pill on their body as a protection did not get harmed by gunshot: bullets were deflected, simply grazing the skin.

Before dying

The pills are very rare and it is considered highly fortunate for someone to be able to take one before dying. Taken at the time of death, they greatly help the chances of liberation of those who are ready. For those who need more spiritual maturation, the power of connection with the Karmapa causes them to be guided by him, in the form of Avalokiteshvara, to an existence favourable for progress.

If it is time to die, Black Pills have this special quality of making the process happen in the best possible way, with Karmapa's support, but they may also prolong life or even bring a cure if it is karmically possible to live on.

In case of life-threatening illness

The pills are a support in case of serious illness, not just by helping the sick to bear their sufferings and live with them positively, but sometimes bringing seemingly impossible results, ranging from a physical improvement, to a significant or even prolonged remission. This extra lease of life gives the person a chance to come to terms with many things in their life, so that death itself becomes less traumatic for them and for those left behind. In case of chronic serious illness, the pills give courage and acceptance, helping to avoid depression and bitterness. One can inhabit a very sick or handicapped body and feel deeply happy and peaceful inside.

How Black Pills Are Made

His Holiness picks very pure and spiritual lamas to help him in the actual making of the pills. On the day, they get up early and wash carefully. Cleanliness is essential for the participants, the objects and the ingredients employed through the whole process. They then do the Guru Yoga of the Eighth Karmapa (*Tunshi Lami Naljor*) which includes the Karmapa's mantra, *Karmapa Khyenno*, which they will keep on saying all day long.

The actual "material" for the black pills is simple: fresh *tsampa* (roasted barley meal) mixed with water that has boiled with the blade of the axe used by Milarepa when building a house for Marpa. The resulting liquid gives the tsampa its black colour. This axe is part of the Rumtek Treasury which also contains some very precious relics of all the previous Karmapas and other holy beings. A small amount of these precious relics is added to the mixture which is then gently stirred to make it into a very workable "dough." However, the main ingredient is the blessing that comes from the Karmapa himself, through his meditative power and prayer.

The lamas spend the day rolling the black dough into minute pills, only a millimetre or so in diameter, while reciting Karmapa Khyenno. The pills are actually incredibly small, so that great care is required when handling them because they tend to "jump" off easily, being so light and tiny. Karmapa himself rolls the larger pills (3–4 mm) known as "mother pills" because they have the capacity to reproduce and make small ones, "babies," when the owner of the pill is a virtuous person. A large bowl belonging to the Third Karmapa, Rangjung Dorje, stands on a shrine in the room. Enough pills are rolled to fill it to about two thirds and, at the end of the day, it is covered with the robe of the Third Karmapa and laid on a cloth where it remains overnight.

In the morning, the bowl is overflowing and the cloth beneath thick with pills. This is due to the extraordinary power of the rilnak to multiply—the "mother pills" mostly but even smaller ones at times. A friend of Ken's, a very rational surgeon, sceptical about the "miraculous" side of Buddhism, was astounded to find that a pill he had been given and had worn for some time had turned into seven of the same size. A very good lama we know carries a few mother pills around with him in a small case and has a constant supply of "baby" pills which he gives generously to the very sick and dying. It is said that the pills reproduce in the presence of a virtuous mind.

The Importance of the 17th Karmapa's Return to Rumtek

When the 16th Karmapa was alive, it was customary to give sponsors of a Black Crown Ceremony little packets of small sacred pills and blessed substances, including seven small black pills. Mother pills were sometimes given to individuals by their guru. Some lamas had mother pills and, due to the goodness of their being, these could produce babies in plenty, so that they could help their students or any one in need. They were also given to dying animals. We did realize the extraordinary value of the *rilnak* and it was amazing to be able to get them whenever needed. Today, it is a sad fact that His Holiness the 17th Gyalwang Karmapa, Ogyen Trinley Dorje, has no access to the Rumtek Treasury which contains the Black Crown and the relics necessary to make black pills. Therefore there have been no new ones since the passing of the 16th Karmapa in 1981, making them even rarer and more precious.

Karmapa's Freedom

Going back in time to the period I was in Rumtek, I will never forget an interview I interpreted for a French group taking place in His Holiness' summer house, in a pleasant ground-floor room opening onto the garden. His Holiness presented all of us with a set of newly-minted Bhutanese coins as a souvenir which, I felt, was also a blessing of prosperity.

During the interview, Bernard Lebeau, the lawyer who had helped with the land donation in France, asked Karmapa a ques-

HH Karmapa at Rumtek.
(Copyright Lars Gammeltoft)

tion. Did he sometimes think of Tibet and feel any wish to return?
I remember the Karmapa's reply: when he lived in Tibet, he had
had the great good fortune to be outside of politics, which meant

he was very free to act. Furthermore, he had no intention to become involved in politics, which would mean the end of his freedom.

So often, in recent years, given the present circumstances, have I thought of that limpid morning and of Karmapa in his Rumtek abode, speaking of freedom, as free as he was then to come and go, and to act as he pleased or deemed fit, performing the activity of the Karmapas.

May the passing obstacles to the fullness of activity of the buddhas' representative in our world, the great Karmapa, Ogyen Trinley Dorje, soon be removed! And may he have the freedom to perform the sacred activity of the Karmapas! Convinced that our own ignorance and negativity is a key factor in this removal, I wish and pray that we may all progress in that direction. *Karmapa Khyenno!*

Parinirvana of His Holiness the 16th Karmapa

by Norma Levine

KARMAPA ASKED ONE PERSON who cried when he saw him, "Why are you crying? Death is an illusion."

One of the greatest teachings of the 16th Karmapa was to demonstrate that what dies is only the body. There were witnesses, both Eastern and Western, who attested to his miraculous passing into parinirvana, like the Buddha.

This way of passing is called *tukdam* in Tibetan, a post-death meditation state in which the mind merges with the clear light. It is as if the person were still alive with a pulse, warmth at the heart, supple limbs and no decay. The meditation may last up to a week and when it ends, and only then, does the body become a corpse. During the final meditation it is important not to disturb the body in any way, not even to touch it.

The Karmapa predicted his death at the age of 58 (1981), ten years before he died, and also referred to it several times. When asked if he needed a new robe, he responded, "I don't need any more robes. This is the last." To a very close disciple, His Holiness said, "I will come as a little boy. Take care of that." He also knew he would die in the West. "I will breathe out (my last breath) in a Western country, and then I will breathe in a new fresh breath.[1]" His death in America signified that his activity encompassed the whole world.

Tai Situ Rinpoche, one of his four heart sons, explained the way of passing of the 16th Karmapa in an interview on November 7th, 1981, forty eight hours after the clinical death of His Holiness in Zion, Illinois, while he was still in the post-death meditation state.

"*Such a death as the passing of His Holiness, the Karmapa, is... very different from ordinary death. ... It is not just a loss. Of course we lost him and his body, but we never lose him... The present state of his body is a sign of the present state of his mind. He is presently in contemplation or state of awareness, more than just the wisdom of mahamudra or the ultimate truth. Another way to say it is dharmakaya. For this reason there is heat on his heart; his skin and flesh and everything is just like that of a living person. ...we are waiting for him to complete that contemplation. Then his body will show signs of death...*

The dharmakaya is all the time; when he is alive, or just as he is now, and after, when he will be re-born. Ultimately the nature of his mind is in the state of dharmakaya..."

Dr Mitchell Levy, the American doctor who attended the Karmapa at his death, gave a graphic description of what happened on the day of his clinical death.

"*... the electrical impulses through his heart had altered in a way that indicated that it was starting to fail... we knew that something was imminent. Then his heart stopped for about ten seconds. We resuscitated him... and then he was stable for about twenty-five, thirty minutes, but it looked like he had had a heart atack. Then his blood pressure dropped all the way down. We couldn't get it back up at all with medication... then his heart stopped again... at that point*

---

1 Tai Situ Rinpoche, «What Dies is Only the Body», November 7th, 1981.

I knew that this was it. Because you could just see his heart dying in front of you on the monitor."

Nonetheless they kept the resuscitation going for 45 minutes, administered two amps of intra-cardiac epinephrine, adrenaline, then calcium, but to no avail. Fifteen minutes passed before they started to take out the tubes, when suddenly his blood pressure registered vigorously.

"Then a nurse literally screamed, "He's got a good pulse!"

Dr Levy described the scientifically impossible occurrence that he witnessed.

"His Holiness heart rate was 80 and his blood pressure was 140 over 80, and there was this moment in that room where I thought that I was going to pass out. And no one said a word. There was literally a moment of "This can't be." A lot had happened with His Holiness, but this was clearly the most miraculous thing I had seen... This was not just an extraordinary event. This would have been an hour after his heart had stopped and fifteen minutes after we had stopped doing anything....

To me in that room, it had the feeling that His Holiness was coming back to check one more time: could his body support his consciousness? Just the force of his consciousness coming back started the whole thing up again... this is just my simple-minded impression, but this is what it actually felt like in that room."

"Shortly after we left the room, the surgeon came out and said, "He's warm. He's warm."... After all that had happened, they just accepted it. As much as all that had happened might have gone against their medical training, their cultural beliefs, and their religious upbringing, by this point they had no trouble accepting what was actually occurring."

This miraculous post death response made it possible to keep the body undisturbed in the hospital until the meditation was complete. The doctors understood that they were not dealing with an ordinary death.

On the second day after His Holiness death, Tai Situ Rinpoche described the doctor's reaction.

"I took the doctor to His Holiness and he examined His Holiness by gently pulling his skin and touching his heart. The doctor was amazed. He said he never saw anything like that before. He said, "When a person dies, you pull the skin and it should stay stretched. His Holiness skin reacted just as would the skin of a normal live body." The doctor also felt heat from His Holiness' heart, just like a live person. The doctor cried for maybe twenty minutes. Other than the attending Lamas, this doctor is the only person who touched him. If the doctor had not been convinced, which he was, we would not have been able to keep His Holiness' body there."[2]

The final meditation of the 16th Karmapa lasted for 3 days. During this time the body showed no sign of decay. Towards the end, perspiration appeared on his brow, a sign that the meditation was complete.

Cremation stupa of HH Karmapa, on roof of Rumtek Monastery, Sikkim, 1981.
(Copyright the late Madhusudan Singh, courtesy of Meera Madhusudan)

The coffin with His Holiness' body

2 Tai Situ Rinpoche, ibid.

arrived at Rumtek Monastery in early November 1981. He was seated in the meditation position, sacred syllables were placed on his body and he was dressed in his monks robes, adorned with a crown of the five Buddha families. Around him was displayed a vast array of offerings. Monks and Lamas performed pujas day and night for forty nine days.

A great multitude gathered from all over the Himalayas and the West to pay final respects.

I was fortunate to be able to attend the cremation of the 16th Karmapa and somehow found a seat on the roof of the monastery near the stupa enclosing his body. At mid-day the sky was perfectly blue with not a cloud in sight. The Indian army fired a 21 gun salute to commence the final rite.[3]

As a flame was lit to burn the body inside the stupa, a rainbow

Cremation of HH Karmapa at Rumtek, 1981.
(Copyright the late Madhusudan Singh, courtesy of Meera Madhusudan)

---

3 The Indian Government sponsored the 49 days puja.

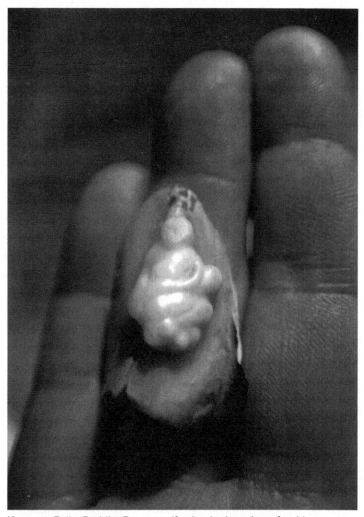

Karmapa Relic: Buddha Bone manifesting in the ashes after his cremation and taken to Tsurphu by Drupon Dechen Rinpoche (Copyright Ward Holmes)

appeared circling the sun.

Many miracles occurred and one is reported in a story in this book—the form of the Karmapa cradled by a rainbow. After-

Jamgön Kongtrul Rinpoche and Bokar Rinpoche at HH Karmapa
cremation, Rumtek, 1981.
(Copyright the late Madhusudan Singh, courtesy of Meera Madhusudan)

wards I heard that there were birds flying in formation circling
the gompa, then heading north. From the ashes appeared a bone
shaped like a buddha.

I was close enough to the stupa to witness perhaps the most
significant event. The Karmapa's four heart sons were sitting in
the four directions around the stupa.

Each made an offering at the door of the stupa. When Tai Situ
Rinpoche made his offering, the heart of the Karmapa came out
from the fire. It is now in a memorial stupa at Rumtek and it is
said that whoever makes a wish there, will have it fulfilled. Such
was the ceaseless activity and loving compassion of the Wish Fulfilling Jewel.

KARMAPA BECOMES VEGETARIAN
by Gelongma Ani Ea

I took Refuge with Ven. Tenga Rinpoche in 1979, ordination with the 16 Gyalwang Karmapa in Rumtek, Sikkim in 1980, and then took Gelongma ordination in Hong Kong in 1983 after which I did 3 years retreat under Ven. Kalu Rinpoche in France in 1984–88.

I helped start the new dharma centre in Denmark in 1993 for the 17th Gyalwang Karmapa after his enthronement in Tsurphu, Tibet.

Since 1996 I officiate at Buddhist funerals with official permission from the Danish Government and care for dying people and animals.

In 1980, I came to Rumtek from Copenhagen after being Tenga Rinpoche's cook for one year. Tenga Rinpoche was my guru and I was on the way to Nepal to stay with him, but I was going via Rumtek to ask His Holiness Karmapa for ordination. His four heart sons were there because His Holiness was quite ill with cancer. He was so weak he couldn't walk well. He could only walk up the hill to Rumtek very slowly.

I talked with HE Situ Rinpoche and shared with him what I had learned about alternative cures for cancer in the best cancer clinics in America. They treated people for cancer when Western

HH Karmapa when he was ill with cancer, in a pet store with a green Amazon parrot, 1980. (Photographer unknown)

medicine had given up on them. The heart sons all thought it was great. His Holiness told them to ask me to stay and cook for him and serve as his health nurse.

I started cooking for His Holiness up in the little house at Rumtek where they had a kitchen. When I do something, I do it properly. I changed his whole diet, took away all the fat, sugar, butter tea, biscuits, white bread, and allowed very little meat. I put him on carrot juice, papaya, the whole number. I kept telling him to drink the carrot juice and eat the papaya. They were all shocked at my uncompromising insistence. He did it and he started getting better. It changed so that he could walk up the hill. This was just before his last trip to America.

He said he wanted me to come with him on his tour to America. I went with him to Calcutta, and stayed at the Oberoi Hotel. The morning before we were flying out, one of his servants came to my door at 4 am and said, "His Holiness wants you." I went to his room and saw him sitting there in his petticoat, bare-chested with a tie around his head. (It could have been red). He put out his hand and put a skull mala into mine. Then he sent me away again. I still have it on my shrine.

We all got on the plane and got off in New York where Trungpa Rinpoche greeted him. We went straight to the Shambhala centre where they offered up the mandala in English. I had the impression they were really offering the whole universe. I had never heard it in English before. It was a fantastic, heart-felt offering.

We then went to KTD in Woodstock, NY. I stayed in the same house as His Holiness, and cooked for him. He would come out in the morning when I was preparing his tsampa and thump me on the back three times. I remember once when Ole and Hannah Nydahl came to visit, he called me in and said to me, "You have the same problem with your liver as they have." We all used to smoke dope. I had never told him anything about it.

He wanted me with him on the whole tour. But some of the Lamas were jealous because I was a woman, a nun and close to him. Then he told me they were jealous and he had to start eating meat again. He sent me back to Tenga Rinpoche in Kathmandu. When he finished the tour, he went back to Rumtek and became even more ill. They took him to Hong Kong where the doctors opened him up and said the cancer was everywhere.

Lopon Tsechu Rinpoche came to my door when I was in Kathmandu and said Jamgön Kongtrul Rinpoche wanted to find me because His Holiness wished me to come immediately to Hong Kong. They offered me the ticket. In Hong Kong I stayed in a flat with Bardor Tulku, Jamgön Rinpoche, Shamar Rinpoche. Drupon Rinpoche, Kalu Rinpoche—all in one tiny flat with 6 or 10 Chinese people. We went back and forth to the hospital where His Holiness was lying in a green room in a metal bed with tubes going in and out. But he was just the same as if he was giving a Black Crown ceremony, a golden Buddha, and had no pain.

It was a frantic few weeks. Traleg Rinpoche came in the middle of the whole thing to see His Holiness and say he was sorry because he had run away from Rumtek. Ole and Hannah were forbidden to come. Some Japanese doctors had been there and said it was too late. But I kept insisting that he go to America.

Because I had been in America where many people came in with terminal cancer and walked out again, well, I was very stubborn. My ex-husband, Bosley and I were really into health food, fasting on carrot juice, colonic irrigation. I wanted desperately to get him to the clinic there. Tobgya Rinpoche was the only one who supported me in this. They all wanted him to go back to Rumtek to die.

Bosley, who is a Gelong, called around in America to find a clinic which would take His Holiness. Many clinics didn't want to do it because his condition was too advanced. Then we finally found a doctor in complementary medicine who agreed to fly to Hong Kong and examine His Holiness.

The Zion clinic in the US agreed to take him. It was where all the big actors and famous people like Steve McQueen had gone and many got better there. The way they treated people was to heat up the body to a certain degree to burn the cancer cells. They also had a proper medical staff. Of course, it cost a lot of money.

His Holiness did a mo. "We go to America, it's the best," he said. So they all prepared for it.

He went on the plane, got off in Chicago and then the Trungpa people took over. They took the credit for it.

Because of my ticket I had to fly the other way round to Chicago via Copenhagen. A few days later Tenga Rinpoche said, "you better hurry to Chicago." And a few days after that Jamgön Rinpoche phoned me and said, "You don't have to come. His Holiness has passed away."

He knew I would get him to America and he wanted to die in America. I am sure he had me with him to create merit. He didn't die of cancer. It was the kidney that collapsed because the drip feed didn't go in. They never got the kidney functioning again.

When His Holiness died in Chicago, Shamarpa called me and said I should not feel guilty at all, that His Holiness passed away in a very good place and a good clinic. I thought the whole Tibetan race would be angry with me because I pushed through to get him to America, but they weren't angry at all.

Many magical moments happened after that. You think of him and he appears in front of you. There were many such astonishing moments.

The last time I saw His Holiness he took my hand and said, "I have so much more to do. Next time I will be much more powerful and will learn all the languages." And this is what he is doing now. I spent the last year of his life with him.

Nothing Happens
by Madeleine Schreiber

Madeline is from New York; she became a Zen student in 1966. Ten years later she moved to Colorado to study with Trungpa Rinpoche. In 1982, accepting Trungpa Rinpoche's invitation to his many students, she moved to Nova Scotia Canada to help build the community there. Madeline now divides her time between urban life in Halifax and retreat time at her place on Cape Breton Island.

At the time when His Holiness Karmapa was dying, many of Trungpa Rinpoche's students were able to visit with him in the hospital. Foremost among them was the Vajra Regent Osel Tendzin. He had very deep feelings of devotion for His Holiness and was weeping quite a lot. At some point His Holiness expressed compassion for his grief and told him not to be bothered by death, that "nothing happens." For several years after His Holiness passed away, bumper stickers could be seen on the backs of cars all over this continent that said, "Nothing Happens."

THE LAST BLESSING
by MJ Bennett
(Ani Jangchub Wangmo)

I was in a hotel room in Delhi with my mother and father, when I received a phone call telling me that His Holiness Karmapa had died. Involuntarily I sobbed huge waves of anguish. It was grief so deep and a loss so great. I had lost my Guru. He meant more to me than the entire world.

My parents were supportive and helped me cancel my flight. I had planned to leave with them for America the next day. Bryan and Patti Miller came by the hotel to pick me up. It had been decided that we would join the party flying with His Holiness' remains back to Sikkim. We went to arrange the special visa. All doors opened, such was the devotion of the Indian authorities for the 16th Karmapa. The grief in that government office in Delhi was palpable.

The following morning I said goodbye to my parents, and then met Bryan and Patti to join the party escorting His Holiness back to Sikkim. He had lain in state for one night at Sikkim House in Delhi. Now he was going back to his monastery the Dharmachakra Centre, "the monastery wreathed in a thousand rays of rainbow light" in Rumtek, Sikkim.

Karmapa at Rumtek, 1980.
(Courtesy of Katia Holmes)

A special plane had been chartered by the Indian government. Once inside, I noticed it was empty except for Jamgön Rinpoche, Gyaltsab Rinpoche and their attendants seated in the front. We filed to the back of the plane in respect; there were four of us— Brian, Patti, myself and a Western monk from Australia. Everyone was quiet, as the plane took off. We were still in shock and grief.

At Bagdogra a small group was on the tarmac to meet the plane. It appeared to be members of the Bhutanese royal family, Sikkimese noblemen and West Bengal officials all dressed in their finest, bearing offering scarves. Everyone prostrated and placed their scarves on the coffin as it was unloaded from the plane. Tai Situ Rinpoche came out onto the tarmac and greeted Jamgön Kongtrul and Gyaltsab Rinpoche. It was an incredible moment.

My spirits lifted slightly. It was comforting to see the respect shown to Karmapa exactly as if he were there in person, being greeted just like he had been 9 months ago on his return from his last world tour.

A helicopter and several official cars were waiting. His Holiness and the Rinpoches were taken to Sikkim by helicopter. The main party got into the cavalcade of cars and Jeeps and began the drive back to Sikkim. A bus took the rest of the party including us. We stayed discreetly in the back of the bus as we went through the check points with official permission, but not the official papers. There had not been enough time.

As our cavalcade wound through the verdant valleys along the Teesta River getting ever closer to the monastery, my grief began to lift. Sikkim is like a magical kingdom. The feeling on arriving in Rumtek was profound. I felt as if the Karmapa had not died. For the first time in months, my sense of separation and impending loss was transformed into a subtle joy. I experienced a deep feeling that the Karmapa had come back to life. He was back in Rumtek, back at his seat, in the place that he loved.

Rumtek was alive with activity. It was the full moon, the clearest of full moons I had ever experienced. We were the only Westerners there. All the lights of the monastery were on and it looked like a jewelled palace against the outline of the mountains behind. I knew that the rinpoches and lamas were preparing His Holiness' body. He was being placed in vajra posture and wrapped in silks. After this preparation, the "kudung" would be packed with salt. I was certain that the Karmapa had come back to life that night. Of course not in his previous form, but his presence was filling the air, the town, my heart and those of everyone present.

Not only the monastery, but the whole village was awake. All night the stoves in the villagers' houses were lit and the women were stirring salt in their large woks over the open flames to take out the moisture. The monks were filing up and down the road to each house, and taking the salt up to the monastery. The lamas were preparing the Karmapa's body in the upper shrine room, where he bestowed the Vajra Crown ceremonies, the blessing of "tongdrol" or liberation by seeing. This evening had all the power and energy of a Crown ceremony. A distinct feeling of liberation permeated the air.

I had not travelled to Hong Kong or Chicago to say goodbye.

Thangka painting of HH Karmapa in Rumtek.
(Artist unknown)

I had stayed in India to await my parents' arrival. But for my last blessing, nothing could have been more profound than being present for the Karmapa's return home.

As dawn rose slowly behind the mountains, I fell into a deep sleep, contented and peaceful. Yishin Norbu, the Wish-Fulfilling Jewel, was still with me. He was blessing all of us with his presence.

As He Is
by Dorzong Rinpoche

The 8th Dorzong Rinpoche was born in 1943 in Tibet amidst many auspicious signs. Rinpoche underwent a thorough training and transmission in philosophy and meditation from many different masters of various lineages.

Dorzong Rinpoche left Tibet with HE Khamtrul Rinpoche in 1958. In 1969 he moved to Tashi Jong, established by Khamtrul Rinpoche. When H. E. Khamtrul Rinpoche passed away in 1980 he became President of the Tashi Jong Community. He performed all the consultations and arrangements for recognition of the reincarnation of the present 9th Khamtrul Rinpoche in conjunction with His Holiness the 16th Karmapa and His Holiness Dilgo Khyentse Rinpoche.

He is an authentic holder of the Drukpa Kagyud lineage. Rinpoche also practices the teachings of other Tibetan Buddhist lineages. Currently, Rinpoche's main project is the creation of the Dorzong Monastic Institute, Jangchub Jong. This is near the village of Gopalpur in the Kangra valley about twenty kilometres from Dharamsala, northern India.

I have four root gurus. His Holiness Karmapa was one of them. I have very strong faith and devotion whether he shows miracles or not. If miracles are there, usually people think he's so great. Whether he shows miraculous activities or not, for me it's the same.

He asked me if I could polish boots. I said yes. He had everything ready and told me to go ahead. So I did and he said, "You have to do it like this," and he took the brush and whisked it back and forth energetically, like professional Indian boot polishers.

He asked if I could sew and I said no. He said he could sew and he came with needles to show me. When I was with him, only this kind of thing happened. I didn't have any kind of expectation. He was very special. I have unshakeable faith and devotion.

Some of my Western students ask me, "What kind of teachings did your root guru give you?" I say, "Nothing. When I go to see my root guru, I just sit there. Whatever he does is a teaching for me."

Some people say His Holiness has miraculous activities and they have more faith and devotion, more confidence. But I say whether he shows these things or not, for me it's the same. Usually when gurus say something nice to us we feel happy. When they are not so happy with us, we feel sad. I don't have that kind of feeling. Any way it happens, I have great feeling for him.

He kept so many birds in Rumtek. He would explain to me about the habits of some of the birds, what they like to eat, which one is expensive. He took great care of them. One time Dilgo Khyentse Rinpoche told me that he himself saw that when some of the birds passed away, they sat upright in meditation. Because of his love, power and compassion, when the birds died they sat in meditation.

When he was dying I heard he would go to Chicago. I didn't really know when to go so I just went and because of our karmic connection, I landed there five minutes after His Holiness. When I went to see him in hospital he was smiling and joking. I said I would like to go there every day to serve him. There were 16 of his attendants there and he didn't need me but I went anyway.

Every day he was very charming, smiling, joking as usual. Sometimes the doctors came to look at him but sometimes there was nobody except me.

The doctors were not Buddhist. They would say, "This man is very strange. He has so many problems, heart, tuberculosis, and so on, and he's always very happy. He must have a lot of pain but he always says, I'm fine, I'm fine." The doctor told his attendants he would not live long, maybe five days or one week. His Holiness laughed and said I will have another fifteen days. And he lasted for exactly fifteen days. I returned to India knowing they would bring his body to Rumtek.

In Tantric teaching it's said that if you have great faith and devotion in the guru you will get blessings; if not, you won't get anything. One bhikshu spent twenty-four years with Buddha and didn't get any kind of blessing. Real faith and devotion is difficult to explain. It's not strong love, not strong attachment. It's some special feeling.

In Guru Yoga practice usually they say your guru should transform into Vajradhara (the primordial buddha), Guru Rinpoche or Buddha Sakyamuni. Then you can say the prayer. For some people, who see the guru as a human being, then maybe it's better for them to transform him into Vajradhara. If I change him into Vajradhara, my guru yoga disappears. I see him as he is. That's good.

As HE IS. Get it?

Thangka painting of HH Karmapa.
(Artist unknown)

Acknowledgments

The idea to collect memories of the 16th Karmapa came entirely through my own devotion. I am deeply grateful to the contributors who entrusted me with their personal experiences without any letter of introduction from the 17th Karmapa or his administration.

I would like to express my deepest gratitude to my agent Jessica Woollard; to Jo Gibson for her tireless and skilful editing; to Lama Surya Das, and Ken Holmes for the invaluable cultural perspective given in their introductions; and Achi Tsepal, MJ Bennett and Steve Roth for their generosity with their contacts and reference material. Thanks also to Janis LaPorte at the Oberoi Hotel for her assistance to Mrs Goodie Oberoi. At the last minute Jeffrey Fuller came to the rescue by re-scanning old photos. Ward Holmes has been a friend throughout helping with last minute requests for archival photos.

The kindness and effort of all the contributors has made this book possible. Without them an important part of the 16th Karmapa's activity would have been lost to future generations.

About the Author

Norma Levine has travelled both East and West to record the stories of the 16th Karmapa and the impact he had on the people who met him.

She is a lifelong Buddhist practitioner and the author of *Blessing Power of the Buddhas: Sacred Objects, Sacred Lands*; *A Yearbook of Buddhist Wisdom*; and *Chronicles of Love and Death: My Years with the Lost Spiritual King of Bhutan*.

Her website can be found at *www.earthmudra.com*.